HOW TO BLOG MADE EASY

This is a **FLAME TREE** book
First published 2014

Publisher and Creative Director: Nick Wells
Project Editor: Polly Prior
Art Director and Layout Design: Mike Spender
Digital Design and Production: Chris Herbert
Copy Editor: Anna Groves
Proofreader: Dawn Laker
Screenshots: Richard N. Williams
Special thanks to: Laura Bulbeck, Emma Chafer, Esme Chapman, Molly McAnany, Rob Zakes

This edition first published 2014 by
FLAME TREE PUBLISHING
Crabtree Hall, Crabtree Lane
Fulham, London SW6 6TY
United Kingdom

www.flametreepublishing.com

14 16 18 17 15
3 5 7 9 10 8 6 4 2

ISBN 978-1-78361-231-4

A CIP record for this book is available from the British Library upon request.

Printed in China

All non-screenshot pictures are courtesy of Flame Tree: 152, 153, 154, and Shutterstock and © the following photographers: Africa Studio: 6, 156, 184; Ermolaev Alexander: 92, 224; alexskopje: 31; arka38: 201; aslysun: 218; auremar: 48; BONNINSTUDIO: 102, 230; Diego Cervo: 181; Jacek Chabraszewski: 209; De Visu: 90; Denphumi: 130; Greg Epperson: 222; JIANG HONGYAN: 190; Hasloo Group Production Studio: 228; Pavel Ignatov: 159; Amy Johansson: 6, 124; Teresa Kasprzycka: 182; kazoka: 176; mimagephotography: 170; ollyy: 16; OtnaYdur: 215; William Perugini: 7, 220; Peshkova: 210; Gunnar Pippel: 30; Pincasso: 3; polaris50d: 234; racorn: 14, 126; RedDaxLuma: 35; steveball: 5, 86; ; Singkham: 7, 188; StockLite: 100, 109; supergenijalac: 178; Syda Productions: 8, 22, 153; Thinglass: 58; Alfonso de Tomas: 145; Vima: 5, 46; wavebreakmedia: 165; yanugkelid: 151

HOW TO BLOG MADE EASY

RICHARD N. WILLIAMS

FLAME TREE
PUBLISHING

CONTENTS

INTRODUCTION........................... 8

GETTING STARTED 14

New to the world of blogging? Start here. Learn why people blog, what subjects blogs feature, and what kind of posts appeal most to readers. You will be familiarized with the different types of blog and discover what it takes to produce a successful one of your own. Finally, you are given a 'New Bloggers' Checklist' to give yourself a head start.

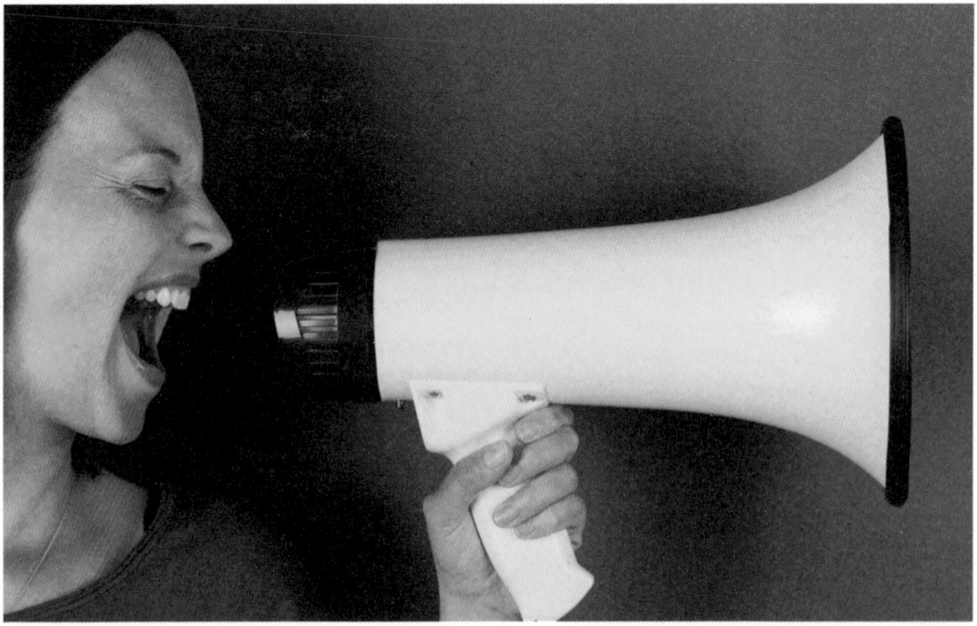

When starting your blog, the software you choose is of critical importance. Here, you will find the ins and outs of blogging software, including how to pick the program to best fit your goals. You will be taught the differences between popular hosted and self-hosted blogs, including Google's Blogger, WordPress and SquareSpace, as well as how to work through the basic features of each.

One of the most exciting parts of blogging is the social network you create through self-expression. This chapter teaches you how to construct an exciting blog post and suggests creative ways to engage with readers. Here, you will also find out how to effectively structure your blog, from its layout and formatting to the importance of proofreading and keeping language interesting.

If you are looking to generate income through blogging, look no further. This chapter teaches you how to make money through advertisements, sponsorship acquisition and affiliate marketing. There is also valuable information on how to sell your own products and services through your blog. Finally, you will read about common problems experienced with funding, as well as how to steer clear of them.

The final chapter of this book discusses ways to keep the momentum of your blog going once it is established. You'll learn where to turn once you've exceeded your goals and how to take your blog to the next level. Advanced bloggers require knowledge of the nitty-gritty technical details. As the book concludes, you will learn how to troubleshoot and come to understand the many technicalities needed to ensure that your blog reaches its maximum potential.

INTRODUCTION

Knowing how to set up, write and develop a blog is not easy. This book is designed to help those new to blogging get started, as well as provide useful information to experienced bloggers so they can develop their blog and reach a wider audience.

WHAT IS A BLOG?

The term 'blog' comes from the phrase 'web log'. Blogs are simply websites consisting of written posts. Blog posts appear in reverse chronological order, so the latest post appears at the top.

Blogging and Bloggers

The act of maintaining or writing a blog is called blogging, while somebody who blogs is known as a blogger. The great thing about blogs is that they can be about anything and everything. Unlike other forms of publishing, a blogger doesn't need an editor or any experience in the publishing industry. In fact, all you need to start a blog is a blogging platform and something to write about.

A Brief History of Blogging

The first blogs appeared in the late 1990s. These early blogs resembled diary entries and were usually kept by people who

wanted to share their life and experiences with other people. Many of these blogs were very basic and resembled simple websites, and were mainly text-based. As blogs became more popular, people started blogging about all sorts of topics and blogs became more advanced. Different blogging platforms were developed that allowed blogs to include multimedia and interactive features, which made it possible for people to leave comments or visit links on posts to other blogs.

THE BLOGOSPHERE

Today, there are an estimated 180 million blogs on the internet. People now refer to this online community of blogs and bloggers as the Blogosphere. Blogs have gone from being basic diary entries addressed to an interested few to a worldwide communication platform. Many newspapers, news organizations and journalists now maintain blogs, while businesses, authors, celebrities and even politicians keep blogs as a means of interacting with people.

Blogging on the Go

Blogging used to be something you could only do on a computer. These days, with smartphones and tablet computers such as the iPad, you can both write and read blogs anywhere. This has made blogging extremely flexible and immediate.

Google Official Blog
Insights from Googlers into our products, technology, and the Google culture
Hulu Plus now works with Chromecast
Posted: Wednesday, October 02, 2013
Tweet
Hulu has added Chromecast support to their Hulu Plus app—just in time for the fall television season. Now you can easily enjoy your favorite shows, such as "Modern Family," "New Girl" and "Parks and Recreation," on your big-screen TV by casting from Hulu Plus on your mobile phone or tablet. It's the same intuitive, remote-free experience you've come to enjoy with the other Chromecast-supported apps, and is as simple as pressing the Cast button which will now appear in the app.
Chromecast: For Bigger Awesome
Google+ Followers
Google
Follow
2,366,016 have us in circles
View all
Archive

Right: Many blogs, like Google's, include multimedia and interactive features.

THIS BOOK

This book has been designed as a guide to help all bloggers. It is not a book that you may want to read from cover to cover, more a book that you can use as a reference when you need help with your blogging. We have tried to cover all aspects of blogging, from setting up blogs and choosing the right blogging platform to helping you make the most of your blog by increasing your audience size or making money from it.

Hot Tip

Throughout this book, we have inserted lots of hot tips. These are designed to help you find some simple yet effective methods for getting the most out of blogging.

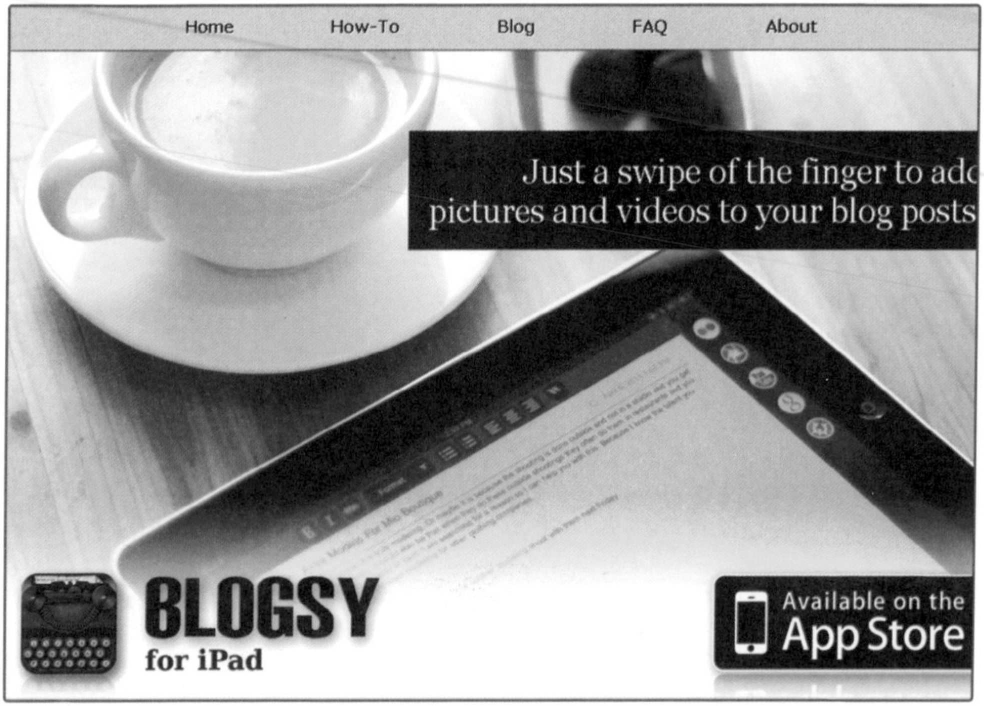

Above: Blogsy, an iPad blogging app, makes blogging on the go effortless.

Advanced Bloggers

This is not just a guide for beginner bloggers. For those experienced with blogging, we have included some useful information that can help you make the most of your blog, from making money to taking your blogging to the next level.

BLOGGING TIPS

One of the first questions we address in this book is the reason to blog. What the point of blogging is, what it can do for you and what it cannot do for you. Furthermore, we discuss the things you should perhaps not blog about, some of the commonest blogging pitfalls and how to avoid problems with the information that you post, such as libel and copyright infringement.

Coming Up With Ideas

One of the hardest aspects of blogging is finding things to blog about. We have tried to provide some advice on keeping your blog posts fresh and interesting, helping you come up with ideas and new angles to blog about. We have also provided you with some handy ways to encourage comments and discussion on your blog posts.

Blogger
Blogger Buzz: The Official Buzz from Blogger at Google
You can do some amazing things with Blogger
Posted: July 28, 2011
+1 237
Tweet 110
Like 245
Guest post by David Kutcher
Editor's note: We invited David Kutcher, an innovative web developer from Northampton MA, to write a guest blog post to share how he uses Blogger to create robust, beautiful and easy to use websites for his clients.
Hi, my name is David Kutcher. I own Confluent Forms LLC, a graphic design and custom web-based software development firm in Northampton, MA. We specialize in creating gorgeous and engaging websites with custom content management systems. As curious as it made sound, we've found that Blogger can be a great platform for web development when a custom CMS isn't needed. Blogger provides a ton of functionality and design freedom for our clients, and not just for blogs!
You're probably thinking: "what? using blog software for a website?". I know - it sounds a bit unconventional, but it's true.
Blogger
Your central hub for Blogger news & tips, direct from the B...
Follow
+1

Above: Blogging offers many outlets for users, depending on what they hope to accomplish.

Researching Blog Posts

We have also included some handy hints on researching topics for your blog, to ensure you can sound authoritative on whatever you are writing about, how to link to sources and how best to keep your audience interested and happy.

Blog Writing

This is not a writing guide, but we have included tips and strategies to make your blog posts more appealing and better to read. We have also included some handy hints on how to proof your blogs, the different software you can use to write blog posts, as well as how to incorporate multimedia, such as images and videos, to make your posts more engaging.

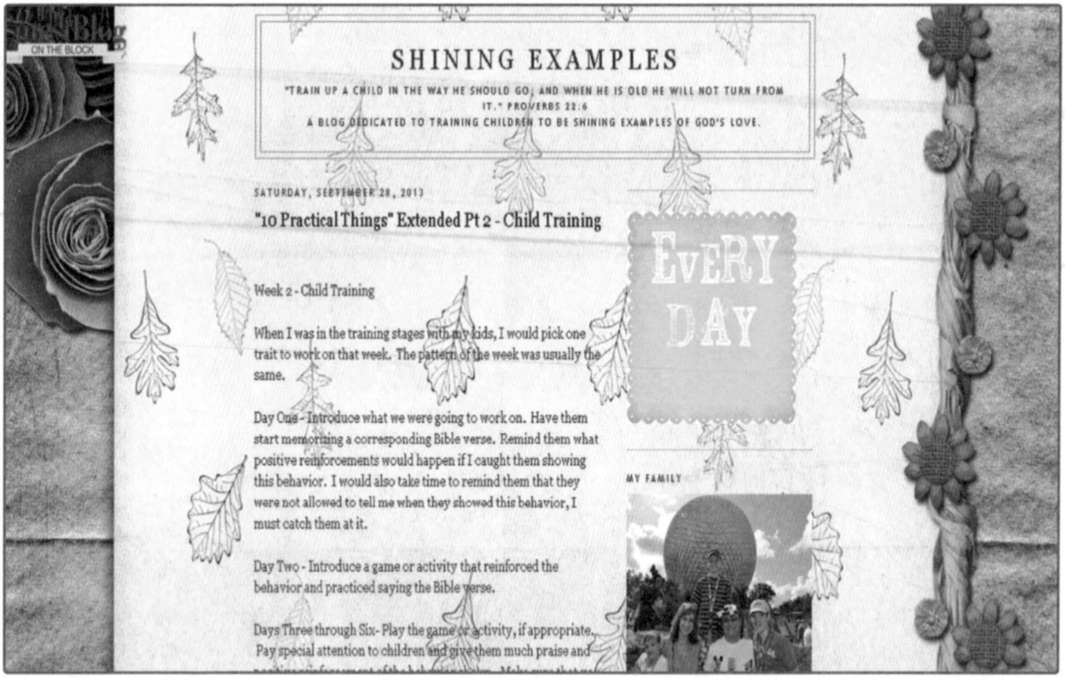
ON THE BLOCK
SHINING EXAMPLES
"TRAIN UP A CHILD IN THE WAY HE SHOULD GO, AND WHEN HE IS OLD HE WILL NOT TURN FROM IT." PROVERBS 22:6
A BLOG DEDICATED TO TRAINING CHILDREN TO BE SHINING EXAMPLES OF GOD'S LOVE.
SATURDAY, SEPTEMBER 28, 2013
"10 Practical Things" Extended Pt 2 - Child Training
Week 2 - Child Training
When I was in the training stages with my kids, I would pick one trait to work on that week. The pattern of the week was usually the same.
Day One - Introduce what we were going to work on. Have them start memorizing a corresponding Bible verse. Remind them what positive reinforcements would happen if I caught them showing this behavior. I would also take time to remind them that they were not allowed to tell me when they showed this behavior, I must catch them at it.
Day Two - Introduce a game or activity that reinforced the behavior and practiced saying the Bible verse.
Days Three through Six- Play the game or activity, if appropriate. Pay special attention to children and give them much praise and
EvERY DAY
MY FAMILY

Above: Blogging is the perfect way to voice opinions and interact with peers and followers on the internet.

Reaching an Audience

One of the hardest aspects of blogging is building an audience. Obviously, the secret to attracting large numbers of people is to write engaging blog posts that people want to read. We have included plenty of strategies to market your blog, spread the word about your posts, and build and interact with an audience.

Software

All sorts of blogging platforms exist. We have tried to cover a number of different software options, but because of the sheer number available, it is not possible to explain how to post blogs on all of them. Instead, we have concentrated on the most popular blogging platforms, as well as providing some information for people wanting to build their own blog from scratch.

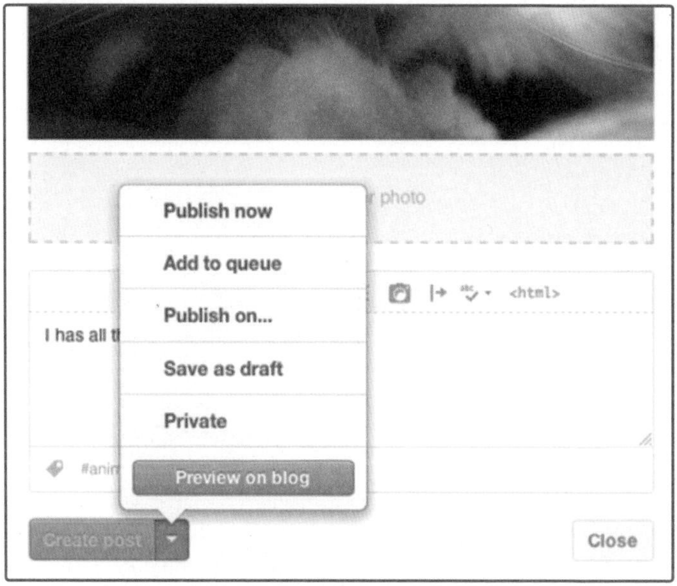

Above: Different blogging websites can be utilized for different purposes. Tumblr, for example, is the perfect way to display images and graphics.

STEP BY STEP

Throughout this book, we have included step-by-step guides to steer you through some of the more technical aspects of blogging, such as including a social media widget, so people can follow your posts on Twitter, Facebook or subscribe to live feeds of your blog.

Jargon

As with the rest of the internet, the Blogosphere is full of its own jargon and terminology. However, where possible, we have provided instructions and information using the simplest possible terms.

Help and Further Reading

No book on blogging can possibly cover every conceivable aspect. Because of this, we have included helpful websites and other books for those wanting more information on certain aspects of blogging.

GETTING STARTED

BLOGGING BASICS

Blogs are a great way to express yourself, pass on information and get involved in an online community. However, starting a blog can be daunting. In this section, we take you through the basics, helping you get to grips with the concept of blogging.

WHY BLOG?

People blog for an almost unlimited number of reasons. Some people just enjoy sharing their thoughts and opinions. For others, blogging is a way to discuss subjects in which they have an interest. In fact, a blog can be anything you want it to be. However, blogging can be a lot of work and requires a degree of commitment and dedication. Posting regular articles can be time-consuming, and not everybody is cut out to be a blogger.

Is Blogging For You?

Many people start blogging but end up giving it up after a few weeks or months. Before launching into the Blogosphere, it is perhaps best to decide whether blogging is really for you and what you hope to get out of it.

Why People Blog

If you are thinking of starting blogging, it may help you decide whether it is for you by understanding some of the reasons why other people blog.

- **Self-expression**: If you have something to say, a blog is a great way to express yourself.
- **Sharing a passion**: If you have a hobby or interest, a blog is a great way to connect to other like-minded people.
- **Sharing your expertise**: If you have skills or knowledge on a particular subject, a blog is a great way of establishing yourself as an expert.
- **Helping others**: Many people who have been through a difficult experience blog about it to help others in similar situations.
- **Promotion**: Blogging is a great way to market a product, business or service.
- **Connecting with people**: A blog can help you connect with people. For example, writers, artists and musicians often blog to connect with fans.
- **Enjoyment of writing**: If you enjoy writing, blogs are a great way to practise and showcase stories, articles and other writings.

Home
Get Your Ex Girlfriend Back
Treatment for Depression without Medication is Possible With A Strong Relationship
There is actually nothing worse in a relationship like having your partner suffering from depression.It is really heart aching watching them go through this dark period of life.Usually many relationship fail or end because of it.Especially when the situation start wearing on both parties.
Read more »
SEARCH THIS BLOG
NEWS & UPDATE
Subscribe here for latest tips on relationship dating delivered directly in your mail box
Enter your email address:
Subscribe
Delivered by FeedBurner

Above: Some people blog as a means of offering help and advice to others.

COMMITMENT

Whatever your reason for deciding to take up blogging, you need to ensure you can give the necessary commitment. Successful blogs require regular postings, so you need to have enough free time to write. How many blog posts you write each week or month will depend on you and your blog (more on this later), but if you are somebody with very little free time, blogging may not be for you. Blogs also take time to promote and manage, so you need to be prepared to spend some time each week on your blog.

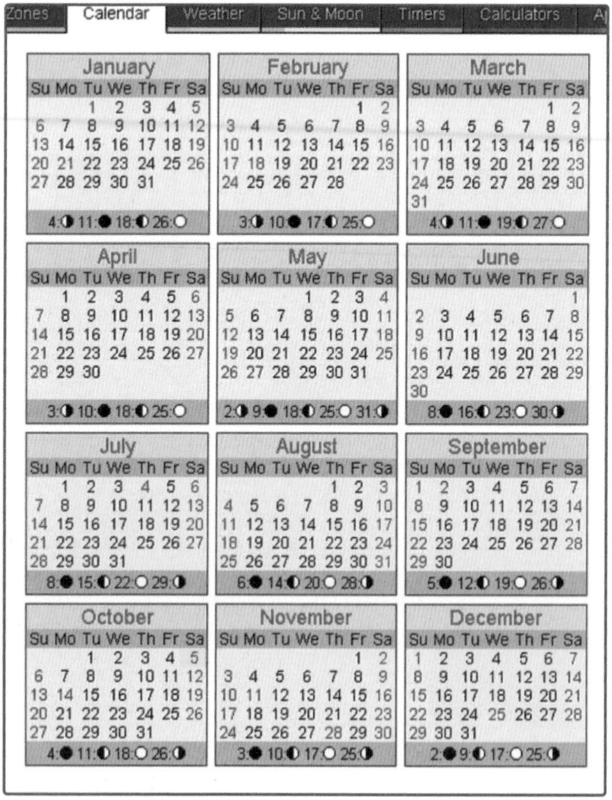

Above: You may want to use an online calendar to plan when, and how often, you intend to blog.

Requirements

The great thing about blogging is that you really do not need much to get going. As long as you have access to a computer and the internet, and you have something to write about, you can make a start. Many blogging platforms are free, so blogging does not even have to cost you anything. Of course, as blogging is mainly about writing, you will need a reasonable grasp of the English language. However, tools and software programs are available to help you.

Hot Tip

If you are thinking of embarking on blogging, start by putting aside at least one or two hours a week as your blogging time. Choose a time when you will not have any distractions.

UNDERSTANDING BLOGGING

Before you start blogging, it is a good idea to understand what a blog is and is not. While blogs are a great way to promote businesses and services, a blog is not a sales platform. People visit blogs because they want information. A blog set up simply to push products is unlikely to be successful. A blog is also not a website. Blogs need to be updated regularly. Without regular fresh information, people will lose interest and stop visiting.

Prepare For Confrontation

While most people in the Blogosphere are generally friendly, you may encounter those who are less so. People may not always agree with your thoughts and opinions and may say so, not always tactfully. Sometimes, negative comments about your blog can be quite hurtful, and even personal, so if you are unsure whether you can take criticism, blogging may not be for you.

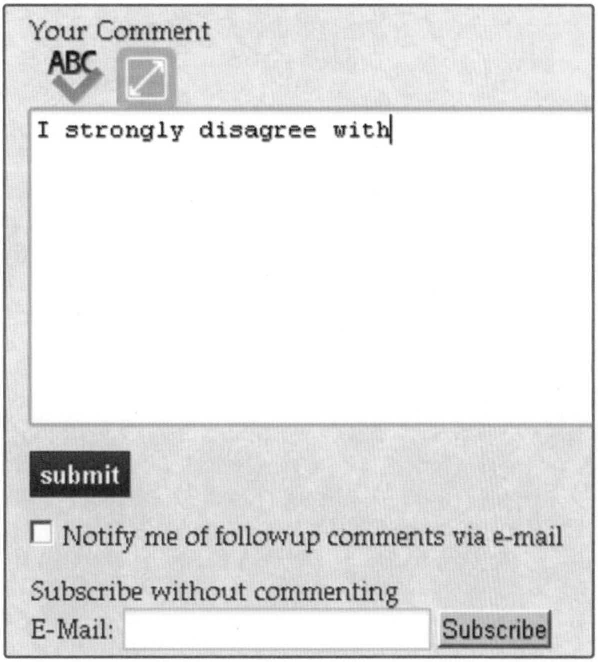

Above: Be prepared that there may be some people who do not agree with what you say on your blog.

TYPES OF BLOG

Blogs fall into a number of categories. Blogs differ in the type of content they provide, but also how that content is delivered.

Personal Blogs

The majority of blogs on the internet are personal blogs. These are normally kept by an individual and may encompass online diaries, a forum in which to share thoughts and opinions, or be centred on a specific interest or pastime.

Above: Corporate blogs, such as this blog by Coca Cola, are a great way for companies to increase visibility and communicate with customers.

Corporate Blogs

If you run a business, blogging is a great way to reach out to customers, suppliers and those in the same industry. Many business websites now have a blog. Corporate blogging can bring several benefits.

- **Brand awareness**: A corporate blog is a great way to boost your company's profile and demonstrate you are an authority in your field.
- **Improve visibility**: You can boost your internet presence with a business blog.
- **Promote new products**: While a blog is not a sales platform, blogging is a great way to let people know when you have a new product or service.

Academic Blogs

Scientists and those in the academic community can find blogging a useful way to connect to other people in their field. An academic blog is a great way of sharing ideas and research.

Hot Tip

Before you start blogging, look around the internet at blogs that cover a similar subject. See what you can do that is different while appealing to the same audience.

Commentary Blogs

Many blogs provide social commentary and opinion. Often, these blogs are maintained by experts or journalists and include such subjects as politics and health. Some political blogs have now become more popular than conventional news publications, and these bloggers have developed good reputations among the mainstream media industry. In addition, most news organizations now maintain a blog.

Microblogs

Microblogs entail the posting of small pieces of content. These have the advantage of being less time-consuming than regular blogs. Twitter is perhaps the most famous microblogging platform.

Vlogs and Photoblogs

Vlogs, also known as video blogs, contain videos rather than written articles, while a photoblog comprises just pictures and are often maintained by photographers.

Hot Tip

Before you commit to blogging, try writing a few articles on a subject to get an idea of how much work is involved. You can also show these to people you know to get feedback.

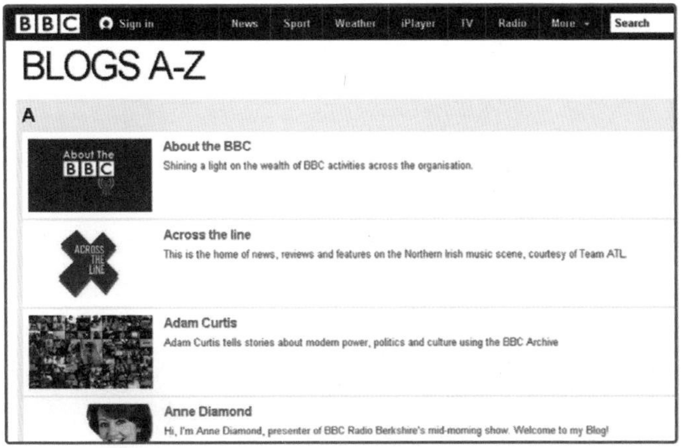

Above: The BBC News blog is an example of a commentary blog, which provides readers with more opinion than a traditional news website. .

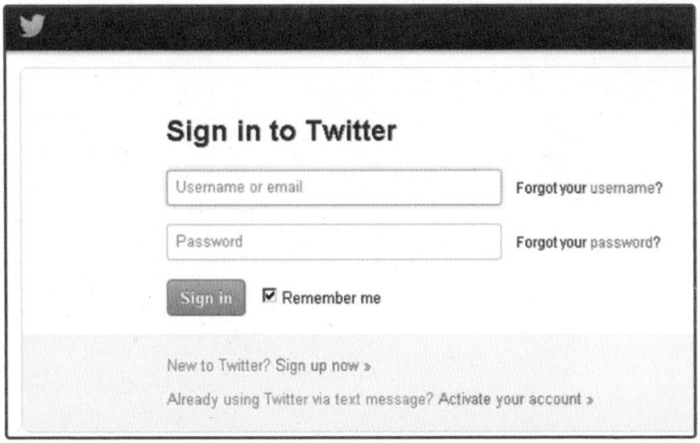

Above: Twitter is a microblogging platform where members can only post small pieces of content at a time.

WHAT MAKES A GOOD BLOGGER?

There are good bloggers and bad bloggers. Simply being able to write well or having knowledge on a topic does not necessarily mean you will be a good blogger. Successful bloggers are those who can generate large numbers of readers and create discussion on a subject. While there is no easy way to achieve this, good bloggers share some similar traits.

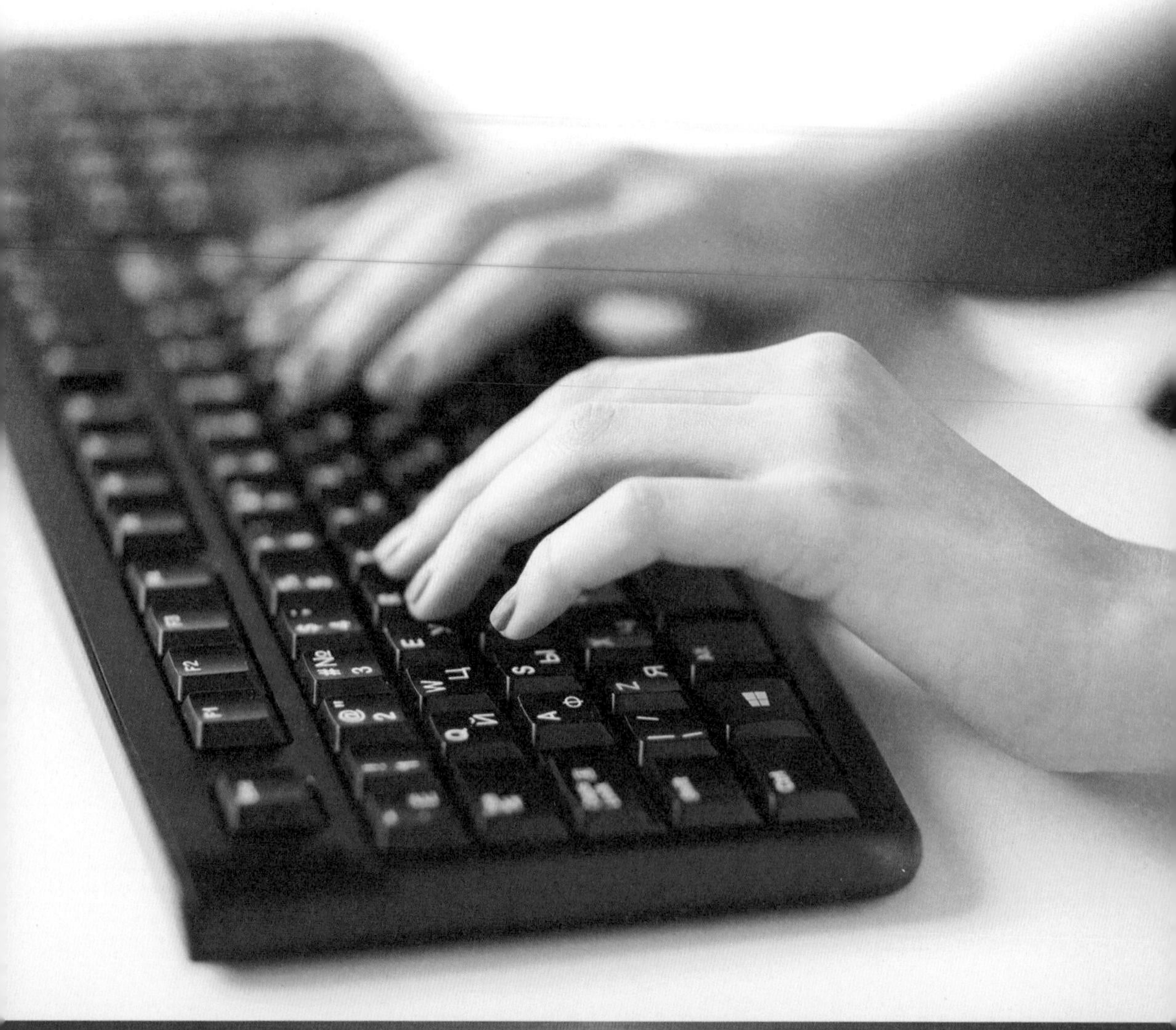

- **Subject has broad appeal**: Just because you are interested in something does not mean anybody else will be. The most successful bloggers are those who write about subjects that have wide appeal.

- **Passion for a subject**: A blogger who can demonstrate passion about a subject will engage readers with their enthusiasm.

- **Experimentation**: There are no hard and fast rules as to what will be successful and what will not. A good blogger is not afraid to try different things.

- **Continuous learning**: The internet never stands still. Blogging is changing all the time and a good blogger needs to understand and keep up with these changes.

- **Ability to network**: You cannot rely on people coming to you. You need to market and promote your blog, as well as interacting with your audience.

- **Encouraging debate**: A good blog is one that encourages debate. Do not be afraid of controversy or allowing people to voice opinions that you may not necessarily agree with.

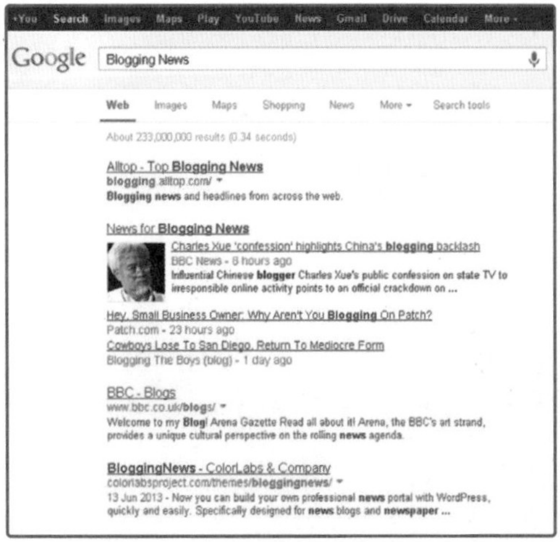

Above: Keeping abreast of news in the blogging world is a great way to build networks and gain inspiration.

- **Love of research and writing**: If you do not enjoy writing and research, your blog may become a burden and not something you can maintain.

- **Knowing your audience**: You need to understand what your audience wants to read and find topics that will appeal to them, not confining your writing to your own interests.

WHAT TO BLOG ABOUT

Before you can begin blogging, you have to establish what you are going to write about. Blogs can be about everything and anything, but you need to find a subject that is not only interesting to you, but will also appeal to other people.

FINDING A TOPIC

Knowing what to write about is the first hurdle on the path to becoming a blogger. While you can write about anything and everything, each blog has to have a common theme or subject that connects all the posts. People need a reason to visit your blog, and if you are not writing about anything in particular, it will not attract much of an audience.

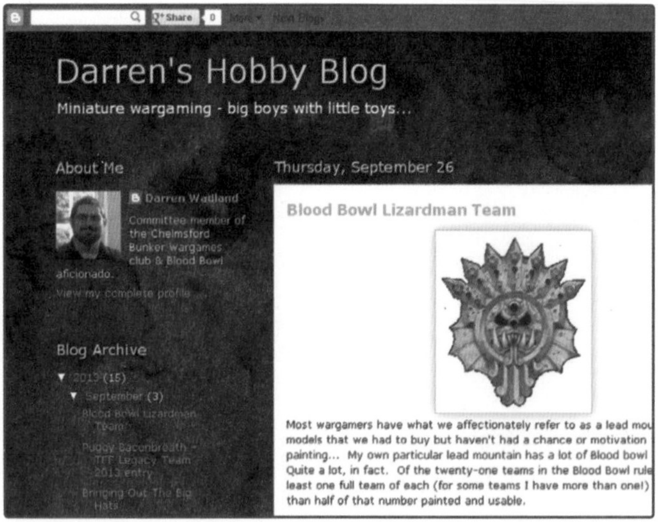

Darren's Hobby Blog
Miniature wargaming - big boys with little toys...
About Me
Thursday, September 26
Blood Bowl Lizardman Team
Blog Archive
Most wargamers have what we affectionately refer to as a lead mou
models that we had to buy but haven't had a chance or motivation
painting... My own particular lead mountain has a lot of Blood bowl
Quite a lot, in fact. Of the twenty-one teams in the Blood Bowl rule
least one full team of each (for some teams I have more than one!)
than half of that number painted and usable.

Above: Hobbyist blogs allow you to share your passions and interests with other people, and can be very enjoyable to write.

Purpose of Your Blog

The reason you are blogging in the first place will go some way to defining your blog's topic. For those writing a business blog, topics about your industry will be the obvious choice. If you have something to promote, such as a product or service, you should blog on something suitably related.

What Interests You?

Finding a topic can be difficult because you need to find something that is both interesting

> ## Hot Tip
> **If you wish to make money from a blog, you may want to find a topic relevant to advertisers and sponsors (see Chapter Six for more information about funding your blog).**

to you and something you know a lot about. Writing post after post on a topic that you do not find appealing will bore you and most likely bore your readers.

Passion

Simply being interested in a topic may not be enough. You need to find something about which you can write enthusiastically. Do not forget, you will have to write countless posts on the same subject, and unless you can demonstrate passion in your writing, you will struggle to engage your audience.

Authority

You also need to choose a topic that you know a lot about. People like to read from authoritative sources, and your readers will soon notice if you sound uninformed.

Above: If you want to build a blog offering expert advice, make it a topic you know a lot about and can communicate clearly to those less informed.

WHAT DO READERS WANT?

Just because you have an interest and passion in a subject does not mean other people will. All blogs need an audience, so you need to ensure the subject you are writing about appeals to other people. Understanding what readers want from blogs is not easy. However, looking at the reasons people visit blogs in the first place can help you narrow down your choice of topic.

Offer Something

Quite often, people visit blogs because they want to learn something. Many blogs provide practical information, such as recipes, DIY tips or 'how-to' advice. If you can provide a benefit to your blog visitors, you are sure to attract an audience.

Above: If you have come through a difficult life experience that you think others may be struggling with, then a blog is an ideal way to offer advice.

Learn From Your Experience

People also visit blogs to learn from other people's experiences. This can range from film reviews that tell people whether the latest blockbuster movie is worth seeing, to how you made a success in a certain field. If you have skills or experience that you can share, you can build a solid audience.

Entertain People

Popular blogs are also those that entertain. You can entertain readers in a number of ways. Some people write witty blog posts, while others link to amusing videos or websites on the internet.

Hot Tip

Some of the most popular blogs are those that provide help with specific problems. Fitness and health advice blogs often attract large audiences.

TOPICS TO AVOID

Just because you have the freedom to blog about anything does not mean that you should. Some subjects may be worth avoiding. For instance, you may think that people will find your diary entries about your friends and family amusing, but the people you are writing about may not take kindly to being discussed in this way. You may also want to avoid giving out too many personal details, such as your address.

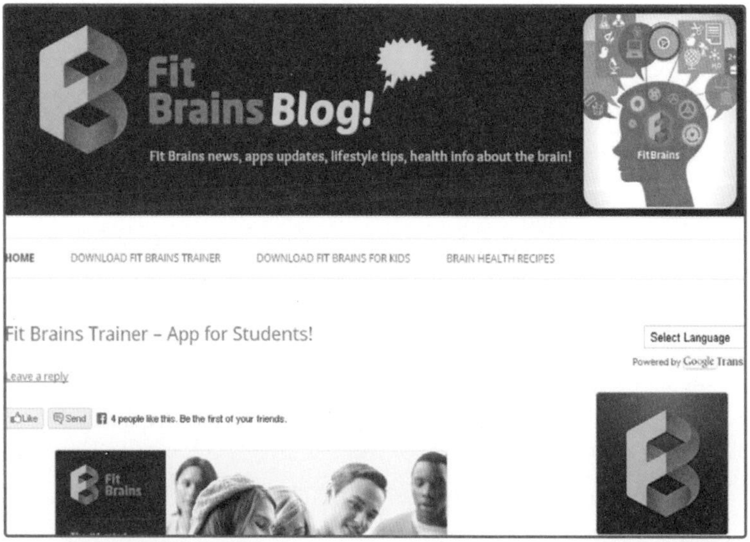

Above: For blog topics, think about the areas you are most interested in and the people with whom you would most like to connect.

In addition, some subjects, such as politics and religion, can be extremely divisive, so unless you have a thick skin and can handle heated debate and strong opinions, you may be best avoiding controversial subject matter.

INDENTIFYING YOUR BLOG TOPIC

The best way to come up with an appropriate subject for your blog is to compile a list of topics in which you have an interest. Think of those things that get you excited or that you feel strongly about. In particular, think about the sort of things you read about when you have time on your hands. Try to identify subjects you are knowledgeable about and have a good understanding of. Perhaps you have a hobby or a particular skill you could blog about.

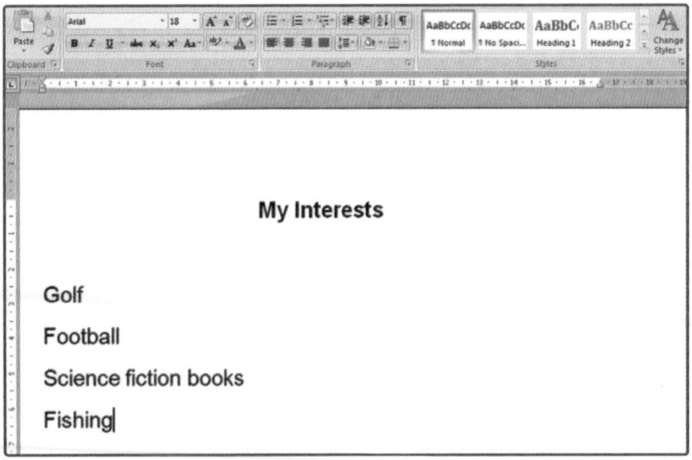

Above: Compiling a list of your interests can help you come up with a topic to base your blog around.

Scope

Whatever topic you decide on, you need to ensure you can maintain a steady stream of posts. Make sure there is enough scope in your topic to write about it consistently. Do not pick a subject that is too narrow or one where you are going to struggle to come up with ideas. Blog posts need to be fresh, so avoid anything that will cause you to repeat yourself.

WHAT DO OTHER PEOPLE BLOG ABOUT?

Some blog subjects are particularly common and prove very popular.

- **Special interest**: Hobbies and interests make for great blogs, as you can attract a niche audience interested in the same pastime. These can vary from stamp collecting and gardening to sports, DIY and astronomy.

- **Internet and technology**: Being technology-based, it is no wonder that the internet is packed full of technology blogs. These usually centre on specific gadgets or internet practices, such as social media or web design.

Hot Tip

If you are struggling to think of a topic for your blog, why not ask your friends and family? You may find there are particular subjects you discuss quite a lot without realizing it.

- **News aggregation**: These blogs are quite easy to manage, as they simply pull in news stories on a particular topic from various sources. These blogs cover topics such as a particular sport, a type of music or are sometimes location-based. These blogs save readers time, as they can get their news in one place without having to scour the internet.

SEP
20
2013
Blogging To Make Money Online - An Easy Way To Profit
Business Opportunities
by James Fairley
Share 1
Share 1
Like 2
Tweet 3
MLM Traffic Formula
How To Generate Endless Leads And Instant Cash For Any MLM
Blogging Your Way To The Top
The truth is that there is not one way to earn money while blogging, but several. For instance, keeping your blog up to date with fresh information may attract the attention of those looking to buy advertising space on niche sites. That said, you would have to have pretty high traffic for this to work successfully, so are there other ways to create an income from blogging where you don't have to wait for this to happen?

Above: Blogs about making money are always popular; check out the competition to make sure yours stands out.

- **Making money online**: People love to make money. Blogs that provide investment tips and money-making hints and advice often do well.

IDENTIFY THE COMPETITION

Once you have a topic in mind, you need to study what other blogs exist on the same subject. Competition for an audience is fierce and you may find there are dozens, even hundreds of blogs on the same topic. Do some background research to find out the most common blogs in your subject area. Become part of the community and read forums and other blogs to establish what attracts the most readers. Then ask yourself what it is these blogs are doing to make them so successful.

Find a Niche

Simply mimicking another blog and providing the same information is not going to get you much of an audience. You need to establish what you can do that is better or different in

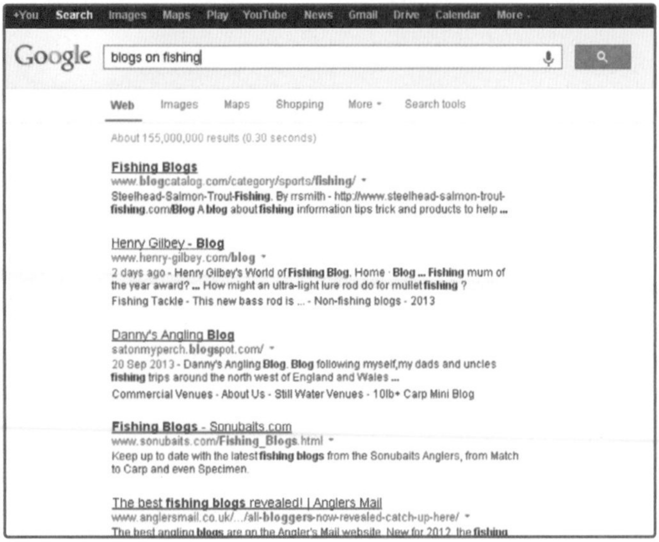

Above: Searching for existing blogs on your topic allows you to assess the competition and find your own unique niche.

order to stand out from the crowd. A good way of doing this is to target a specific niche area on the subject. This is not easy, as you have to remain focused, and your niche has to have enough scope that you can provide regular content on it.

Identifying Your Niche

Narrowing down your topic and finding a specific angle may require a lot of thought. Try to see what subject areas are written about a lot, and which are the most popular with readers. A good indication as to the popularity of subject areas is the number of comments they generate. Think of specific areas you would like to read about. For instance, if you are writing about a sport, concentrate on a specific team, or even a certain player. The more you can narrow your focus, the more unique your blog will be.

Test the Water

A good way of seeing if your niche area is worth developing a blog about is to test out your ideas. Approach existing bloggers in the same subject area and ask if you can

provide a guest blog. Many bloggers are happy to post articles by others and often have a simple procedure for doing so. This also gives you a great opportunity to try out your blogging skills before you take the plunge.

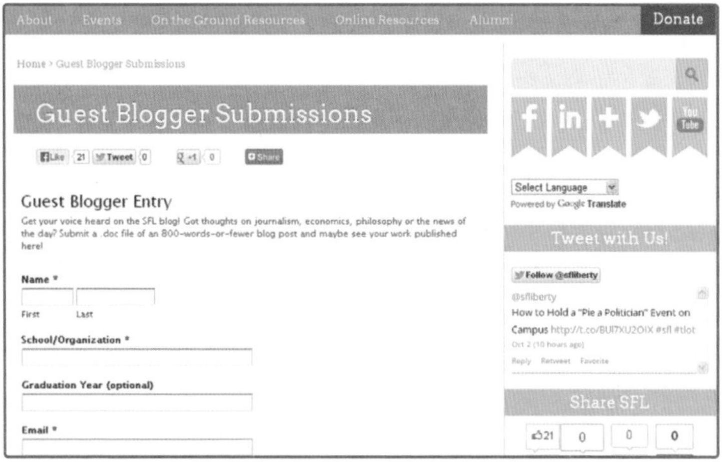

Right: Guest blogging for a blog in the subject area you intend to enter is a good way to test out your ideas and improve your writing style.

HOW AND WHEN TO BLOG

Once you have established the subject you are going to write about, you are nearly ready to begin blogging. But before you can start, there are certain things you need to do first.

BLOGGING PLATFORMS

In order to create a blog, you will need a blogging platform. A platform is the software needed to create and maintain a blog. We'll go into more detail about the various types of blogging software in Chapter Three, but for now, it is worth understanding the different types of blogging platform available. They fall into two categories.

- **Hosted**: This is blogging software that is hosted on a platform's server. You create and post your content online. These are easy to start and maintain, and many of them are free.

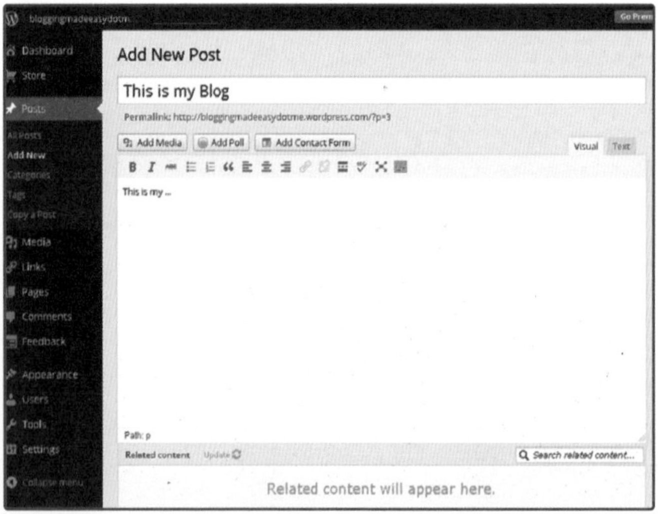

- **Self-hosted**: Sometimes called non-hosted, this is where you have to provide your own server to host your blog. This may mean paying for third-party hosting. Self-hosted blogs are more difficult for beginners, but they do offer more control over the blog and its layout.

Left: WordPress is a popular blogging platform which will host your content online for free.

YOUR BLOG AND DOMAIN NAME

Regardless of which type of blogging platform you opt for, you will have to decide on a name for your blog and obtain a domain name. A domain name, often called a URL (uniform resource locator), is the web address for your blog. While you can choose any name for your blog, because of the popularity of blogging, your desired URL may already be taken. In addition, with a hosted blog platform, you will be more restricted as to the URL you can choose. Hosted blogging platforms usually include their own suffix on a domain name, so if you opt for a WordPress blog, your URL will end with .wordpress.com.

Hot Tip

Try to come up with your URL first. This way, when you find one that is available, you can match the name of your blog to the domain name.

Relevance

For a new blogger, it is a good idea that your URL and blog name match and have some relevance to the subject the blog is about. If your desired domain name is taken, you may wish to rethink your blog name.

Thisismyblog.com
THIS IS MY BLOG
AFTER A FASHION, ANYWAY.
TUESDAY, MARCH 26, 2013
Cake (picture-heavy)
For reasons too complicated to explain, I found myself committed to baking a cake for a friend in another country who isn't going to be here to eat it any time soon. The only relevant part of the backstory is that I was meant to make a cake some months ago and made a bloody great mess on the floor instead. It's almost like I got DLA for a reason.
Nevertheless.

Above: It is a good idea to try to match your blog name and URL; this may mean thinking creatively to find a domain name which isn't already taken.

Keywords

A good way to find a unique but relevant blog name and URL is to search the popular keywords people use when looking for information relevant to your blog's topic. Using relevant keywords will also help people find you in search engines.

Hot Tip

When you type the most obvious keywords into Google, you can then check the bottom of the results page and find searches related to your keyword that people have typed in when looking for articles on the topic.

Above: Looking at related searches on Google is a useful way of discovering what else your intended audience is interested in.

Being Creative

Because of the unavailability of many domain names, some bloggers decide to come up with a unique name for their blog that has no connection with a keyword or the subject matter. While this will make it more difficult for people to find the blog, it does mean you can get the URL of your choice. In addition, it offers you the opportunity to develop a brand. Many of these blogs use made-up words (such as Mashable or Squidoo), portmanteaus (two words spliced together, such as Digerati or Hackintosh) or keywords with random words attached (such as Blogspot).

STYLIZING YOUR BLOG

Most blogging platforms, whether hosted or self-hosted, have a basic blogging template. However, to stand out from the crowd, you need to personalize your blog and make it look unique. In Chapter Three, we will discuss how to utilize themes and lay out your blog to make it user-friendly. Hosted blogs are more restrictive in how you can make them look, and the most individual-looking blogs tend to be self-hosted or built from scratch.

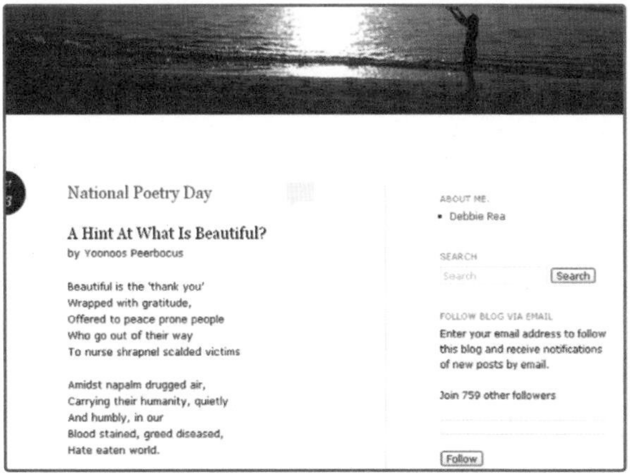

National Poetry Day
A Hint At What Is Beautiful?
by Yoonoos Peerbocus
Beautiful is the 'thank you'
Wrapped with gratitude,
Offered to peace prone people
Who go out of their way
To nurse shrapnel scalded victims
Amidst napalm drugged air,
Carrying their humanity, quietly
And humbly, in our
Blood stained, greed diseased,
Hate eaten world.
ABOUT ME
Debbie Rea
SEARCH
Search
FOLLOW BLOG VIA EMAIL
Enter your email address to follow this blog and receive notifications of new posts by email.
Join 759 other followers
Follow

Above: Think about when to schedule your posts. Co-ordinating them with significant dates or events in your subject area is a good idea.

24 HOURS CABLE
MEDIA DEBATES
SOCIAL NETWORK
FRIENDS
BLOGS

POSTING CONTENT

The basic role of a blogging platform is to provide a system where you can post your content on a regular basis. Blogging software works in reverse chronological order, so when you upload a new post, it always appears at the top. Your earlier posts will still exist and readers can scroll down and read them. This does mean, however, that if you upload two or three posts at a time, only one will get prominence at the top of the blog.

Scheduling Posts

If you choose to write several blog posts at one time, you do not have to post them all simultaneously. Blog posts can be scheduled, so you can upload multiple posts and have them appear at certain dates and times. This is useful if you wish to write all your posts in one go but want to have regular content appearing on your blog throughout the week.

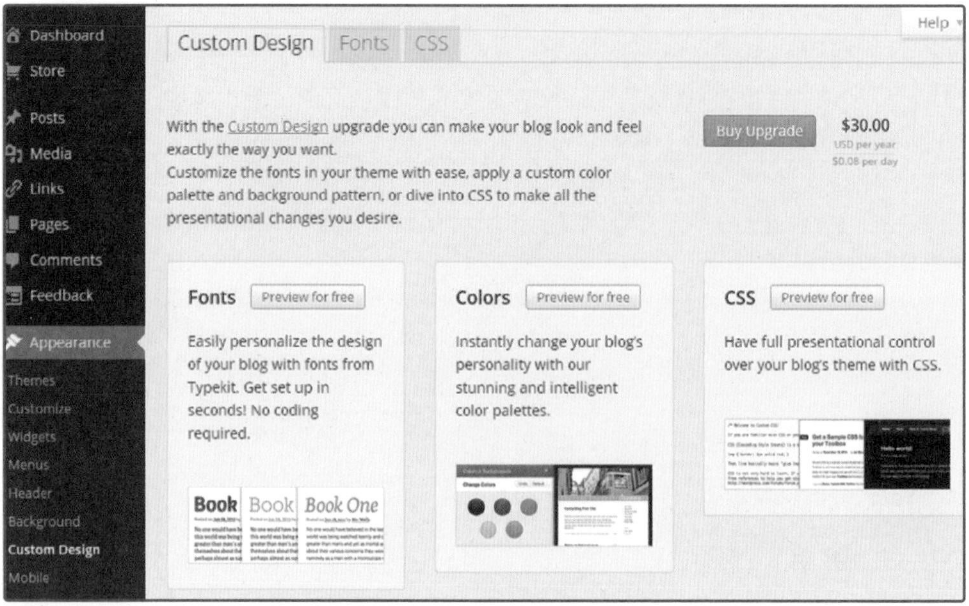
Dashboard
Store
Posts
Media
Links
Pages
Comments
Feedback
Appearance
Themes
Customize
Widgets
Menus
Header
Background
Custom Design
Mobile
Help
Custom Design
Fonts
CSS
With the Custom Design upgrade you can make your blog look and feel exactly the way you want.
Customize the fonts in your theme with ease, apply a custom color palette and background pattern, or dive into CSS to make all the presentational changes you desire.
Buy Upgrade
$30.00
USD per year
$0.08 per day
Fonts
Preview for free
Easily personalize the design of your blog with fonts from Typekit. Get set up in seconds! No coding required.
Book
Book
Book One
Colors
Preview for free
Instantly change your blog's personality with our stunning and intelligent color palettes.
CSS
Preview for free
Have full presentational control over your blog's theme with CSS.

Above: WordPress allows you to customize the appearance of your blog, including altering colours and fonts.

HOW OFTEN SHOULD YOU BLOG?

To attract and maintain an audience, you need to blog regularly. How frequently will depend on your subject, blog and the amount of free time you have. Some bloggers manage to post something every day, others post something weekly, while some blogs manage to maintain readers with fortnightly or even monthly posts. The key is to ensure you are always posting useful, informative and relevant content. There is little point in posting for the sake of posting. Readers will soon get bored if you are uploading weak content. In short, only blog when you have something to say.

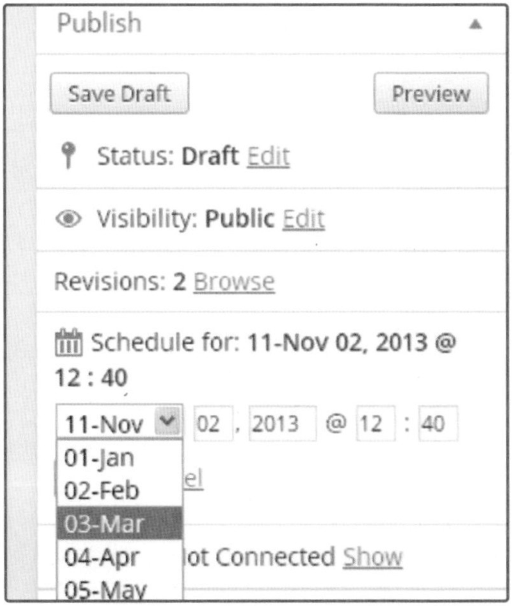

Above: Scheduling your blog posts allows you to write a chunk in one go when you have spare time, and then release them gradually.

When to Post

When to upload or schedule blog posts can make a difference when it comes to attracting an audience. Uploading a new post when nobody is likely to read it may mean your content goes stale. People like to read new content, so a post that is a few days old may be deemed old news. Unless you are keeping a corporate blog, your audience is more likely to visit your blog in the evening or at the weekend, and this is also when there is more social media activity, which is important when it comes to generating an audience, as you want people to talk about your blog and share links.

Hot Tip

Remember to consider time zones. Your main audience may not be in the same country as you, so do not post when they are at work or asleep.

Regularity

Perhaps more important than when you post is the frequency. People like blog posts to be regular. If you are posting every day, try to

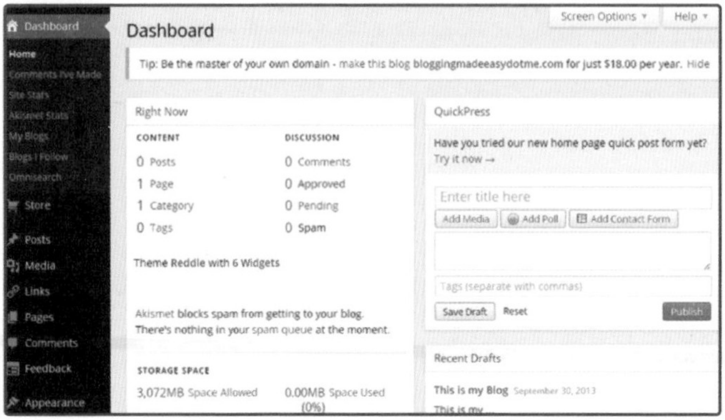

Above: The WordPress dashboard allows you to keep track of information such as how many posts you have written and published.

schedule your content for the same time, while for weekly posts, ensure they go up on the same day.

Breaking News

Another good idea is to ensure that your blog posts coincide with events connected to your subject matter. For instance, if you are maintaining a blog on a sports team, posting a blog after a big match will help generate a larger audience. This is because people like to read match reports and opinion soon after watching a game. This may be challenging, but blog posts like this do not have to be detailed. You can simply express your opinion on the event or match and ask others what they think. People like to discuss what they have seen and this is a good way of generating interest in your blog.

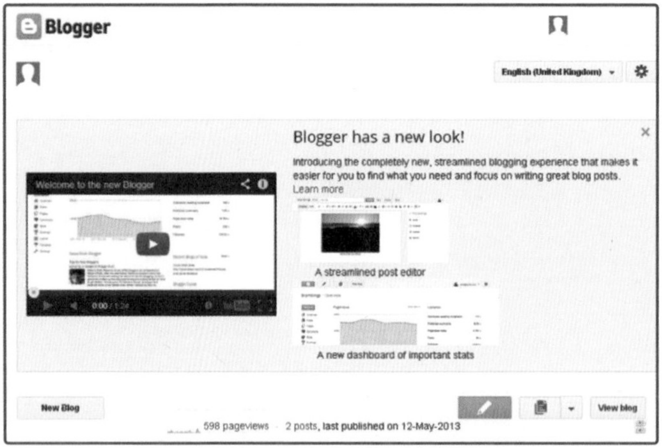

Above: Blogger is another free hosting platform, which you may wish to choose for your blog.

What Other People Are Saying

Another good time to blog is when other people are. People like to visit several blogs at a time, so if your content coincides with other blogs on a subject, you can tap into the same audience. Also, take note of other bloggers' opinions. Perhaps you have different views. This can help create debate and discussion and build up your audience.

GETTING YOUR VOICE HEARD

Once you start posting on your blog, you need to build an audience. Successful blogging means you have to market your blog and let people know who you are.

JUST THE BEGINNING

Creating a blog and then posting content is only the first step to blogging. Many new bloggers have to face the disappointment of realizing all their hard work has gone unrewarded because nobody is visiting their blog. There is a good reason for this. There are millions of blogs on the internet, so you cannot just sit back and hope that people will stumble across yours. Even the most successful bloggers had to start somewhere. Audiences have to be grown and maintained, and this is perhaps the hardest aspect of blogging.

Acorns to Oaks

You should never expect your blog to become successful straightaway. Audiences take time to grow. For most bloggers, this means starting small and building a steady but loyal following. Once you have a few regular visitors, you will be surprised at how quickly things can develop.

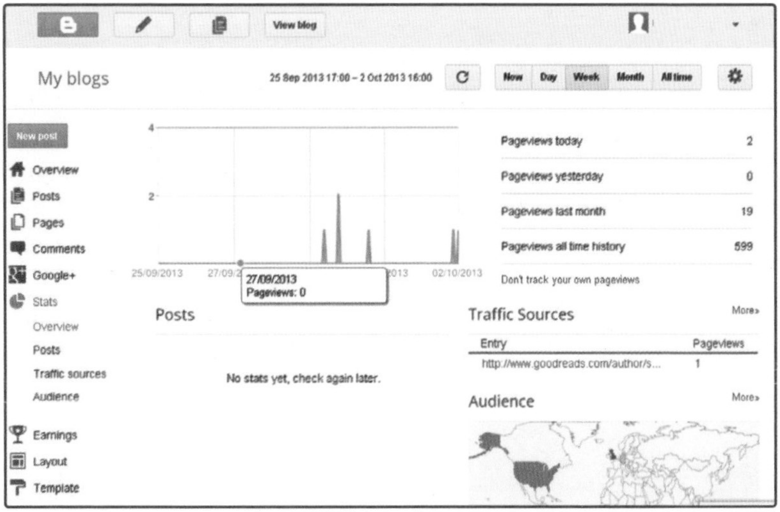

Above: Page view counters, such as this one on Blogger, allow you to see how many people are looking at your blog.

Above: Twitter is a useful way of letting your audience know when you have published a new blog post.

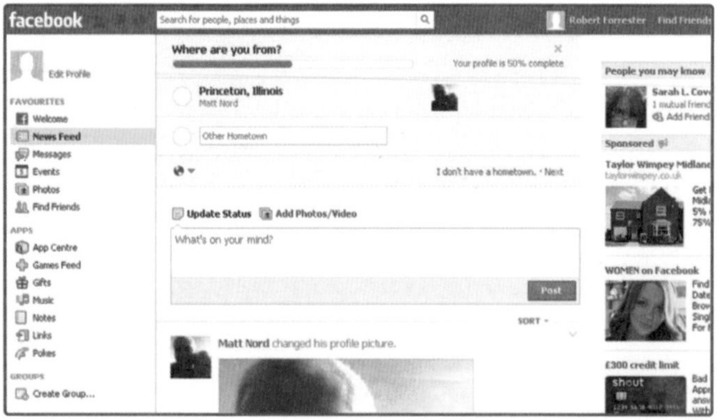

Above: Facebook is another good environment for promoting blog posts.

SPREAD THE WORD

The secret to building an audience is to let your readers build it for you. If a person likes your blog, they may very well tell somebody else about it, who in turn may tell somebody else. The best way to start this chain is to tell people you know about your blog. Start with friends, family and social network followers. However, do not expect everybody you know to take an interest in your blog. Everybody has different interests.

Feedback

Getting feedback is an important part of the process. While you may think your blog looks amazing, not everybody may agree with you. Ask for other people's opinions on both the layout and the content. Do not be defensive about your blog.

Hot Tip

Send people links to your blog on Twitter and Facebook and ask them to forward it on to their friends and followers.

Listen to criticism and make changes. After all, when it comes to building an audience, it is not your opinions that count, but those of your readers. If they do not like your blog, they will stop visiting.

CONTENT

The biggest factor that will determine a blog's success is the content. No matter what subject you are writing about, unless you can produce engaging and interesting posts, you will not build an audience. Think about the sorts of things that you enjoy reading. Even if you are writing on a specialist subject, do not bamboozle your audience with jargon and complicated ideas. Not everybody who reads your posts will have the same level of knowledge as you.

Be Useful and Unique

The key to engaging readers is to ensure you are writing content that is worth reading. It may sound simple, but you need to give people a reason to visit your blog. This may mean providing advice and information that people will find useful, or entertaining your readers.

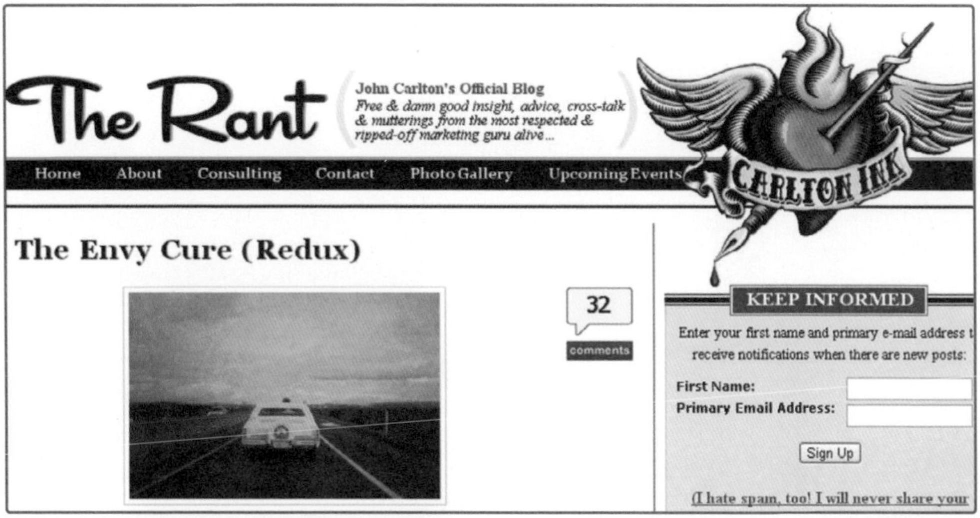

Above: The Rant is a good example of a blog with a clear and distinctive voice.

Do not just write the same sorts of things as everybody else. Try to be distinctive and have your own voice. Keep the tone and style of your writing consistent so you can become a recognizable voice on the topic.

> **Hot Tip**
>
> **Include relevant keywords relating to the topic in your posts, especially in the title and first paragraph, as this will help people find it on search engines.**

Short and Sweet

When it comes to blog posts, people do not like to read pages and pages of text. Try to be concise and put all the important information in the first few paragraphs. Make sure your title sums up what the blog post is about. Do not try to fool readers with a snappy headline that has little to do with the content. Finally, make sure you include images and headings to help break up the text (more on this later).

RESEARCH YOUR READERS

Only write what you think other people will want to read. While a blog can be a platform for your own opinions and ideas, if these are not consistent with those of your readers, you risk alienating them. Research websites, blogs and forums in your subject area and look out for things people are discussing.

Guest Blogging

One of the easiest ways to build an audience quickly is to guest blog. Guest blogging is very common and many blogs encourage others to participate. The great thing about a guest blogging slot is that you can tap into an existing audience, which should help steer people to your own blog (most blogs allow guest bloggers to link to their blog). Of course, this means you have to find the right blogs on which to guest blog. You may find guest slots on the most popular blogs are difficult to obtain, so maybe start with less popular blogs and work your way up.

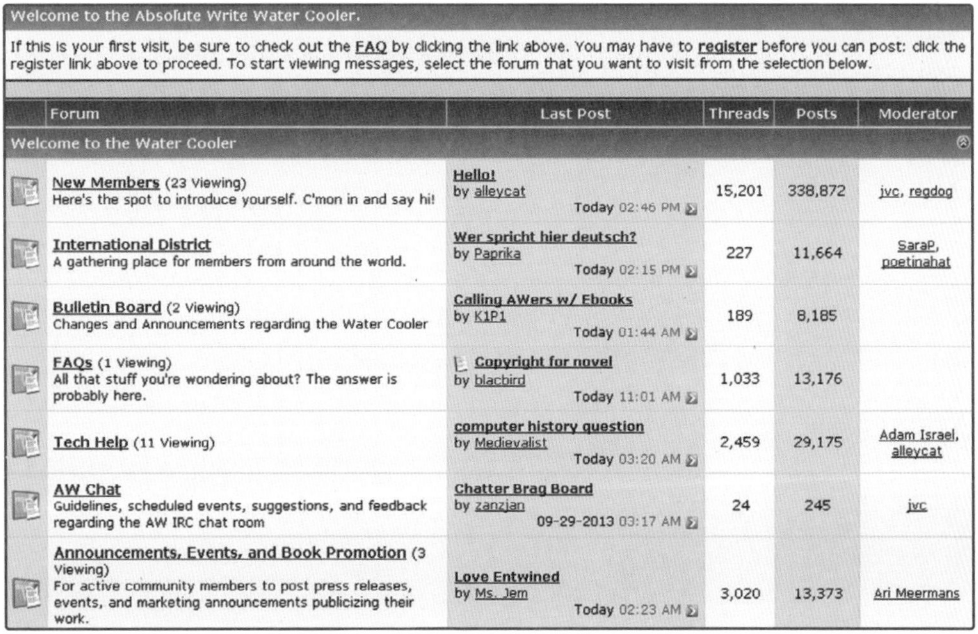

Welcome to the Absolute Write Water Cooler.

If this is your first visit, be sure to check out the FAQ by clicking the link above. You may have to register before you can post: click the register link above to proceed. To start viewing messages, select the forum that you want to visit from the selection below.

Forum	Last Post	Threads	Posts	Moderator
Welcome to the Water Cooler				
New Members (23 Viewing) Here's the spot to introduce yourself. C'mon in and say hi!	Hello! by alleycat Today 02:46 PM	15,201	338,872	jvc, regdog
International District A gathering place for members from around the world.	Wer spricht hier deutsch? by Paprika Today 02:15 PM	227	11,664	SaraP, poetinahat
Bulletin Board (2 Viewing) Changes and Announcements regarding the Water Cooler	Calling AWers w/ Ebooks by K1P1 Today 01:44 AM	189	8,185	
FAQs (1 Viewing) All that stuff you're wondering about? The answer is probably here.	Copyright for novel by blacbird Today 11:01 AM	1,033	13,176	
Tech Help (11 Viewing)	computer history question by Medievalist Today 03:20 AM	2,459	29,175	Adam Israel, alleycat
AW Chat Guidelines, scheduled events, suggestions, and feedback regarding the AW IRC chat room	Chatter Brag Board by zanzjan 09-29-2013 03:17 AM	24	245	jvc
Announcements, Events, and Book Promotion (3 Viewing) For active community members to post press releases, events, and marketing announcements publicizing their work.	Love Entwined by Ms. Jem Today 02:23 AM	3,020	13,373	Ari Meermans

Above: Looking at forums in your subject area is a good way of finding out what people will be interested in reading about on your blog.

Inviting Guests

Guest blogging can work both ways. If you are struggling to get a guest blogging spot, invite other bloggers to post on your blog. The great thing about hosting another blogger is that they will bring their audience with them.

Guest Blog: John Bennion

John has blogged for us before. He teaches at BYU and leads some amazing writing classes. He's smart, kind and funny. He has a book of short stories and a novel published, both with Signature books. He's also published a TON of short fiction.

Carol wants to know about my writing struggles and how I'm overcoming them. Am I overcoming them? What a novel idea! I think she really just wants to pour alcohol in my wounds.

My struggles:

I feel so good when I write. I'm in my natural space when I'm wrestling with words and ideas, imagining characters or reimagining real people. It's satisfying work. You can feel the "but" coming and here it is—but so much else gets in the way. My daughter's divorce hearings, my mother's heart problems, the psychological and moral struggles of my children that I want to fix. Then there is my teaching, the designing of questions and the reading of papers, both of which I love, but which take time. The peaches and tomatoes that need to be bottled before they rot. The blog I need to write two weeks late for my friend. All these things that want my attention. I know that when I write for myself first that these things will still work out.

Join 92 other followers

Follow

RSS for TUW

RSS - Posts

RSS - Comments

Recent Posts

Right: Inviting guests to post on your blog is helpful for increasing your followers, as they will bring their own audience with them.

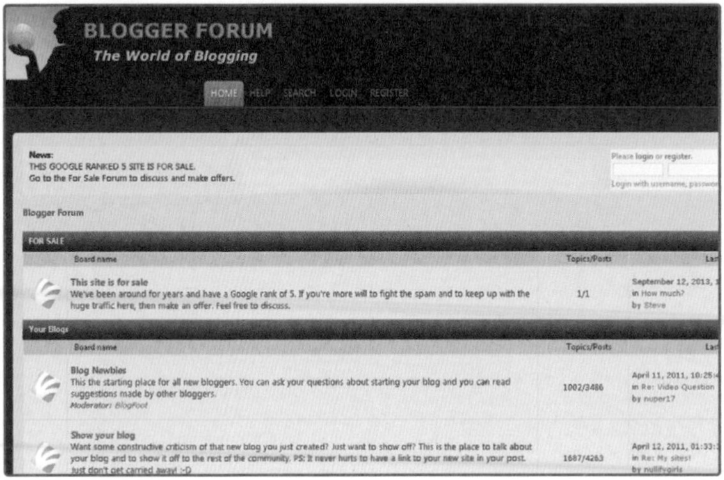
BLOGGER FORUM
The World of Blogging
HOME
HELP
SEARCH
LOGIN
REGISTER
News:
THIS GOOGLE RANKED 5 SITE IS FOR SALE.
Go to the For Sale Forum to discuss and make offers.
Blogger Forum
FOR SALE
Board name
Topics/Posts
This site is for sale
We've been around for years and have a Google rank of 5. If you're more will to fight the spam and to keep up with the huge traffic here, then make an offer. Feel free to discuss.
1/1
Your Blogs
Board name
Topics/Posts
Blog Newbies
This the starting place for all new bloggers. You can ask your questions about starting your blog and you can read suggestions made by other bloggers.
1002/3486
Show your blog
1687/4263

Above: Blogging forums are a good way to participate in the blogging community, enabling you to establish a name.

Not all bloggers will agree, especially if you are yet to establish an audience, but you may find somebody willing to help a new blogger.

Become Part of the Community

One way to secure guest blogging slots and entice other bloggers to your blog is to participate in the community. Become a regular contributor to the comments sections of other blogs. Think of this as microblogging, as it gives you the opportunity to advertise the sort of content you have on your blog. You can also earn a reputation as an authority on a subject, which may encourage people to visit your blog. Forums are also great places to get yourself known and find an audience for your blog.

Hot Tip

Follow popular bloggers in the same subject areas as your blog on social media such as Twitter and Facebook.

NEW BLOGGERS' CHECKLIST

Now you have decided to become a blogger, it is worth going over some of the key steps to starting a blog.

1. You have chosen a subject to blog about that you are both interested in and passionate about, and one that has lots of scope for writing regular posts.

2. You have researched other blogs of the same subject and come up with your own angle.

3. You have researched your readers and know what sort of things they like to read about.

4. You have chosen a good name for your blog that is appropriate to the subject you are blogging about.

5. You have chosen a blogging platform and selected an appropriate URL.

6. You have started networking and become part of the community relating to your blog.

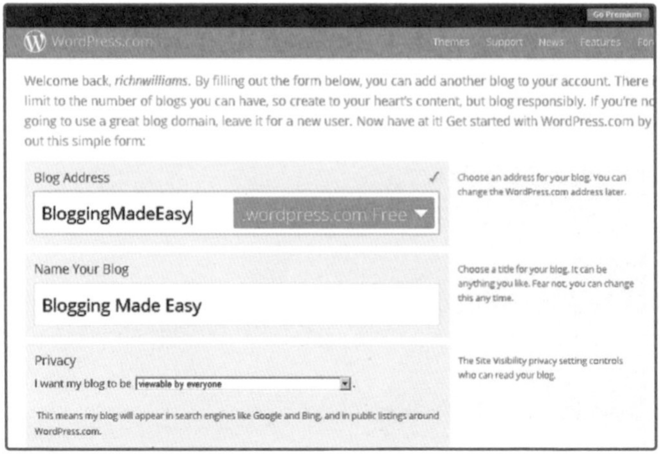

Go Premium
WordPress.com
Themes Support News Features
Welcome back, richnwilliams. By filling out the form below, you can add another blog to your account. There
limit to the number of blogs you can have, so create to your heart's content, but blog responsibly. If you're n
going to use a great blog domain, leave it for a new user. Now have at it! Get started with WordPress.com by
out this simple form:
Blog Address
BloggingMadeEasy
.wordpress.com Free
Choose an address for your blog. You can change the WordPress.com address later.
Name Your Blog
Blogging Made Easy
Choose a title for your blog. It can be anything you like. Fear not, you can change this any time.
Privacy
I want my blog to be viewable by everyone
This means my blog will appear in search engines like Google and Bing, and in public listings around WordPress.com.
The Site Visibility privacy setting controls who can read your blog.

Above: When you choose your blog name and URL try to keep it as relevant as possible to the subject you are blogging about

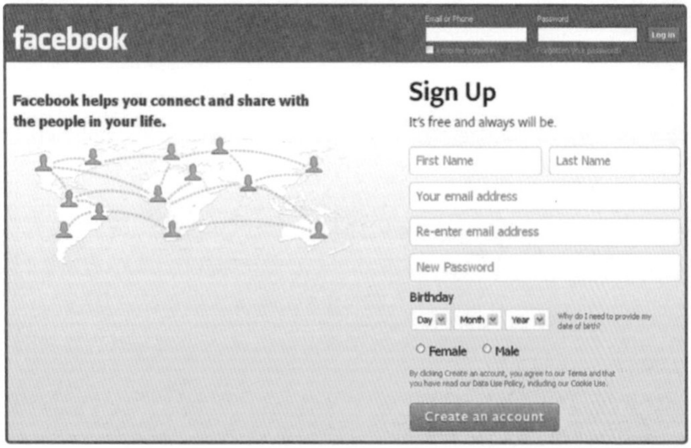

facebook
Log in
Facebook helps you connect and share with the people in your life.
Sign Up
It's free and always will be.
First Name
Last Name
Your email address
Re-enter email address
New Password
Birthday
Day Month Year
Female Male
Create an account

Above: Follow other bloggers in your subject area by using networking sites such as Twitter and Facebook.

GET BLOGGING

Now you understand the basics of blogging, it is time to start looking in depth at other aspects. In the next chapter, we will look at the different blogging platforms available. We will discuss the advantages and disadvantages of different platforms, and you'll find how-to information to create your blog and personalize it, as well as how to upload your posts and use the various tools available to make your blog appealing and attractive to readers.

BLOG

CREATING YOUR BLOG

BLOGGING SOFTWARE

Blogging software provides you with the tools you need to blog. Choosing the right platform for your blog can be quite confusing. Blogging software can vary tremendously, but if you understand what you want from your blog, it can help you decide which is best for you.

BLOG MANAGEMENT

Blogging platforms are software programs that enable you to create and manage a blog. Sometimes called blogware, these programs are specialized Content Management Systems (CMS), which enable the writing and publishing of blog posts, as well providing tools to stylize and manage a blog.

Design and Layout

Few people that go into blogging are experienced web designers, but with blogging software, you do not need to be. Most platforms provide a simple way to personalize and lay out a blog, enabling you to make it different to the millions of other blogs in the Blogosphere. The amount of freedom you have to get creative with your blog layout will depend on the platform you use and your technical experience.

Scheduling and Posting

The main function of blogging software is to enable you to publish what you write. Most blogging software provides the facilities to draft and edit blog posts, schedule them to appear on a certain date, as well as insert images and other multimedia. Nearly all blogging CMS work to the principle that the newest blog posts will appear at the top of a blog, while older posts appear below.

Hot Tip

You can write blog posts on word processing software and paste them into the blog platform. This enables you to take advantage of the advanced proofing tools offered by programs such as Microsoft Word.

Control

Blog platforms also allow you to categorize blog posts, insert links and tag posts. You can also set up blogs to accept comments from readers, with the software allowing you to moderate what people post. Furthermore, many blog platforms allow you to keep track of the number of visitors you get on your blog and find out which are your most popular posts.

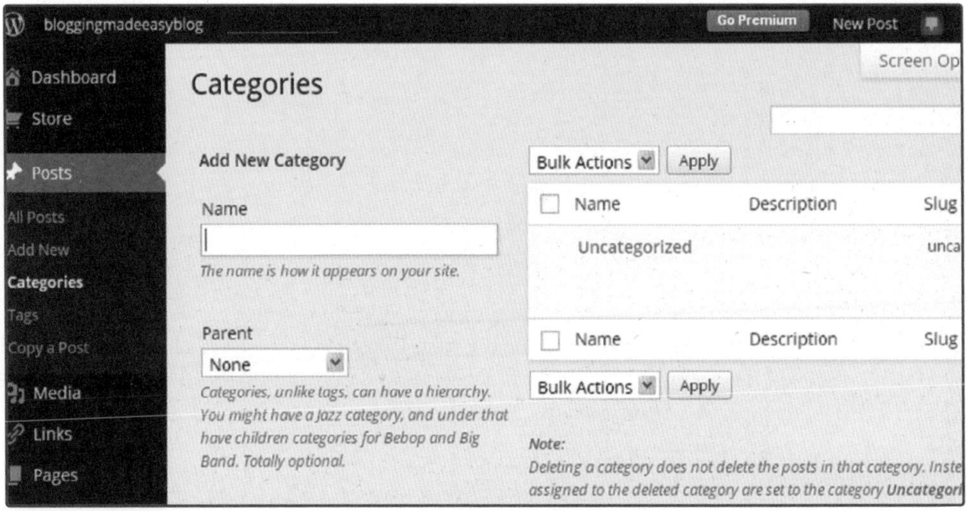
bloggingmadeeasyblog
Go Premium
New Post
Dashboard
Store
Posts
All Posts
Add New
Categories
Tags
Copy a Post
Media
Links
Pages
Categories
Screen Op
Add New Category
Name
The name is how it appears on your site.
Parent
None
Categories, unlike tags, can have a hierarchy. You might have a Jazz category, and under that have children categories for Bebop and Big Band. Totally optional.
Bulk Actions
Apply
Name
Description
Slug
Uncategorized
unca
Note:
Deleting a category does not delete the posts in that category. Inste
assigned to the deleted category are set to the category Uncategori

Above: Blogging platforms such as WordPress enable you to sort your posts into categories.

HOSTED OR SELF-HOSTED

The first decision you have to make when choosing your blogging software is whether to opt for a hosted or self-hosted platform. Hosting is simply the term used to describe where your blog will be located. All websites need to be hosted somewhere. A hosting company will store your blog on their servers and ensure it is visible on the internet.

Hosted Blog Platforms

Hosted blog platforms are the simplest way to get blogging. These online services provide everything you need to get started: a domain name, a location for your blog, and the software and tools to

Hot Tip

You can start on a hosted platform to see if blogging is for you, and then transfer your content to a self-hosted system later on, as it is possible to export all your blog posts.

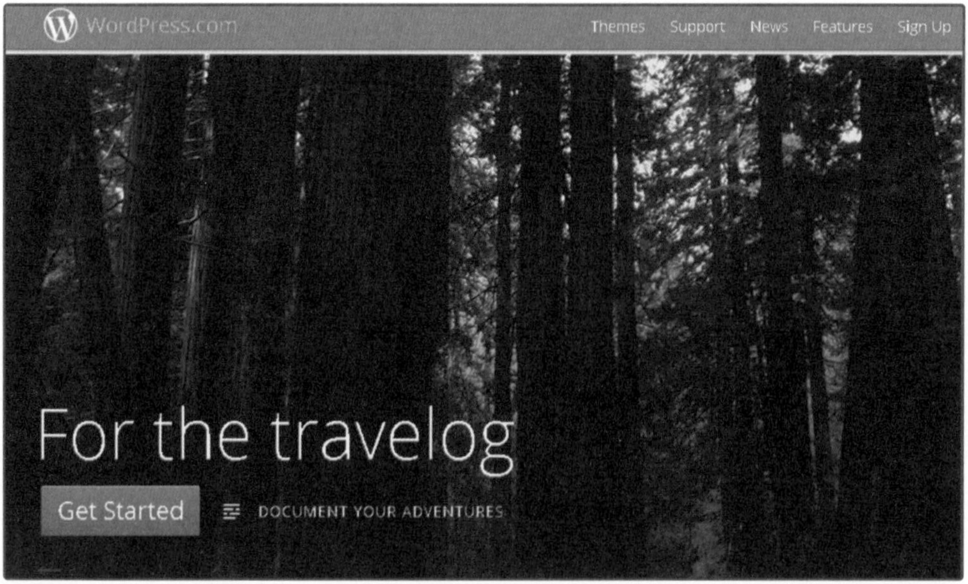

Above: Hosted blogging platforms, such as WordPress, have both advantages and disadvantages.

upload your posts. Some of these platforms are free too. However, what you gain in simplicity, you lose in control. With a hosted system, you may be tied to the platform's subdomain (such as www.myblog.wordpress.com). In addition, some hosted blogs do not permit advertising on their blogs and have strict rules as to the type of content they permit. Furthermore the customization features are often limited.

Self-hosted

Self-hosted blogs offer far more freedom. With these platforms, you may have to pay for the blogging software (although some do offer it free) and may also have to pay a third-party website to host your blog. The big advantage of these platforms is their flexibility. You are not tied to a particular domain name, so can purchase your own, and there are no restrictions on advertising or content. Furthermore, the customization features are far more advanced. However, you do need some technical knowledge to get the most out of them.

CHOOSING YOUR BLOGGING SOFTWARE

Understanding what you want from your blog is key in deciding your software platform. If you have specific goals and requirements, you may find self-hosted software your best option, but if you are lacking in technical skills, you may struggle with the added complexity.

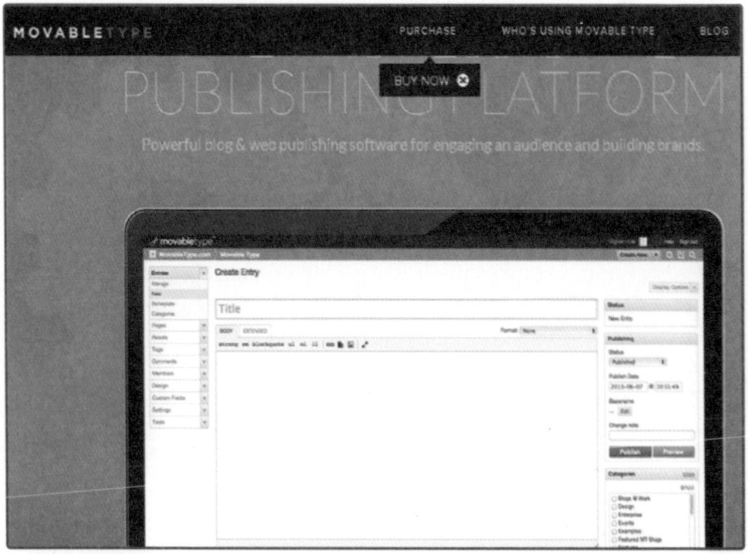

Above: Moveable Type is an example of non-hosted blogging software, which can meet more complex requirements.

Establish Your Goals

If you are starting a corporate blog or wish to make money out of blogging, a self-hosted platform will be the best option. A corporate blog should really be tied to a business' website with the same domain name. Your customers may regard a hosted domain as unprofessional or amateurish.

Customization

With any type of blog, it is important to stand out from the crowd. While most blog software allows you to change the layout, background colours, fonts and other elements on your blog, you may want something more bespoke. If this is the case, a self-hosted platform will be better for your needs.

Budget

Hosted blogs allow you to blog for free. Unless you can afford licence costs and subscription charges for the software, domain and hosting service, you are better off opting for a hosted service.

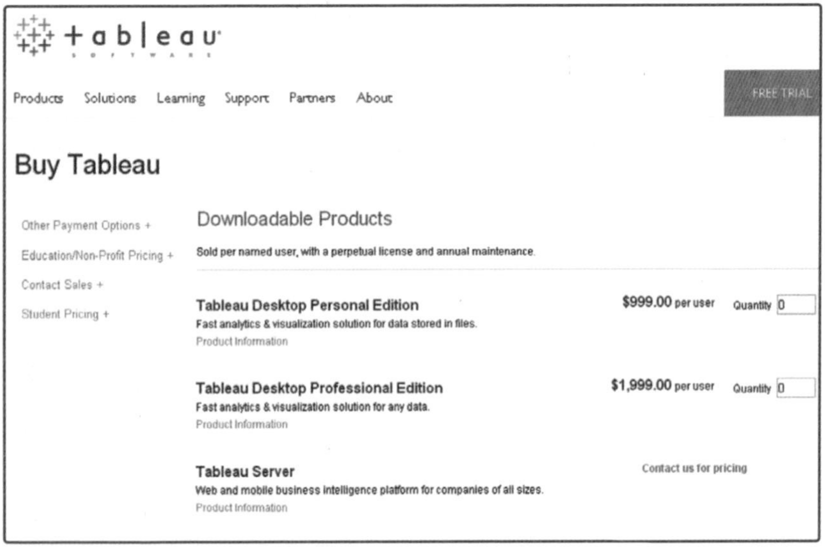

Technical Skills

Unless you have a basic understanding of blog software, you may find a self-hosted solution a little daunting.

Left: Different packages for non-hosted blog software will come at different prices; consider which one is most appropriate for your needs.

PAYING FOR THIRD-PARTY SERVICES

If you opt for a self-hosted blogging platform, there will be things you will need besides the blogging software.

- **A domain name**: The website address for your blog.
- **A web-hosting service**: The third-party company that hosts your blog on their servers.

Hot Tip

For a corporate blog, upload your blog to a subdomain of your company website using the suffix 'blog', for example, www.mybusiness/blog.com. This will save you having to pay for a new domain name and incurring hosting fees.

Domain Names

Domain names, also known as URLs, have to be both purchased and registered. There are numerous companies that make it easy to buy and register domain names, such as www.123-reg.co.uk and www.godaddy.com, but because of demand, you may find your chosen domain name has already been taken.

Web Hosting

Web hosting does not have to be expensive. Many hosting companies, such as www.gatorhost.com and www.1and1.com, offer hosting for less than £5 ($7) a month, although business users pay extra.

Above: Go Daddy is a hosting and domain service where you can buy and register domain names for your blog.

HOSTED BLOGS

For many people, hosted blogs offer the simplest and easiest way of getting involved in blogging. These all-in-one packages provide everything you need to create and maintain a blog, and there are many different options available.

MOST POPULAR HOSTED BLOGS

Hosted blogs vary in their complexity. Some hosted blogging platforms are extremely simple, aimed at new bloggers and those with little technical know-how, but they are quite limited in their functionality. The more complicated hosted blogging platforms do have more scope to create unique blogs, but have a steeper learning curve.

Above: Webnode offers free hosted blogs for business and personal purposes.

Free Versus Subscription

Some hosted blogging platforms are completely free, providing both the software and hosting facilities at no cost. However, some of these blogs do run their own advertising. Other platforms charge for hosting, but you have to pay for the software and for additional functions, such as extra themes. While some blogging hosts charge for their services, they do tend to offer a premium blogging experience with more features and flexibility than comparable software.

Hosted Blog Services

The number of hosted blogs available are too numerous to mention, and many new platforms arrive on the internet each year. However, some of the most popular include:

- **Blogger**: Google's Blogger has to be the easiest blogging platform to use. With a template designer and all the basic tools you need, Blogger is perfect for beginners.

- **WordPress**: This is the most popular blogging platform available. WordPress provides both a free hosted service and a free open-source software platform for self-hosted blogs.

- **SquareSpace**: Aimed at professional bloggers and businesses, SquareSpace charges a monthly subscription, but offers a very easy-to-use interface for designing and laying out your blog.

- **TypePad**: Requires a monthly subscription. TypePad is popular with business bloggers and corporate blogs.

Above: SquareSpace blogging software offers excellent customer support in return for a subscription.

- **LiveJournal**: LiveJournal combines blogging and social media. More suited to personal blogs, you can exchange photos and have more direct conversations and interactions.

- **Tumblr**: A free microblogging platform where users share links, pictures and videos.

- **Blog.com**: A free hosting platform powered by WordPress's CMS. Many people use it for its simple subdomain (yourname.blog.com). Blog.com also provides the ability to earn money from advertising.

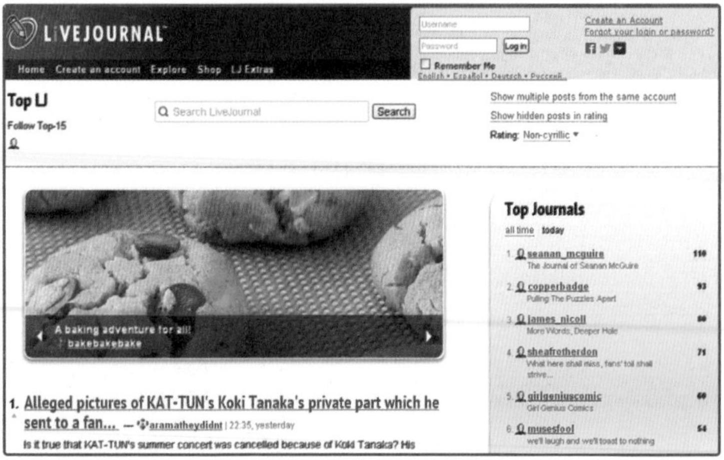

Above: LiveJournal combines blogging and social media to give an interactive experience.

Hot Tip

Most subscription services offer a free trial. Make sure you take advantage of these to ensure the blogging platform is suitable for your needs.

Making Your Choice

If you are thinking of opting for a hosted blogging platform, make sure it can handle all your requirements. Check the availability of domain and blog names when you sign up to ensure you can get something relevant to your blog. Do not be afraid to experiment and upload test posts before you begin marketing your blog. Make sure you are aware of all the terms and conditions attached with each platform, especially if you intend to monetize your blog or post content that could be contentious.

GETTING STARTED

Because of the sheer number of hosted blogs available, it is impossible to provide a guide to creating a blog in each one. However, in the next section, we will explore how to create blogs on two of the most popular hosted blogging platforms available.

BLOGGING ON BLOGGER

Google's Blogger is one of the easiest blogging platforms to get to grips with. Free to use, all you need is a Google email account to get started, making it an ideal platform for those new to blogging.

SIGNING UP

Anybody can start a blog on Blogger, but you will need a Google account.

1. You can sign up for a Google account in a number of ways, but perhaps the easiest is to visit www.blogger.com and click the **Sign In** button in the top right corner.

Hot Tip

Your Google username will also become your Google email address, so choose something that relates to either your name or your blog.

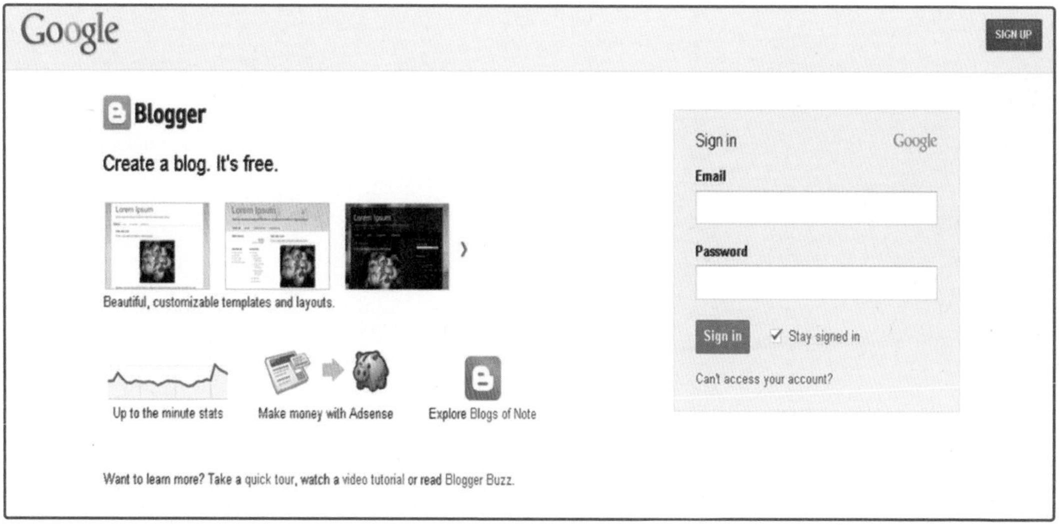

Above: Click the 'Sign Up' button in the top right corner to create an account and start using the Blogger platform.

2. You will then be asked to fill in your details, as well as creating a username and password. Once you have entered these details, click **Next Step**.

3. You can then update your profile, such as by uploading a photograph of yourself, but you can skip this if you so wish by clicking **Next Step**, which will complete the sign-up process.

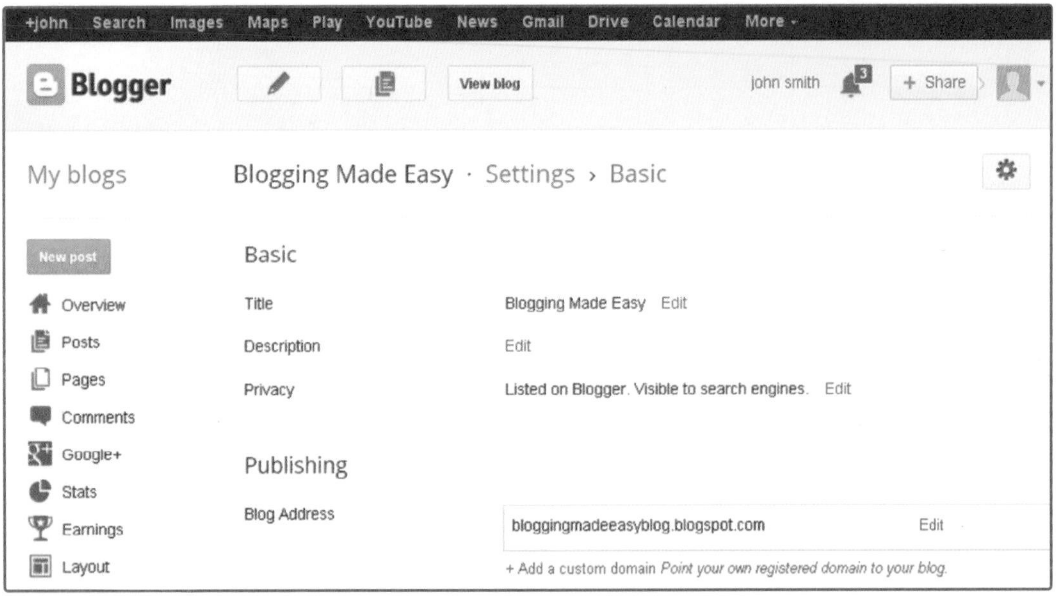

Above: The Blogger dashboard is the starting point when it comes to building your blog.

STARTING YOUR BLOG

Once you have created your account, you can use your username and password details to log in to Blogger, where you can start creating your blog by clicking the **New Blog** button.

1. Choose a name for your blog where it says **Title**.

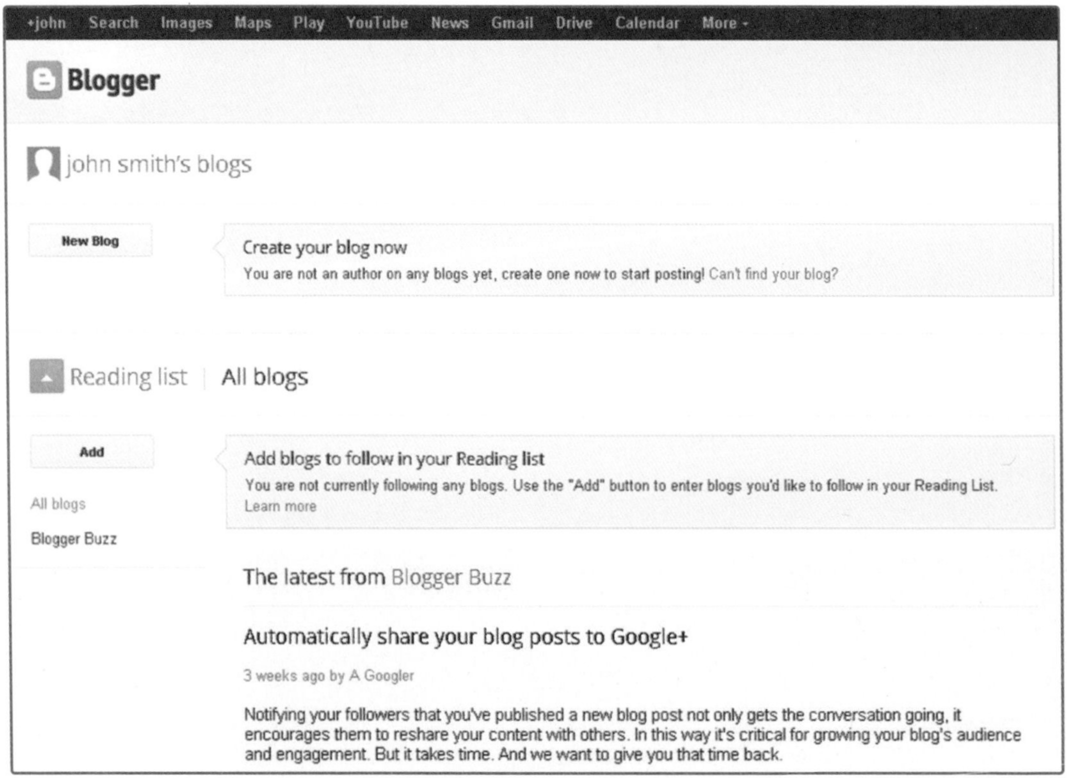

+john Search Images Maps Play YouTube News Gmail Drive Calendar More
Blogger
john smith's blogs
New Blog
Create your blog now
You are not an author on any blogs yet, create one now to start posting! Can't find your blog?
Reading list
All blogs
Add
Add blogs to follow in your Reading list
You are not currently following any blogs. Use the "Add" button to enter blogs you'd like to follow in your Reading List. Learn more
All blogs
Blogger Buzz
The latest from Blogger Buzz
Automatically share your blog posts to Google+
3 weeks ago by A Googler
Notifying your followers that you've published a new blog post not only gets the conversation going, it encourages them to reshare your content with others. In this way it's critical for growing your blog's audience and engagement. But it takes time. And we want to give you that time back.

Above: Selecting 'New Blog' allows you to start working on your blog.

2. Where it says **Address**, choose a domain name (URL) for your blog. All blogs on Blogger are hosted under the subdomain of .blogspot, so yourblogname.blogspot.com.

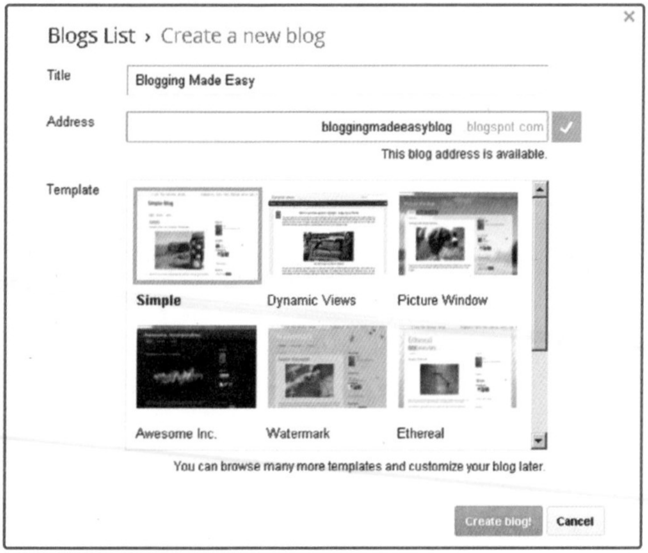

Above: Blogger enables you to create your blog in the style you want by offering template options.

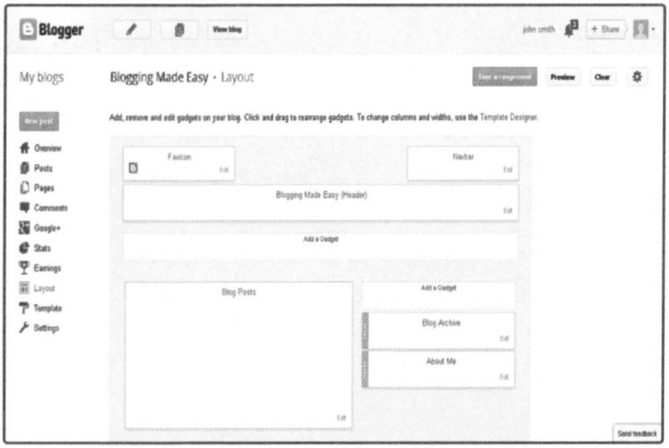

Above: Blogger allows you to rearrange the layout of your blog to suit your preferences and audience.

3. Choose a template for your blog. Templates are basic layouts and designs for a blog. You do not have to worry too much about which template to choose for your blog at this stage, as you can choose and customize your template later on.

4. Once you have selected your template, click **Create Blog**, and you will have set up your first Blogger blog.

Personalizing Your Blog

While Blogger has many different templates to make attractive blogs, to ensure you stand out from the crowd, it is a good idea to customize your blog to make it unique to you.

Customizing Your Template

You can adjust the template you have chosen in various ways, such as by changing the colours of the background and text, and adjusting the layout. You can even choose a new template altogether.

1. To customize your template, click the options arrow on the Blogger homepage and then select **Template** from the drop-down menu.

2. On the next screen, you can choose a new template or click **Customize** to make changes to your existing one.

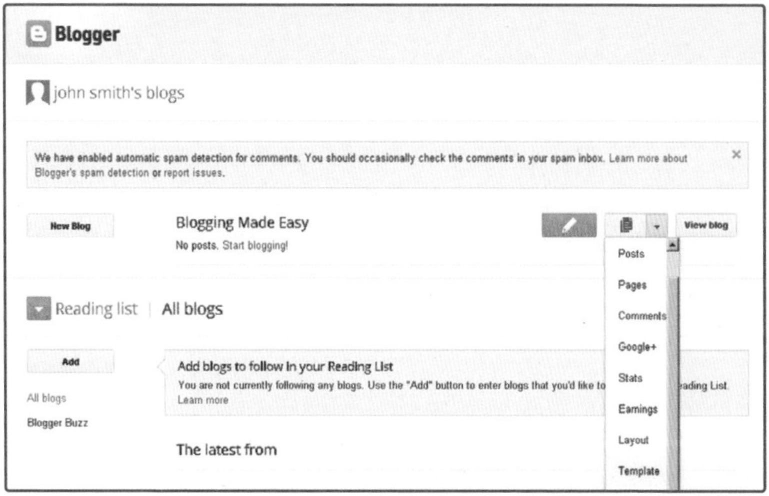

Above: Select 'Template' in the drop-down menu to choose a new template for your blog.

3. If you have chosen to customize your template, you can alter the colours, page width and basic layout of the template in the next screen. If you make changes, do not forget to click **Apply to Blog** in the top right-hand corner to ensure your changes are applied.

Customizing Your Layout

Once you have chosen and adjusted your template, you can make further changes to your blog by going to the homepage and clicking **Layout**. Here, you can add new elements, such as images and social media feeds, as well as fine-tuning the appearance of your blog.

Above: You can alter aspects of each section of text, including fonts and text colour.

Adding and Altering Elements

With Blogger, you can include all sorts of things on your blog page, such as images, headers, information about the blog and social media feeds. You can also remove elements that came with your template and adjust where everything sits on the page.

> **Hot Tip**
>
> **To adjust the position of your different elements, you can drag and drop them in the layout page.**

1. To make changes to an element, click **Edit** in the bottom right-hand corner.

2. In the editing window, you will be offered all sorts of options, such as changing the text, including images and adjusting the placement of the element on the page. You can also remove it entirely, although this option is not available on all elements, such as the header, as at least one of these has to be included on the blog.

3. To add a new element, click one of the **Add a Gadget** links on the layout page. Here, you can add all sorts of gadgets and applications to make your blog more interesting.

Blogger: Blogging Made Easy - Add a Gadget - Google Chrome
www.blogger.com/choose-gadget?blogID=1338929479280018441&sectionId=cross
Blogger
Add a Gadget
Basics
More Gadgets
Add your own
1 25 of 28
next »
+1 Button
Let visitors quickly recommend your brand and your content.
By Blogger
Google+ Followers New!
Highlight your total Google+ audience (both its size and some friendly faces) and offer visitors the chance to follow you on Google+.
By Blogger
Google+ Badge
Tell your visitors that you're on Google+ and let them follow you with a single click.
By Blogger

Above: Enhance your blog by adding elements such as a '+1 button' and a 'Translate' service, which gives your audience the option to translate content.

Adding New Pages

With Blogger, you can have several pages on your blog. This enables you to add promotional pages, lists of relevant websites related to your blog topic, or a biographical page. To insert a new page, simply click the **Pages** tab on the homepage and use the **New Page** drop-down menu.

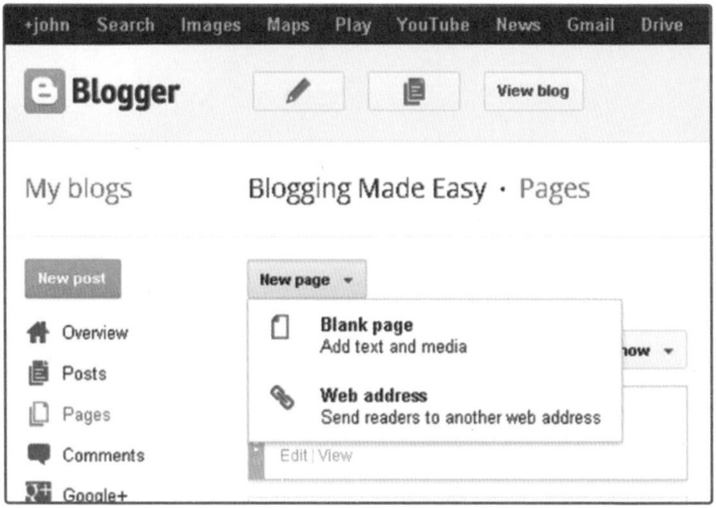

Above: You can add new pages to your blog by selecting 'Pages' from the menu on the left.

POSTING CONTENT

Just as creating a blog on Blogger is incredibly simple, so is posting content. To get started with your first blog post, click the orange **New Post** tab on the homepage.

1. All blog posts require a title, so insert yours at the top of the title page. You can then begin writing your first post.

2. Posts are written in the main window. You can use the tools at the top of the menu to format your text, add headers, change the colours and fonts, as well as add links, images and multimedia (more on this in Chapter Five).

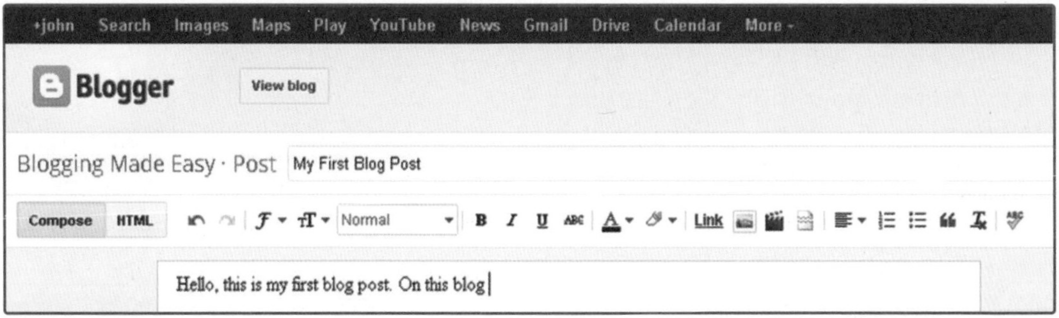

Above: When you write your posts on Blogger, you can use the menu bar for everything from changing text colour to adding links and images.

Hot Tip

To see how your post will look before you publish it, click the Preview button in the top right-hand corner.

3. Blogger automatically saves your posts as you write them, but you can click **Save** in the right-hand corner to save it manually as a draft.

Publishing Your Post

Once you have completed your blog post, you can either publish it straightaway by clicking **Publish** in the top right-hand corner of the page, or you can schedule the post to appear at any time you want by clicking **Schedule**. You can also adjust your time zone, so you can ensure your blog posts appear when your audience is active.

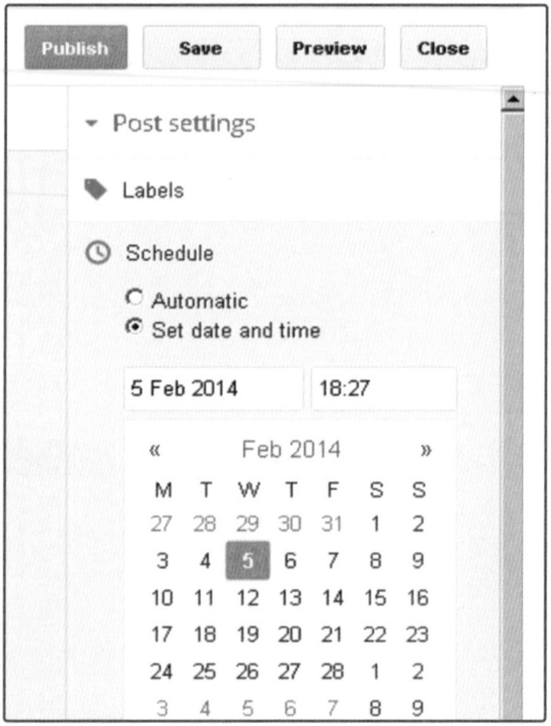

Above: When you decide a post is ready to publish, you can either do so automatically or schedule a date and time in the future.

Editing Your Posts

You can edit and delete blog posts at any time. Simply use the **Posts** tab on the left-hand side of the homepage. Here, you can see all your published posts as well as draft posts, which you can publish or schedule whenever you wish.

Viewing and Editing Your Blog

You can view your blog at any time simply by clicking the **View Blog** tab in the top left corner. You can also make simple edits by clicking the **Tool** icon on the bottom of each post or element.

MANAGING YOUR BLOG

Once you start blogging, you will want to know how well your blog is doing. Blogger provides some useful tools that allow you to monitor the number of views your posts are getting.

Overview

The overview page on Blogger provides all the useful information about your blog, such as the number of posts published, number of page views, how many people are following your blog, as well as any comments awaiting moderation. You will also find useful hints and tips to get more out of your Blogger blog.

Statistics

The statistics page is full of useful information.

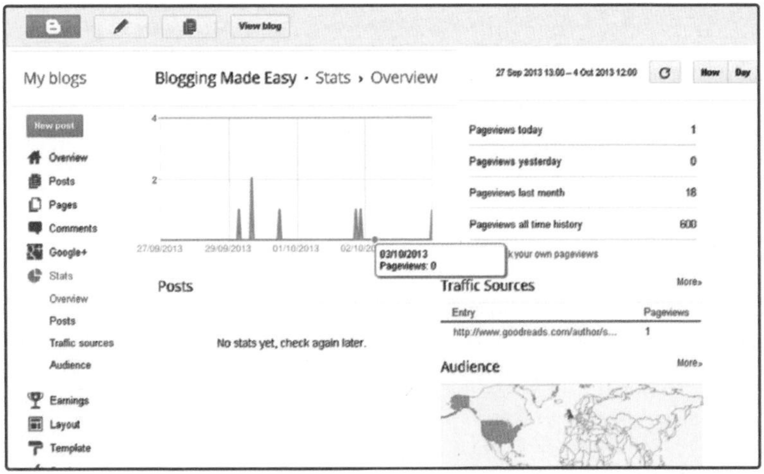

Above: The statistics page is a useful way of keeping abreast of how many people are reading your blog.

- **Pageviews:** See how many people have visited your blog on a daily, weekly, monthly or all-time basis.
- **Audience:** Not only allows you to see in which countries your visitors are based, but also which operating system and internet browser they are using.
- **Traffic sources:** Find out how people are finding you, such as which search engine referred them to your blog, or whether they came from a link on another website.
- **Posts:** Discover which posts are the most popular.

BLOGGING ON WORDPRESS

WordPress is by far the most popular blogging platform around. WordPress provides two options for the blogger: a free hosted service and free downloadable software for self-hosted blogs.

THE WORLD OF WORDPRESS

When it comes to blogging software, WordPress has been the number-one choice for many bloggers since it arrived on the internet in 2003. WordPress is not just a blogging platform, as many websites are built using it. In fact, WordPress powers a fifth of all blogs and websites on the internet.

Popularity

One of the reasons for the popularity of WordPress is that it is open source. This simply means it is free and anybody can help develop and introduce customizations to the platform. The WordPress CMS also provides the basis for many other blogging software systems and its interface has also become quite ubiquitous, so learning on WordPress can help you get to grips with all sorts of other blogging platforms. For anybody wishing to take blog creation seriously in the future, learning to use WordPress is a must.

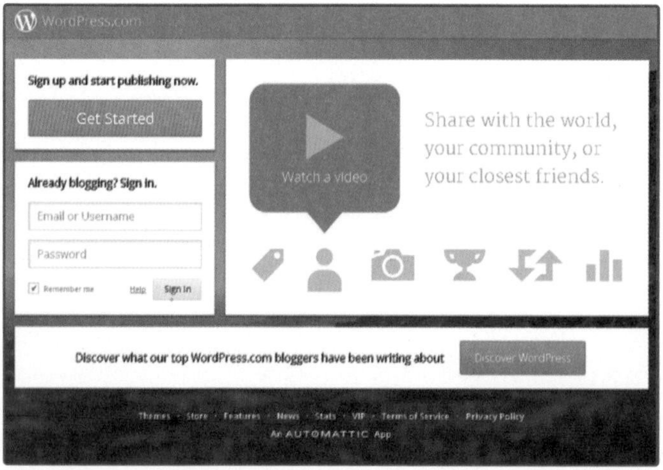

Left: The WordPress homepage gives you the option to 'Get Started'; select this to sign up and start creating your blog.

Hosted and Self-hosted

WordPress has two main websites:

- **www.wordpress.com**: A free hosted service, where you can blog for free under the wordpress.com domain. This online version of WordPress does have limited capabilities, but is a good place to learn to use the platform.

- **www.wordpress.org**: Provides a free downloadable version of WordPress that you can use to create blogs for hosting on third-party servers. This version is much more flexible and allows for more control than the hosted version.

STARTING A HOSTED WORDPRESS BLOG

Many beginners start blogging on a wordpress.com blog. There are restrictions on content and advertising, but you can have multiple blogs. To start one, all you need is an email address.

Signing Up

1. To start a hosted WordPress blog, simply visit wordpress.com and click the **Get Started** button.

2. Enter an email address, username and password. Usernames have to have a minimum of four characters.

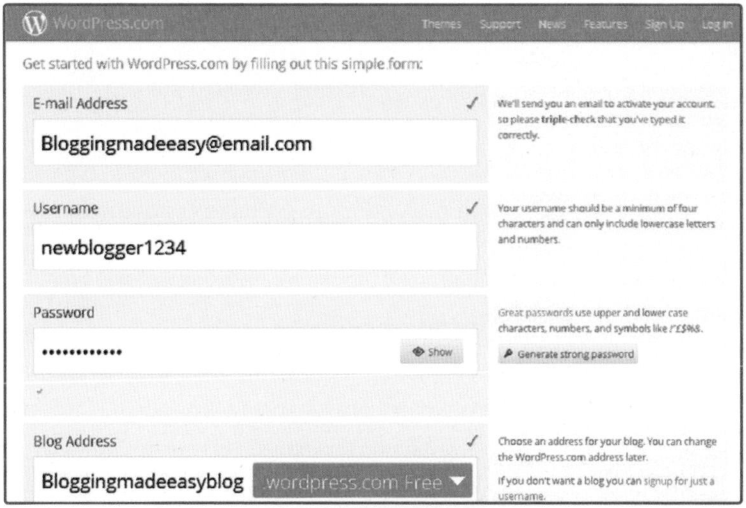
WordPress.com
Themes Support News Features Sign Up Log In
Get started with WordPress.com by filling out this simple form:
E-mail Address
Bloggingmadeeasy@email.com
We'll send you an email to activate your account, so please triple-check that you've typed it correctly.
Username
newblogger1234
Your username should be a minimum of four characters and can only include lowercase letters and numbers.
Password
Show
Great passwords use upper and lower case characters, numbers, and symbols like
Generate strong password
Blog Address
Bloggingmadeeasyblog
.wordpress.com Free
Choose an address for your blog. You can change the WordPress.com address later.
If you don't want a blog you can signup for just a username.

Above: To sign up, you will need to enter your email address and choose a username, password and blog address.

3. Choose a blog domain name and any additional upgrades.

> **Hot Tip**
>
> **WordPress allows you to purchase domain names so your blog does not have to end in .wordpress.com. These URLs are often cheaper than from a third-party provider.**

Upgrades

For an annual fee, you can upgrade your WordPress hosted blog to their premium version, which has several advantages over their free blogs. You can upgrade at any time, so it is probably best to try the free version first before spending any money for the following enhancements:

- **Domain name**: Gives you the chance to have a bespoke domain name that is not under the wordpress.com subdomain.
- **Extra space**: Free users only have 2 GB of space for storing blog posts and multimedia, but premium users can upgrade to 10 GB.
- **No advertising**: WordPress runs adverts on its free blogs, but premium users can avoid this.
- **Added design features**: You get more customization options on the premium version. You can also upload HD videos straight to your blog.

Terms and Conditions

Make sure you read the WordPress terms and conditions carefully. WordPress does have strict rules regarding content and does not permit advertising on its blogs. Your WordPress blog may be taken down if you are deemed to have broken any of the terms of service.

THE DASHBOARD

The main interface in WordPress is known as the dashboard. Here, you can design your blog, write and edit your posts and manage your blog. All of the functions are listed on the left-hand side and it is worth spending some time familiarizing yourself with the dashboard and the different menus.

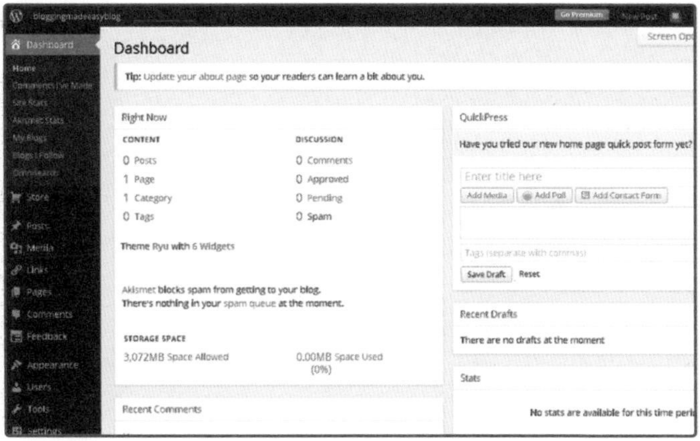

Above: The WordPress dashboard is the interface from which you will build and grow your blog.

- **Home**: Here, you will find an overview of your blogs. You can see how many posts you have made, look up statistics to see how many views you have received, as well as several other features.

- **Store**: Purchase themes, domain names and upgrades for your blog.

- **Posts**: View your posts, add a new one and categorize and tag your posts.

- **Media**: Where you can store images and video in your media library.

- **Links**: Links to other blogs and websites your readers may find useful.

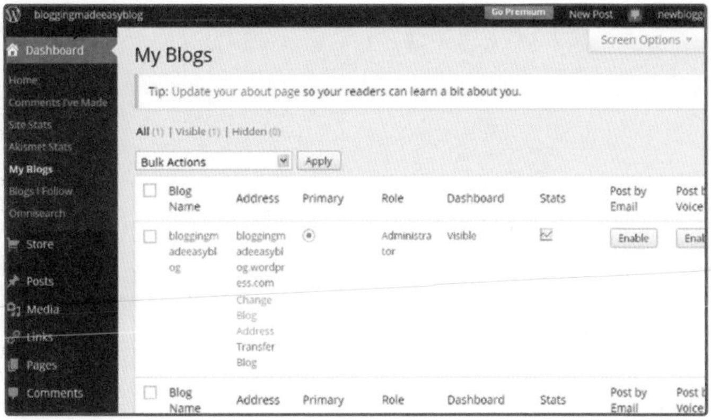

Above: The 'My Blogs' option in the WordPress dashboard menu can be a useful way to navigate between multiple blogs.

- **Pages**: View and add pages to your blog.
- **Comments**: View and moderate the comments others have made on your blog.
- **Feedback**: Where you can provide polls, ratings and request feedback from your readers.
- **Appearance:** Customize your blog to make it unique.

> **Hot Tip**
>
> **To make a quick post, use the QuickPress box on the dashboard. This is ideal for microblogging or posting brief messages.**

- **Users**: Control who has access to your blog. WordPress allows multiple authors and users to make posts.
- **Tools**: Various tools and features that can help you with your blogging.
- **Settings**: Control the functionality of your blog.

CUSTOMIZING YOUR BLOG

While the hosted version of WordPress is quite limited in its customization, there is still quite a lot of scope to personalize your blog and make it unique. In the **Appearance** menu, there are all sorts of options to customize the layout, change colours, add background images and alter the structure of your blog.

Themes

The biggest range of options when customizing a WordPress blog comes with the themes that are available. Themes are templates that provide the background to your blog. WordPress provides many free themes, but you can also purchase additional themes from their store. If you are creating a self-hosted WordPress blog, there are thousands of themes available on the internet.

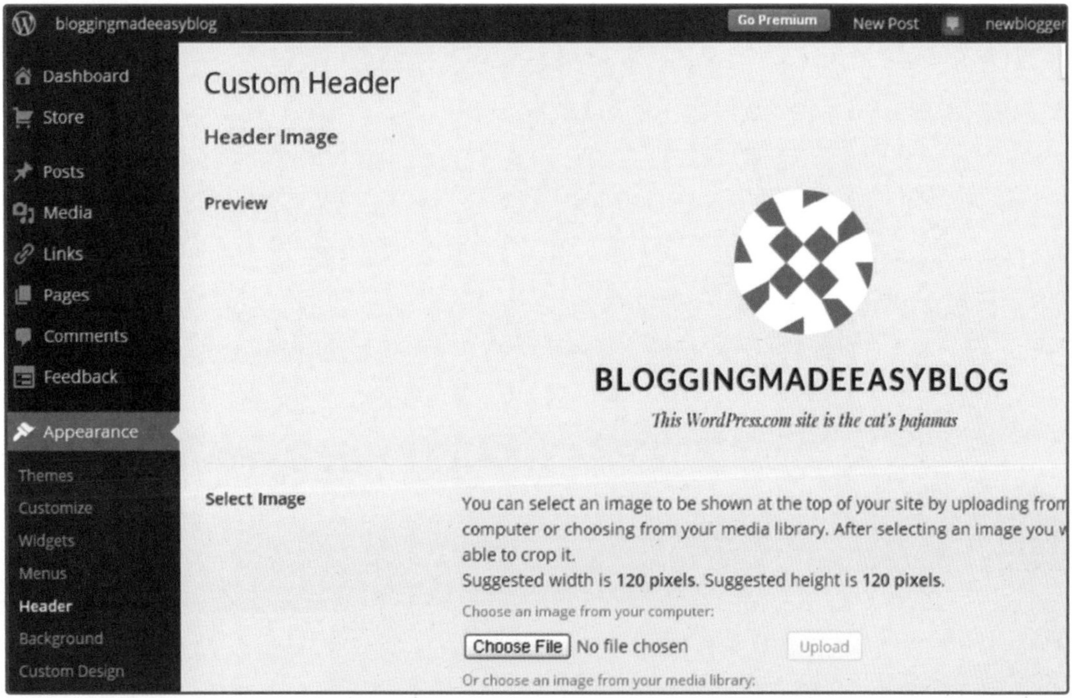

Above: Personalize your blog by customizing the page headers using the 'Appearance' option in the menu on the left.

Customizing Your Theme

Once you have selected a WordPress theme, your blog homepage will appear on screen with a menu down the side allowing you to customize it.

- **Custom design**: This is a paid-for upgrade that allows you more freedom to customize your theme, allowing you to make your blog look exactly how you want.
- **Colours**: Allows all users to change the background colour of the blog.
- **Header**: Change the image behind the header. You can upload any image you like.

- **Background image**: Upload an image to change the main background.
- **Front**: Choose whether to have a dynamic homepage, where your latest blog posts appear at the top, or a static page that does not change.
- **Site title**: Change the title and subtitle of your blog.
- **Logo**: Include an image or logo in the header.

Hot Tip

If you do not want to make changes to your theme now, you can click Cancel, and then use the Customize submenu to make your changes later.

Above: Customize your blog themes to make it match your topic and best appeal to your intended audience.

Adding Widgets To Your Blog

You can add all sorts of features to your blog pages, such as your contact information, an 'Aboute' column and even blog statistics by using widgets. You can select up to four widgets on any one blog page.

1. To add a widget to your blog, click **Widgets** under the **Appearance** menu.

2. Select the widget you want to include on your blog by clicking and holding down the mouse button.

3. Drag the widget to one of the Widget areas on the right-hand side.

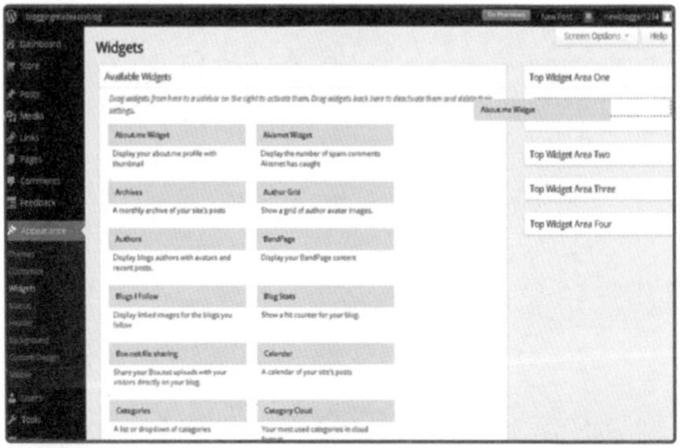

Above: You can select widgets of your choice to enhance the experience of your blog users.

Adding Pages

You can add different pages to your WordPress blog by using the **Pages** menu on the dashboard and selecting **New Page**. You can connect a new page to a main page and include links to it. Simply select the page you want to connect it to under the **Parent** menu.

Hot Tip

You can optimize your blog's theme for mobile readability by clicking Mobile in the Appearance menu and selecting or deselecting various mobile-friendly options.

POSTING CONTENT

It is easy to begin blogging in WordPress.
To start posting, simply go to the **Posts** menu on the dashboard and click **Add New**.

1. Enter the title for your blog post. Try to keep it short and ensure it sums up what the blog post is about. If possible, include a keyword to help people find it on internet searches.

2. Choose a format for your blog post using the **Format** menu on the right. This helps WordPress format the blog post depending on whether it is a standard post, image-based or a video blog.

Above: Enter your text into the box and use the tool menu to adjust as desired.

3. Write (or paste) your blog post in the main window. Use the tools above to bold text, add subheadings, insert links and images, and add features such as readers' polls.

4. WordPress does have an automatic save function, but you can save an unfinished post at any time by clicking **Save Draft**. You can also view your post at any time by clicking **Preview**.

Hot Tip

You can proof your blog posts using the ABC/Tick icon, which provides help with spelling, grammar and punctuation.

Permalink

Under the title of your blog post, you will see your permalink. This is the URL that your blog post will appear under. The permalink is normally your blog URL plus the title of your post, but you can change it by clicking **Edit**. This is useful if you have a long title, so making it easier to share a link to your post.

Publishing Your Post

You can schedule your post to appear at any time using the **Schedule** function to the right. If you want it to appear immediately, click the blue **Publish** button. WordPress also allows for a review process, so if there are other authors writing on the blog, you can approve their posts before publishing them.

Editing Your Posts

You can go back and edit an existing post by simply clicking **All Posts**, then selecting the post you wish to edit. If you cannot find a post, there is a search box. You can also delete a post by selecting **Move to Trash** in the drop-down menu.

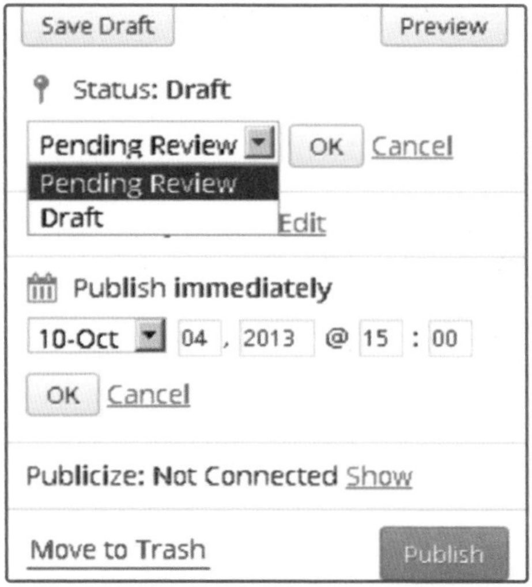

Above: Choose whether to save your post as a draft, publish it immediately or schedule a date for future release.

MANAGING YOUR WORDPRESS BLOG

WordPress provides plenty of tools to enable you to manage and control your blog. In fact, the number of options available to bloggers is one of the reasons so many people prefer it as a CMS. You will find most of the tools and options for blog management on the dashboard.

Site Stats

The **Site Stats** submenu allows you to see how many views your blog has received. Here, you can also see your top posts, what search engine terms visitors have used to find your blog, which websites have linked to your blog and the number of times your visitors have clicked on links on your blog posts.

Comments

You can set comments to be visible immediately or you can choose to moderate them. WordPress also has a built-in spam filter called Akismet that prevents spammers from infiltrating your comments.

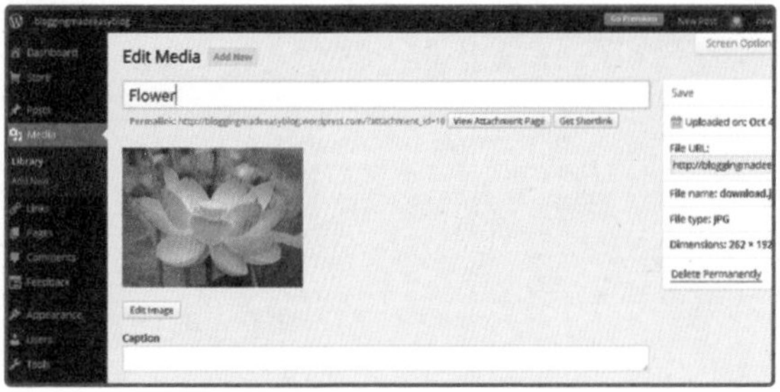

Above: Use the media library to add images.

Library

You can store images and videos in your WordPress media library, which is useful if you intend to use them again. You can also edit your images and multimedia and add captions.

Users

You can have several users on your WordPress account and control how much access each one has. This enables multiple authors to write blog posts. You can also edit your profile and personal settings and nominate somebody as administrator.

Tools and Settings

You can import a variety of plug-ins to help you control and manage your blog, such as search engine optimization (SEO) tools. In the **Settings** menu, you can make all sorts of changes to how your blog works. Some of the most useful features include:

- **Post by email**: This enables you to email posts to your blog and automatically publish them. A great way to blog on the move is to use a smartphone.
- **Email notification**: Receive emails whenever somebody comments on one of your posts or re-blogs what you have written.
- **Social media sharing**: Connect your blog to the most popular social networks and automatically notify your friends and followers whenever you have a new blog post.

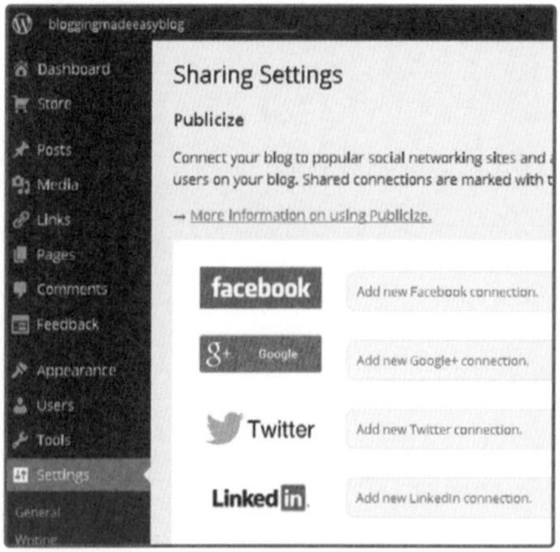

Above: Change your sharing settings so that readers can connect to social media sites through your blog.

DIY BLOGS

Some bloggers find hosted blogs too restrictive. A self-hosted blog provides the freedom to build and customize your own blog as you see fit, as well as choose your own domain name.

SELF-HOSTING

For anybody serious about blogging, a self-hosted blog provides far more freedom. While hosted platforms provide plenty of scope for customization, there is no limit to what you can do with a self-hosted blog. With a self-hosted blog, you can run advertising, monetize your blog, customize the blog exactly how you like it, and you are not tied to the subdomain of a blog hosting company. Of course, there are disadvantages to self-hosting blogs, such as finding somewhere to host it.

Hosting

All websites need to be hosted somewhere. While it is possible to run your own server, this is too impractical for most people, not to mention very expensive. For this reason, most bloggers use third-party servers to host their blogs.

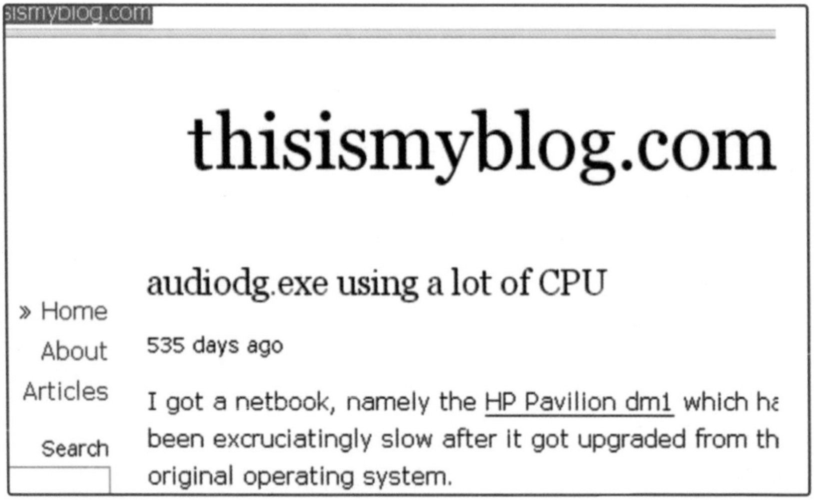
thisismyblog.com
audiodg.exe using a lot of CPU
» Home
About
Articles
Search
535 days ago
I got a netbook, namely the HP Pavilion dm1 which h
been excruciatingly slow after it got upgraded from th
original operating system.

Above: You will need to choose a unique blog domain name.

Attach a Blog to Your Website

If you already have a website, you may want to attach your blog to it. This is what most companies do with their corporate blogs. This means you do not need to register a new URL or find a hosting company.

DOMAIN NAME

If you don't have a website, then you will have to obtain a domain for your blog. A domain is the website address that your blog will be hosted under and that users will type in to visit your blog. Domain names have to be unique. Because of the sheer number of websites and blogs on the internet, your desired name may already be taken.

Choosing Your Domain Name

Your domain name does not have to be the same as your blog name, but visitors will find you more easily if it is. The domain name should be easy to remember and ideally quite short. You cannot leave spaces between words, but you can use hyphens and underscores.

Registration Companies

Once you have come up with a domain name, you will have to see if it is available and for sale. You can then purchase your domain name and register it. To register a domain name, you will need to use the services of a domain registration company. There are hundreds of such companies around, but some of the most established domain registration companies include www.123-reg.co.uk, www.go-daddy.com and www.easyspace.com.

Hot Tip

If you discover your desired domain name is already taken, see if it is available under a different domain extension, for example, under myblog.org or myblog.co.uk instead of myblog.com.

Registering a Domain Name

1. To register a domain name, choose a registration company and see if your domain is available.

2. Select your domain extension (.com, .org, .co.uk, etc.). You may find the price of your chosen domain varies depending on its extension (.com domains are often more expensive).

Above: You will need to check the availability of your chosen domain name.

3. Register your domain by creating an account on the registration website. You will need to enter your name and address to register a domain. Please note, for a business website, the domain should be registered to the business owner or managing director of the company, as it is a business asset.

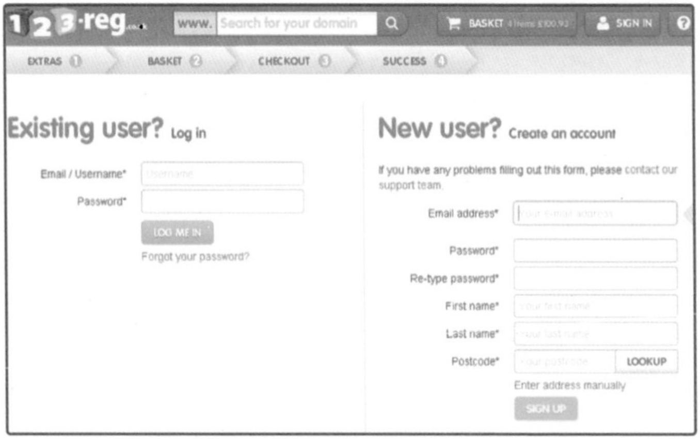

Above: Once you have found an available domain name that you are happy with, you will need to enter your registration details.

4. Pay for your domain name. Once complete, you should receive an email confirming your registration. Many companies also issue a certificate of domain registration.

Re-registering

You can only register a domain name for a limited time. The maximum is ten years. Some companies will register your domain for just a year or two, so you must remember to register the domain again when the time expires.

HOSTING YOUR BLOG

Once you have registered your domain name, you will need to find somewhere to host your blog. A company that offers hosting services is known as a web host. Web hosting can vary in price, speed and the technical help available. You have three options when it comes to web hosting.

- **Shared host**: This is the most common form of web hosting. You share digital space with other blogs and websites. This normally reduces costs, but you may be restricted on the amount of space available to you.

Above: There are different types of hosting available; think carefully about which is most appropriate for the kind of blog you want.

- **Reseller host**: These companies purchase server space from hosting companies and resell the space. This can be the cheapest option, and you often get better support options than going direct to a web host.

- **Dedicated web host**: This is the most expensive option and means you are hiring an entire server to host your blog. Because of this, your blog has to be either very big or very popular to warrant the costs.

> **Hot Tip**
>
> **Research your intended web host carefully. Use forums to see what other bloggers' experiences were using the same company.**

Signing Up with a Web Host

Signing up with a web host is normally straightforward.

1. Select the web host and service that is most suitable for your blog.
2. Give the hosting company your domain name and set up a username and password.
3. Commit to a contract. These can vary from 12 to 26 months.
4. Pay for your hosting service.

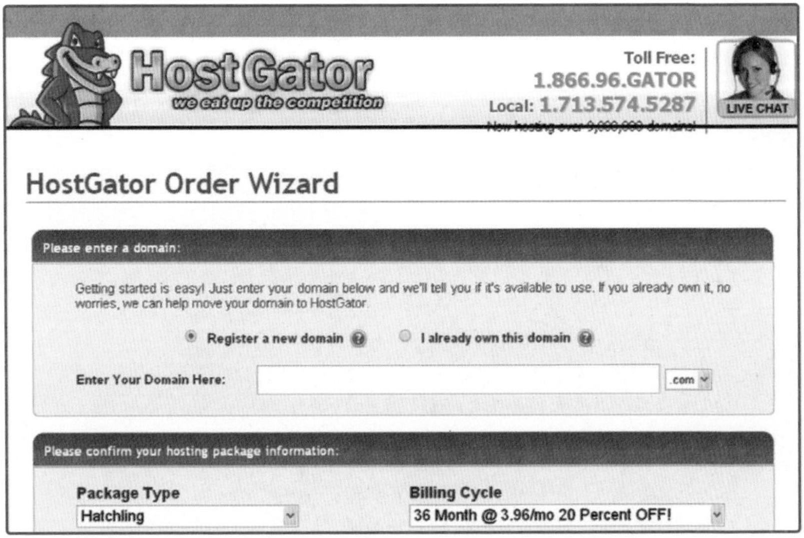

Above: To sign up for web hosting, you will need to commit to a contract and enter payment details.

BLOGGING SOFTWARE

The great advantage of building your own blog is that you can choose any blogging software you like. As with hosted services, self-hosted blogging software can vary from the simple to the complicated. It can also vary in cost, with some software such as WordPress completely free to download and use, while other software comes with a licence fee.

Choosing Blogging Software

When you are deciding on your blogging software, you need to think about several factors.

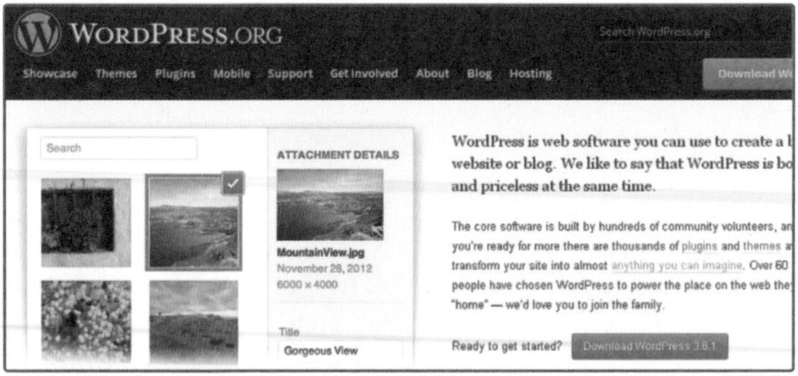

Above: WordPress offers self-hosted software which you will need to install on your computer.

- **Technical experience:** With some blogging software, building your own blog may require some understanding of HTML (HyperText Markup Language) and CSS (Cascading Style Sheets).

- **Costs**: Make sure you can afford the monthly subscription costs. If your licence expires, you will no longer be able to use the blogging software to manage your blog.

- **Your host**: Blogging software is not just used to build a blog, but it also acts as a Content Management System (CMS). For this reason, you need to install your software through your host, so you need to ensure your web host accepts your chosen platform.

Installing Blogging Software

Most web hosting companies make installing your chosen blogging software fairly simple, especially if it is a common platform such as WordPress. Most web hosts provide you with a control panel or dashboard from which you can install your software.

As an example, you install WordPress in HostGator by doing the following:

1. Log on to the control panel on GatorHost and select **QuickInstall**.

2. Under **Blog Software** select WordPress.

3. Click continue.

4. Choose a URL to install WordPress if you do not want it to be on your main domain (for instance, if you already have a website on the domain).

5. Fill in your details and choose an administrator username and password (used to make changes to the blog).

6. Click **Install Now**!.

Above: Choose your domain and administrator details.

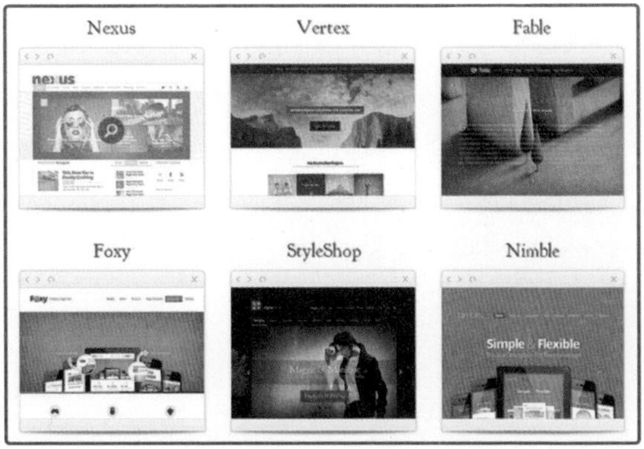

Above: WordPress offers a good selection of themes for your blog.

BUILDING YOUR BLOG

Once you have installed your blog software on your web host, you can begin to build your blog. If you have used a hosted platform such as WordPress before, you will find the self-hosted version very similar. However, you will have far more scope when it comes to customization. Furthermore, there are tens of thousands of themes available for your blog. If you are skilled with CSS and HTML, you can even build your own from scratch.

Downloading Themes

You can download WordPress and other blogging platform themes from hundreds of different websites. Some are given away free, while other must be paid for. Don't forget, whatever theme you choose to download, you can always customize it to suit your needs.

1. Find a theme you would like to install on your blog from one of the many theme vendors on the internet.

2. Pay for it and download it to your desktop.

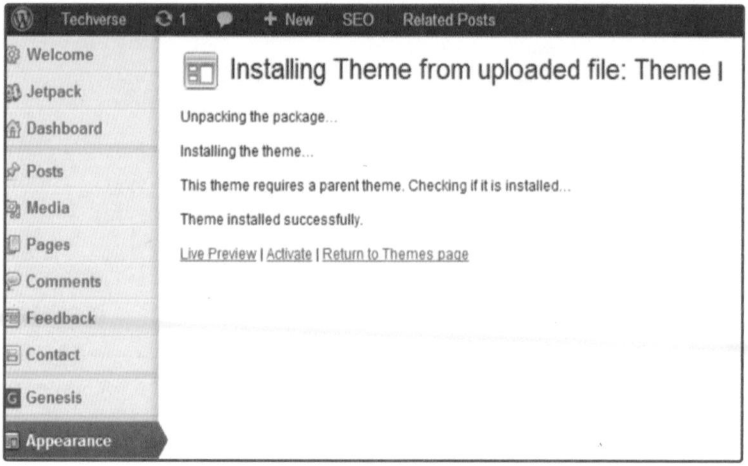

Above: The themes menu allows you to preview a theme and activate it.

3. Using the dashboard on WordPress or other blogging platform, go into the themes menu and click **Install Themes**, then **Upload**.

4. Select **Browse** and find the theme you downloaded to your computer.

5. Click **Install Now**.

6. Once the theme is installed, remember to click **Activate**.

Hot Tip

A simple search for WordPress themes on a search engine will bring up hundreds of results.

Making Your Blog User-friendly

When you build your blog, always keep your readers and visitors in mind. Do not make your blog too cluttered or difficult to navigate. Make sure it is easy on the eye. Avoid dark backgrounds and bright text, as this can cause problems with reading.

Hot Tip

The WordPress Import function allows you to import from many of the most popular blogging platforms directly, without having to download the blog first.

BLOGGING

To add new posts to your self-hosted blog, you simply have to log on to your software platform through your web host. Any new posts you publish will appear live on your blog for the whole world to see.

Using Plug-ins

Most self-hosted blogging platforms utilize plug-ins. These applications allow you to do a great variety of things, from managing advertising to improving your blog's SEO (Search Engine Optimization). As with themes, plug-ins can be bought (or downloaded free) and then uploaded and installed on your blogging platform.

TRANSFERRING A BLOG

If you have already been blogging, perhaps on a hosted blog, and now wish to transfer to a self-hosted blog, transferring your blog is usually straightforward. Most blogging platforms use a simple export/import system. In WordPress, all you have to do is export your content using the **Export** menu under **Tools**. You can export your posts, pages or the entire blog by downloading them as a single file to your computer. Once you have downloaded the files, you simply reverse the process on your self-hosted blog by using the **Import** menu.

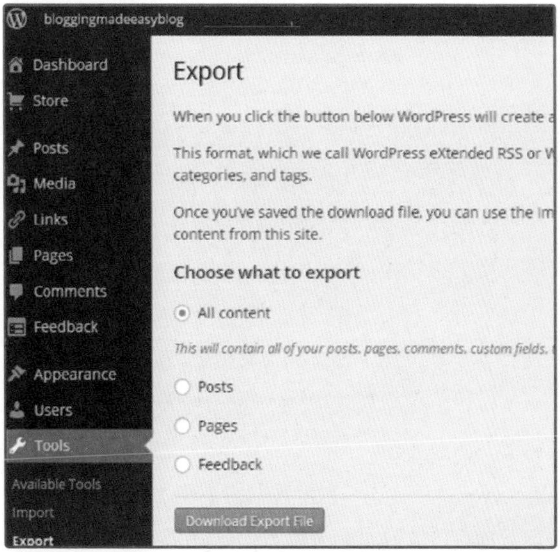

Above: Exporting a blog on WordPress is fairly simple and allows you to transfer your content between different hosting platforms.

WRITING YOUR BLOG

CHOOSING WHAT TO WRITE

A blog is only as good as the content it contains. One of the hardest aspects of blogging is writing good content on a regular basis and choosing what to write about.

BE CURRENT

People do not want to read something they have read or heard about before. Where possible, choose something current to write about. This may seem obvious, but many bloggers fall into the trap of repeating old ideas or regurgitating posts other bloggers have written. Keep your blog fresh and research your ideas carefully.

Read the News

Make sure you stay abreast of what is happening in your chosen area of interest. Pay attention to the news and write about any developments or issues relevant to your topic that you feel your readers will be interested in. However, do not just explain to your readers what has happened, but voice your opinion on it. A blog should not be just a news portal, but a place to express views and invite discussion on your chosen topic.

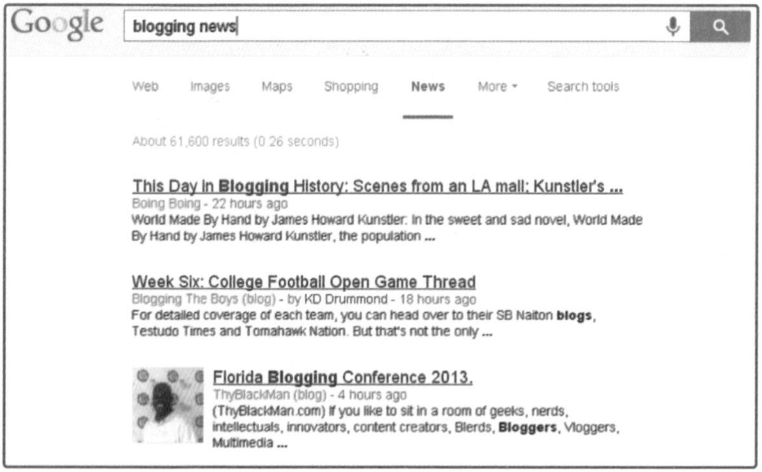

Google
blogging news
Web
Images
Maps
Shopping
News
More
Search tools
About 61,600 results (0.26 seconds)
This Day in Blogging History: Scenes from an LA mall; Kunstler's ...
Boing Boing - 22 hours ago
World Made By Hand by James Howard Kunstler: In the sweet and sad novel, World Made By Hand by James Howard Kunstler, the population ...
Week Six: College Football Open Game Thread
Blogging The Boys (blog) - by KD Drummond - 18 hours ago
For detailed coverage of each team, you can head over to their SB Naiton blogs, Testudo Times and Tomahawk Nation. But that's not the only ...
Florida Blogging Conference 2013.
ThyBlackMan (blog) - 4 hours ago
(ThyBlackMan.com) If you like to sit in a room of geeks, nerds, intellectuals, innovators, content creators, Blerds, Bloggers, Vloggers, Multimedia ...

Left: A Google search is a good way of keeping abreast of news in your area of interest.

Hot Tip

You can use tools such as Google Alerts to keep abreast of what is happening. Google Alerts will send you email updates of the latest Google results based on certain keywords.

Be Critical

Do not be afraid to be critical in what you say. If you have strong feelings or opinions, voice them. While your readers may not agree with your views, being outspoken will encourage comments and discussion. Some of the most popular bloggers are those who are not afraid to speak out and encourage debate.

Opinion

Blogs should be a place to voice your opinions, but make sure you are willing to accept the views of others. People like to engage with blogs. The best bloggers are those who try to interact with their readers. Rather than just voicing your own opinion about an event or news story, seek views from your readers by asking them what they think.

DEVELOP A UNIQUE ANGLE

If you are writing about a news story or event, one way to ensure your blog is fresh and original is to try to approach the subject from a different angle. An angle is really just a term to describe which aspects of a story or event to concentrate on. Try to tailor your angle to suit your readers.

Five Ws

A good way to find a unique angle is to separate a story into its different components. These are often called the five Ws.

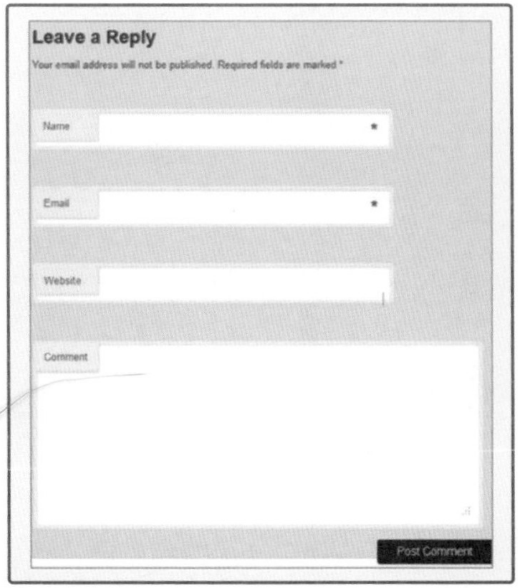

Above: A comments box on your blog is the perfect way to allow readers to offer their opinions on your posts.

- **Who**: Who is the story about?
- **What**: What happened?
- **When**: When did it take place?
- **Where**: Where did it take place?
- **Why**: Why did it happen?

Example

If a well-known person who was connected to your blog topic has just died, you may decide to write about their death. Alternatively, you could come up with a post remembering the person (an obituary), or you may choose to analyse the cause of death and ask questions as to what went wrong.

AVOIDING WRITER'S BLOCK

Writing regular content is not easy. Sometimes you may have no idea what to write about. Of course, you should never post just anything and should only blog when you have something to say. Maybe there are no new developments in your subject area, but that does not mean you cannot come up with blog posts. There are various ways of coming up with fresh, interesting content, even if you cannot think of anything to write.

Conduct Interviews

Blogging has become a lot more credible as a communication medium these days, so you may find people in your subject area are willing to be interviewed by you. You can ask people, politely and professionally by

> **Hot Tip**
>
> **Post interviews in a question-and-answer format. This can be more engaging for a reader and much easier than rewriting an interview into an article.**

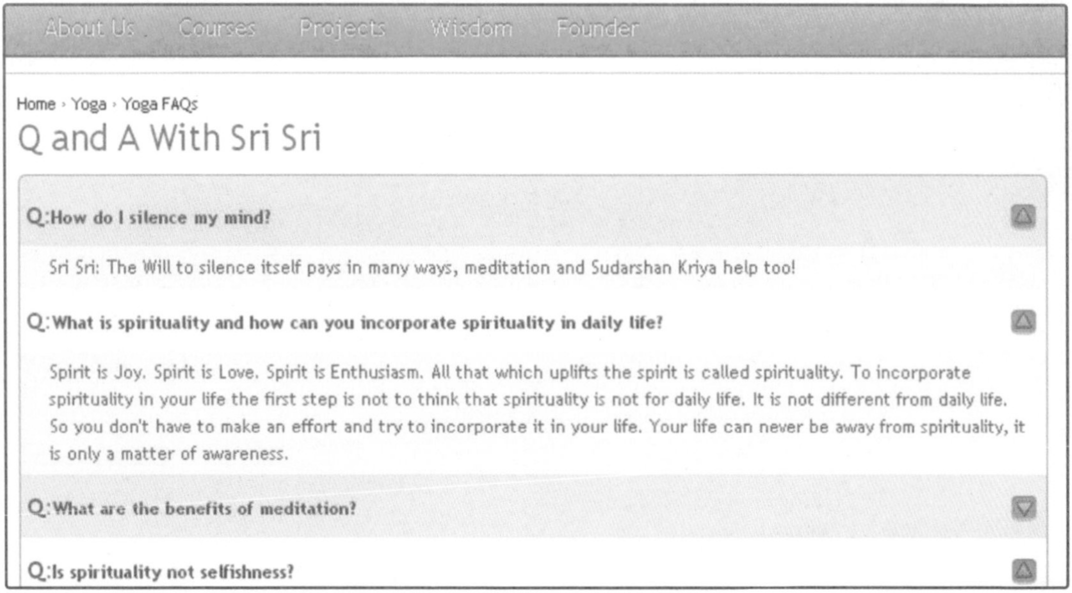

About Us
Courses
Projects
Wisdom
Founder
Home › Yoga › Yoga FAQs
Q and A With Sri Sri
Q:How do I silence my mind?
Sri Sri: The Will to silence itself pays in many ways, meditation and Sudarshan Kriya help too!
Q:What is spirituality and how can you incorporate spirituality in daily life?
Spirit is Joy. Spirit is Love. Spirit is Enthusiasm. All that which uplifts the spirit is called spirituality. To incorporate spirituality in your life the first step is not to think that spirituality is not for daily life. It is not different from daily life. So you don't have to make an effort and try to incorporate it in your life. Your life can never be away from spirituality, it is only a matter of awareness.
Q:What are the benefits of meditation?
Q:Is spirituality not selfishness?

Above: Interviews are now a popular medium of communication to include on blogs in specific areas of interest.

email, if they are willing to take part, and then send them a list of questions. You can even conduct interviews with some of your readers as a way of getting different views and opinions on your blog.

Hold Contests

A great way to encourage debate as well as providing interesting content for your readers is to hold contests. You do not need to give away physical prizes, as readers often enjoy just taking part. You can even ask your readers to judge the winner. However, if you are giving away a prize, ensure you write up a set of rules, including deadlines and how to enter.

- **Quiz**: Run a simple quiz, asking questions related to your topic.
- **Name that thing**: Run a contest to see who can come up with the best name for something related to your topic, for example, the funniest name for a movie.
- **Guess the picture**: Use a close-up photograph and invite readers to guess who/what it is.
- **Predict the result**: Ask readers to predict the results of an event, such as a sports score.

Conduct Polls

Another great way to encourage visitor participation is to hold regular polls. Polls can be on all sorts of things, for example, who is the best or worst at something related to your topic.

Setting up a poll in WordPress is pretty simple.

1. On the writing editor, click the **Add Poll** icon.
2. If it is the first time you have included a poll, you will be invited to create an account with Polldaddy.com. This is an automatic process, just click **Create a Poll Now**.

Right: You can create opinion polls on your blog on absolutely anything – a great way to encourage visitor participation.

Hot Tip

If you withhold the poll results from your readers, you can choose a day to announce them. This will encourage your visitors to come back to your blog to see the results.

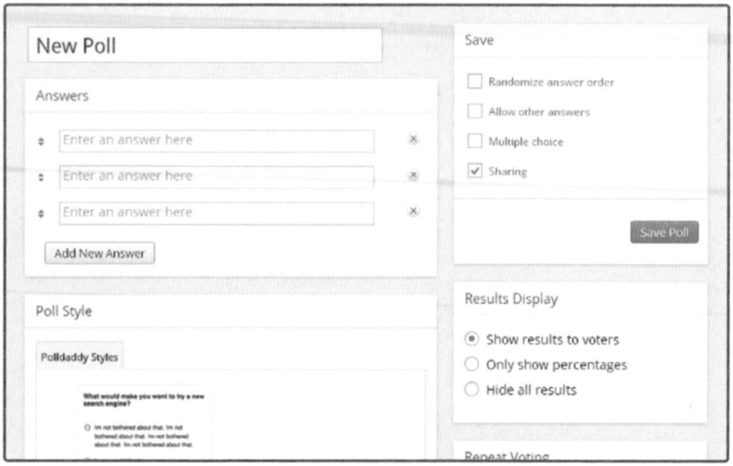

Above: Poll options can be changed to suit your requirements.

3. Configure the poll options to suit your requirements. You can allow voters to see the results, change the style of the results and have different formats for the poll questions.

4. Click **Save Poll**, and then **Embed in Post** to include the poll in your blog post.

Ask for Guest Posts

Inviting your visitors to submit guest posts is a great way to get new content. If you invite prominent bloggers in your subject area to guest post, you can also encourage some of their readers to visit your blog.

Ask for Ideas

Do not be afraid to ask your visitors what subjects they would like you to write about. This is not only a great way to come up with fresh ideas for content, but can also help you understand the sorts of posts your readers like to read.

Post Videos

If you find an interesting video in your subject area, why not include it on your blog? Embedding videos directly from places such as YouTube is not difficult (see Chapter Five on how to do this).

Above: Videos are a popular way to complement your subject area; visit YouTube for an endless supply.

Link to Other Blogs

A good way to come up with content is to refer to what other people are saying. Avoid just linking to another blog, as you run the risk of simply sending your readers elsewhere. Instead, provide your own opinion and views on what the blogger has written. Maybe you disagree, or you think there is another angle to the blog post worth exploring. If you are referring to what somebody else has written, always attribute it and post a link to avoid accusations of plagiarism or copyright infringement.

TAKING RESPONSIBILITY

While blogging enables you to write about anything you like, it does not mean you can say anything. Just as with mainstream publications, bloggers have to take responsibility for what they publish. This means you have to face up to any legal ramifications that could result from your posts.

Legal Issues

The laws on defamation vary from country to country and are very complicated. While it is rare for bloggers to end up in court, if you publish something that is untrue about somebody or something, you could find yourself in a libel lawsuit. Always check your facts carefully before you publish. If you are unsure of the validity of some information, attribute your sources to protect yourself from any legal consequences. You also have to take care not to publish information that is restricted by law. In addition, simply reprinting somebody else's work without permission or using copyrighted images could also have legal consequences.

STRUCTURING YOUR BLOG

Before you write your blog post, you need to plan it out. A good blog post needs structure in order to provide readers with an informative and entertaining read.

COMPONENTS OF A BLOG POST

When you compose a blog post, you should structure it in a way that provides the best possible reading experience and hooks your readers straightaway. You want to make sure that when people start reading, they continue to the end. The best way to do this is to structure a blog to include five basic elements.

From banter to false nines: The top ten most annoying words and phrases in modern day football
Thursday 3 Oct 2013 6:00 am
Share
142
14 comments
Next
By Daniel Jones
Metro Sport Reporter
What's popular on Sport
Khedira: Ozil makes Arsenal the best team in England
Januzaj double seals
Football has always thrown up funny phrases and nonsensical sayings. But as the game has changed in recent years so has the vernacular. Old favourites such as 'stick it down the channel' or 'put in the mixer' have gradually been

Above: A catchy title is vital in getting people to visit your blog.

- **Headline**: Your title needs to explain what the post is about as well as enticing people to read it.
- **Introduction**: Your introductory paragraph should introduce the topic and hook your reader.
- **Body**: This is the main part of your blog post, where you explore the topic and voice your opinions.

- **Conclusion**: A conclusion ensures a satisfactory end to a post. It should either sum up the main points or provide some closing thoughts.

- **Call to action**: At the end of a blog post, encouraging readers to comment, voice their opinions or read further posts helps engage your readers.

Hot Tip

If you find that you have lots of points to make or your post is very long, split it up into a serial and conclude each part by explaining what will be in the next installment.

Headline

We will examine writing a good headline in the next section, but the importance of a good title cannot be stressed enough. The title is what gets people to click on an article and brings them to your blog. A good title has to explain what a blog post is about and make people want to read it. Many people find it best to leave it until they've finished writing the blog post.

Introduction

Your introductory paragraph is by far the most important. A good introduction should explain clearly what the blog post is about as well as hooking your readers. An introduction can be a single sentence or paragraph, but it has to be punchy and well written. If your introduction is flat and boring, visitors will not want to carry on reading.

Body

The body of your blog post is where you go into more detail. Blog posts can be any length, but always ensure you write in short paragraphs. People do not like seeing large chunks of text. Also, break up the body of your blog post with images and subheadings.

The Battle for Social
This small change to Google's search features reveals an evolution of the web that is an early indicator of the growing battle for social that will over time produce winners and losers but will also create a web that will surprise you with its speed and capabilities. The announcement and launching of Google+ saw Zuckerberg respond with a a Skype feature offering free video calls and promising more to come.
The survival of the social species is a digital battle that will create opportunities and disrupt traditional business models for decades to come.
Social is about Sharing
All marketers know that if you can make something so shareable that it goes viral then you will produce results for brands that will sell products, make people famous and maybe even position your agency as part of marketing folklore.
You only have to look at viral videos such as the Old Spice YouTube videos to see the results of that.
Marketers also know that sharing by peers and friends creates more traffic and trust than brand advertising so motivating sharing is the holy grail of social marketing
Find us on Facebook
Like
Facebook social plugin

Above: Subheadings improve clarity within a blog post, allowing the reader to absorb information more easily.

Conclusion

Many people forget about a conclusion, but just as a good introduction will encourage somebody to read the rest of your post, a good conclusion will encourage people to read your other posts. Blog posts that stop abruptly or tail off can leave readers frustrated. Summing up your main points or closing off with a final thought helps to provide a satisfying read.

Call to Action

If you have managed to grab readers' attention long enough to read your blog post, it is a waste to simply let them leave your blog. Encourage them to leave a comment, read further posts in a series or provide buttons so they can share the post with their friends on social networks (more on this in Chapter Four).

– Covers Designed and Finished: 1. Covers finished month-to-date: 1 Covers
For projects finished in the first two months and links to the posts, click on the Wri
tab above.
For projects finished this month and where you can read them, click continue read
Continue reading →
Share
Tweet
Email
ShareThis
Like
0
+1
Pinterest
Posted in Challenge, On Writing, publishing, Writing in Public | Tagged challenge, publishing, Writing, Writing in
comment

Above: Social media buttons are a great way for the reader to share the post on social media sites.

PLANNING YOUR BLOG POST

Before you sit down and write your blog post, it is worth taking time to plan it out. A good way of doing this is to make a list of the main points you want to include. Think about what subheadings to use for each point, and experiment with the order of your points to see which order makes the most logical sense.

Using Subheadings

Subheadings are important for readability. While you can simply embolden your heading, it is best to use the subheadings function on your blogging software, as this helps with formatting your blog properly on different internet browsers and devices.

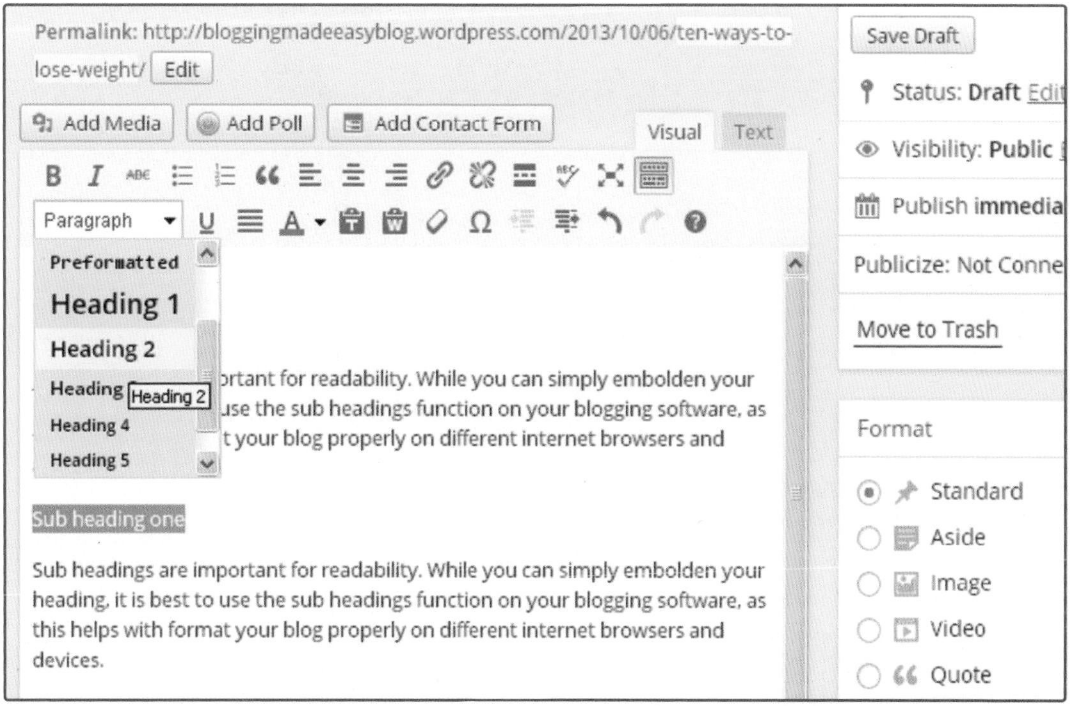
Permalink: http://bloggingmadeeasyblog.wordpress.com/2013/10/06/ten-ways-to-lose-weight/
Edit
Add Media
Add Poll
Add Contact Form
Visual
Text
Paragraph
Preformatted
Heading 1
Heading 2
Heading
Heading 2
Heading 4
Heading 5
ortant for readability. While you can simply embolden your
use the sub headings function on your blogging software, as
t your blog properly on different internet browsers and
Sub heading one
Sub headings are important for readability. While you can simply embolden your heading, it is best to use the sub headings function on your blogging software, as this helps with format your blog properly on different internet browsers and devices.
Save Draft
Status: Draft
Visibility: Public
Publish immedia
Publicize: Not Conne
Move to Trash
Format
Standard
Aside
Image
Video
Quote

Above: Use the heading function on your blogging software in order to ensure your blog is formatted correctly on different browsers.

Inserting subheadings in WordPress.

1. Ensure all your tools are visible by clicking the **Show / Hide Kitchen Sink** button (or pressing Alt + Shift + Z)

2. Highlight the text you want to be your subheading.

3. Click the **Paragraph** menu and choose the type of subheading.

Hot Tip

You can use subheadings within subheadings. The larger the heading number, the smaller the heading will look on screen.

EXPERIMENTING WITH STRUCTURE

Blog posts do not just have to be a series of paragraphs. You can use all sorts of techniques to make a post visually interesting.

Lists

You can structure a post as a numbered list. These are very common with bloggers. Use a title that describes your list, such as 'The Ten Best ...' or 'The Top Five ...'.

Top 10 Best Social Networking Websites
Share This Post
Tweet
Like
+1
3 months ago by Hamza Arif
Internet has made the globe smaller. What is happening where? This is no longer a difficult task to know for any of us now. And with the concept of social networking now it is simpler to stay connected with your friends. Now it is easy to know where your friends are headed, what they having in dinner, how fussy their office was, and how they feel about weekends. Social networking sites help you keep tabs on the current friends and stay in touch with the old ones. Some of these also help you create a social circle that aids you to get contacts to find a job. Life has become more easy and social while staying at home. It may surprise you that not every social networking site is the clone of the other. There are sites that have their own unique styles of sharing your self with your friends and friends of friends. That can be statuses, hash tags, photos or an art piece created by you. Sharing has just become as easy as ABC. After a fussy day at office or school and completing deadlines, all one needs is to relax. And sharing is somehow relaxing. Here is a list of the top 10 best social networking websites which you may want to check out.
10. Friendster
friendster
The pionerr or the father of social networking was Friendster. It is surprising that not very much people know about this social network any more. It was created back in the year 2002. These days the website has been redesigned and revamped and is made a social networking gaming site. Here you can play many games with your friends and have fun. If you have a Facebook account then it would be easy for you to have an account at this site.
9. Tagged
Find us on Facebook
Click Top 10
Like
2,752 people like Click Top 10.
Facebook social plugin
Recent Posts
Top Ten Places to Visit in New York
Top 10 Biggest Earthquakes Since
Top 10 Biggest Firms in the World
Top 10 Popular Tourist Attractions in
Top 10 Deadliest Mountains in the
Top 10 Most Popular Foods in Asia
Top 10 Most Dangerous Roads in th

Above: Using the Top 10 format is a great way to make your post visually interesting.

Steps

If you are writing a how-to article, it is often easier to get the information across by using numbered steps. Number each stage in the process from start to finish. You can then call your blog post 'Ten Steps to ...' or 'How to ... in Five Easy Steps'.

Images

Images can help break up a blog post as well as help clarify your points. Ensure you have the right to use an image before posting it in your blog (see Chapter Five for more information on copyright).

> **Hot Tip**
>
> **When compiling a numbered list, order it in descending order, which will encourage people to continue reading to discover what you think is the best.**

WRITING YOUR POSTS

You do not need to be an expert writer to be a good blogger. What you are writing about is far more important than how you write it. However, sloppy writing, riddled with spelling, grammar and punctuation errors, could put readers off. In addition, good writing will improve the reading experience.

Keep Language Simple

Never use more words than necessary. Making your points simply and concisely will make reading your blog a far easier experience than writing long sentences full of unnecessary words. Remember who your readers are. Not everybody will be as experienced or knowledgeable

Hot Tip

Keep your sentences and paragraphs short. While a few long sentences may add depth to your writing, too many could make reading a chore.

about your particular topic as you are. Avoid too much jargon and make sure you explain any complicated terms and concepts. At the same time, try not to talk down to your audience. While finding the balance can be difficult, you want your blog posts to be attractive to as wide an audience as possible.

Active Versus Passive Voice

One way of keeping a reader engaged is to talk directly to them. Try not to speak in the third person. In addition, avoid using passive sentences. Write in the active voice, with the subject of a sentence before the object. Not only is the active voice more engaging, but it is also more concise.

- **Passive**: The blog post was written by the team's manager.
- **Active**: The team's manager wrote the blog post.
- **Passive**: The blog is visited by a thousand people a day.
- **Active**: A thousand people a day visit the blog.

Strong Verbs

Many blog writers make the mistake of using too many modifiers, such as adverbs and adjectives, to emphasize their points and embellish their writing. While adverbs and adjectives have their place, always try to find a strong verb rather than a modifier.

- **Instead of**: The player ran quickly down the pitch.
- **Try**: The player sprinted down the pitch.
- **Instead of**: It is extremely tiring to run a marathon.
- **Try**: It is exhausting to run a marathon.

Hot Tip

When writing instructions such as numbered steps, try starting with an actionable verb to make the instruction more direct.

JUSTIFYING YOUR POSTS

How your posts look on the page can aid readability. Posts should look neat and well formatted, and one of the best ways of doing this is to ensure they are justified. Justification is when you have a straight edge on both margins so the paragraphs appear as neat rectangles, rather than just being left aligned, which leaves a ragged right edge.

Justifying text in blogging software is extremely simple.

1. To justify your blog posts, select the text you want to justify using your mouse.
2. Click the justification icon (sometimes labelled as **Align Full**).

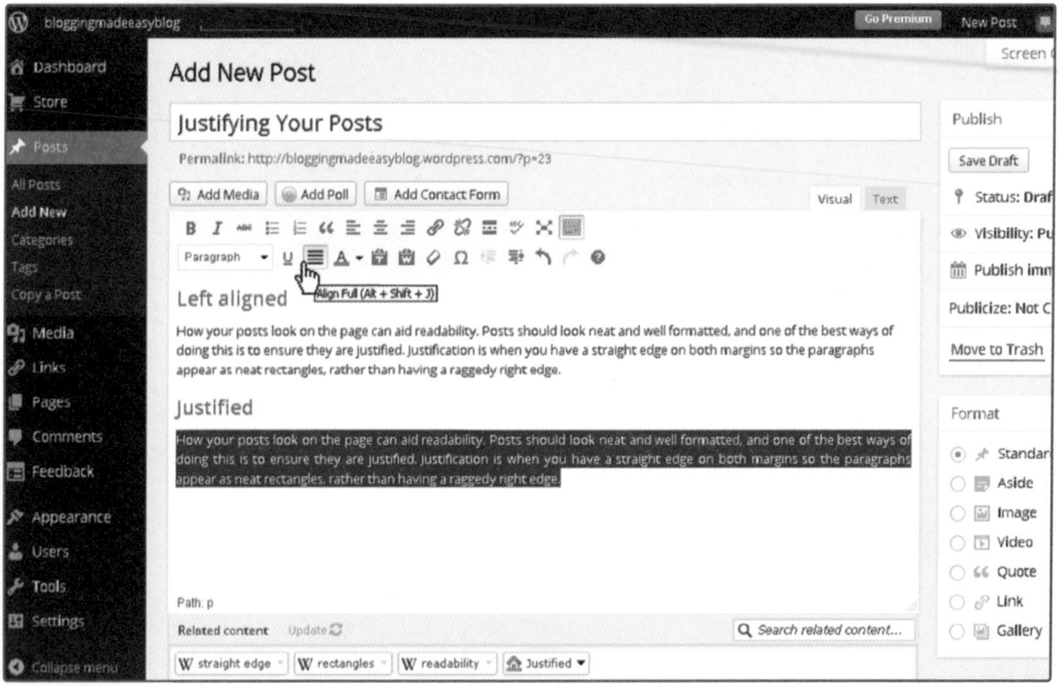
bloggingmadeeasyblog
Go Premium
New Post
Dashboard
Store
Posts
All Posts
Add New
Categories
Tags
Copy a Post
Media
Links
Pages
Comments
Feedback
Appearance
Users
Tools
Settings
Collapse menu
Add New Post
Justifying Your Posts
Permalink: http://bloggingmadeeasyblog.wordpress.com/?p=23
Add Media
Add Poll
Add Contact Form
Visual
Text
Paragraph
Align Full (Alt + Shift + J)
Left aligned
How your posts look on the page can aid readability. Posts should look neat and well formatted, and one of the best ways of doing this is to ensure they are justified. Justification is when you have a straight edge on both margins so the paragraphs appear as neat rectangles, rather than having a raggedy right edge.
Justified
How your posts look on the page can aid readability. Posts should look neat and well formatted, and one of the best ways of doing this is to ensure they are justified. Justification is when you have a straight edge on both margins so the paragraphs appear as neat rectangles, rather than having a raggedy right edge.
Path: p
Related content
Update
Search related content...
straight edge
rectangles
readability
Justified
Publish
Save Draft
Move to Trash
Format
Aside
Image
Video
Quote
Link
Gallery

Above: Align Full is sometimes another name used for justification – when both of the margins have a straight edge.

STRUCTURING YOUR HOMEPAGE

The homepage displays all your recent posts. How people view your homepage is very important. Your blog needs to be easy to navigate. Visitors may wish to scroll through the various posts to see which ones interest them the most.

More Follows

It is often wise to condense the blog posts on your homepage to show just the title and an introductory paragraph with a 'Read More' link on the bottom, so you can fit in more posts and visitors do not have to scroll through every post.

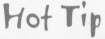

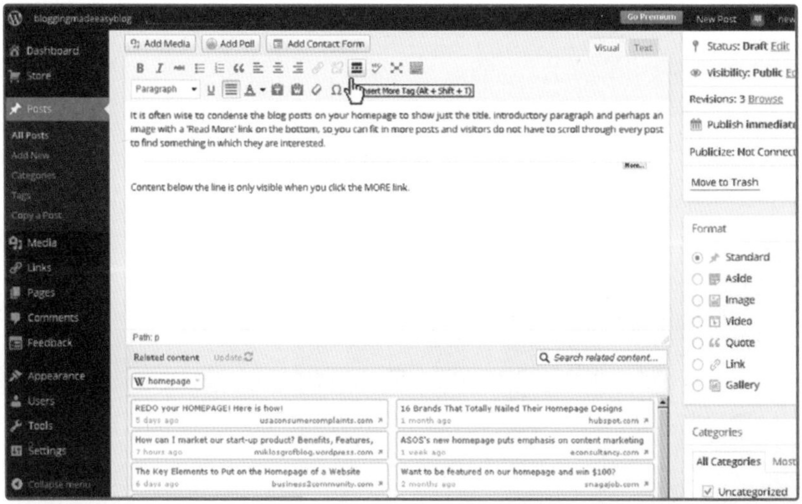

Above: A More Follows tag is helpful, as it condenses blog posts on your homepage to show just the title and introductory paragraph.

You do this by using **More Follows** tags in your posts. To insert a **More Follows** tag in WordPress:

1. Choose a place to insert your tag. It is best to select somewhere beneath the introductory paragraph so visitors can still see what the post is about.

2. Click the **More Follows** icon to insert the tag. Content below the line will now only be shown when visitors click the link.

Hot Tip

If you have an image, insert it high up. You can then insert a More Follows tag just beneath, so visitors will see the title, introductory paragraph and image.

WRITING A HEADLINE

Your headline is the most important part of a blog post. It is what people will see first and determines whether somebody will continue to read the rest of your post.

THE Sun

QE2 IS SET TO SAIL FOR WAR

We told you first

14p

TODAY'S TV: PAGE 17

GOTCHA

Our lads sink gunboat and hole cruiser

SUNK

AN Argie patrol boat like this one was sunk by missiles from Royal Navy helicopters after first opening fire on our lads

CRIPPLED

THE Argie cruiser General Belgrano ... put out of action by Tigerfish torpedoes from our super nuclear sub Conqueror

From TONY SNOW aboard HMS Invincible

THE NAVY had the Argies on their knees last night after a devastating double punch.

WALLOP: They torpedoed the 14,000-ton Argentina cruiser General Belgrano and left it a useless wreck.

WALLOP: Task Force helicopters sank one Argentine patrol boat and severely damaged another.

BATTLE FOR THE ISLANDS

UNION BOYCOTTS WAR

'Folly'

Question

MAJOR

£50,000 BINGO! Today's lucky numbers are on Page 20

Above: Make your headline as compelling as possible, to hook your reader in.

THE TITLE

The determining factor for most people in deciding on whether to read a blog post is the title. Blog titles are just the same as headlines in a newspaper, and are just as important. It has been estimated that for every person who reads a blog post, another four will only have read the headline. This means most bloggers are losing readers, simply because their headline is not grabbing people's attention.

What Makes a Great Headline

Good headlines are hard to quantify. Some headlines are just a few words. Others can be quite long. However, all great headlines share certain aspects.

- **Compelling**: Headlines have to entice readers to want to read the post.
- **Concise**: A good headline will sum up a blog post in as few words as possible.
- **Clarity**: A headline has to establish clearly what the blog post is about.
- **Offer a benefit**: A good headline will offer the reader a reason to read a blog post, such as satisfying a need for information.

Compelling Headlines

Headlines are what appear on search engine results and are what attract readers to a blog. An enticing headline has to be clickable. However, understanding what makes one headline compelling and another less so is not always easy to understand. Headline writing is more art than science and, for that reason, you should do your research. When searching for internet content, think about the links you are clicking and ask yourself what it is about the headline that is grabbing your attention.

Headline Formulae

Some headlines are formulaic, but have been proven time and time again to work. Many of these headlines use a list or numbered format, such as '5 Tips For Writing A Compelling Headline' or '10 Reasons to Blog'. Other headlines use words such as how, what or why: 'How to Write a Killer Headline' or 'Why Headlines Matter'.

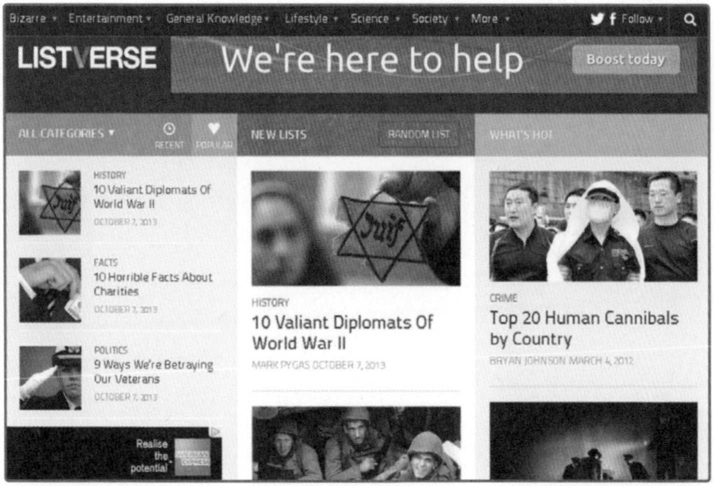

Above: Listverse.com only uses the numbered list format to create headlines.

Hot Tip

Think about using evocative words to spice up your headline, such as 'How to Write a Breathtaking Headline' or '5 Killer Headline Writing Tips'.

Clarity

While headlines should be simple and concise, they have to define what a blog post is about. Failing to convey what you are writing about will deter readers from clicking a headline link. When composing a headline, it is important to separate it into its component parts.

Let's look at the following headline.

'Headline Writing is the Key to Successful Blogging'

This headline has three components:

- **Subject**: What the main subject of the headline is, in this instance, headline writing.
- **Relationship**: The relationship the subject has to an object, in this case 'being key'.
- **Object**: What the subject is relating to: successful blogging.

Some bloggers often miss out one of the components of a headline, which can make the meaning unclear, such as 'Headline Writing is Key'. This will leave a question in readers' minds. In this case, they may wonder what headline writing is key to, which may deter a reader from proceeding to read the blog. Always make sure your headline has all its component parts.

Concision

Headlines have to be concise. A long-winded, wordy headline is going to give the impression that your blog post is long-winded and wordy too. While headlines do have to be well written, they do not have to follow the same grammar rules as sentences. You can sometimes get away with omitting words to make the headline more concise, as long as the main components of a headline are in place.

- **Instead of**: The Top 5 Tips for Writing a Blog Headline
- **Try**: Top 5 Blog Headline Tips
- **Instead of**: How to Write a Great Blog Headline
- **Try**: Writing a Great Blog Headline

Punctuation and Special Characters

A good way to make a headline more concise and compelling is to use special characters.

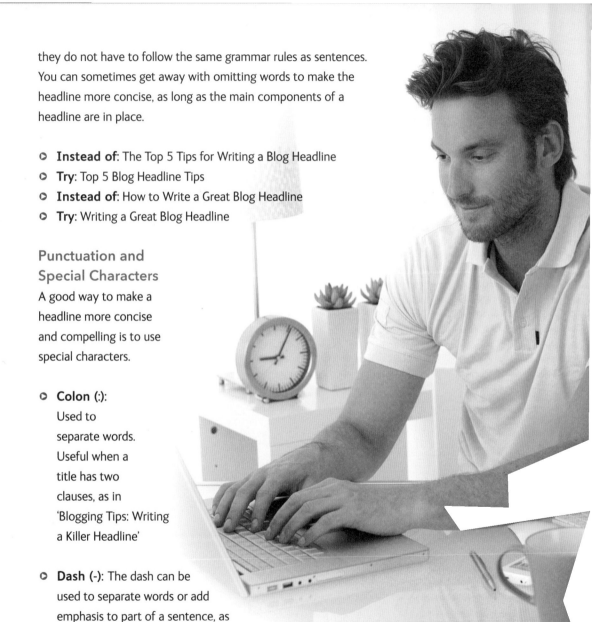

- **Colon (:)**: Used to separate words. Useful when a title has two clauses, as in 'Blogging Tips: Writing a Killer Headline'

- **Dash (-)**: The dash can be used to separate words or add emphasis to part of a sentence, as in 'Five Blogging Tips – That Work!'

- **Question mark (?)**: Used when your headline is asking a question, as in 'Does Your Blog Need More Visitors?'

- **Exclamation mark (!)**: Used to emphasize importance, as in 'Why Your Headline Matters!'

> **Hot Tip**
>
> **Certain symbols should always be avoided in headline writing: &, #, <>, " and some others are used in HTML code so may not display properly.**

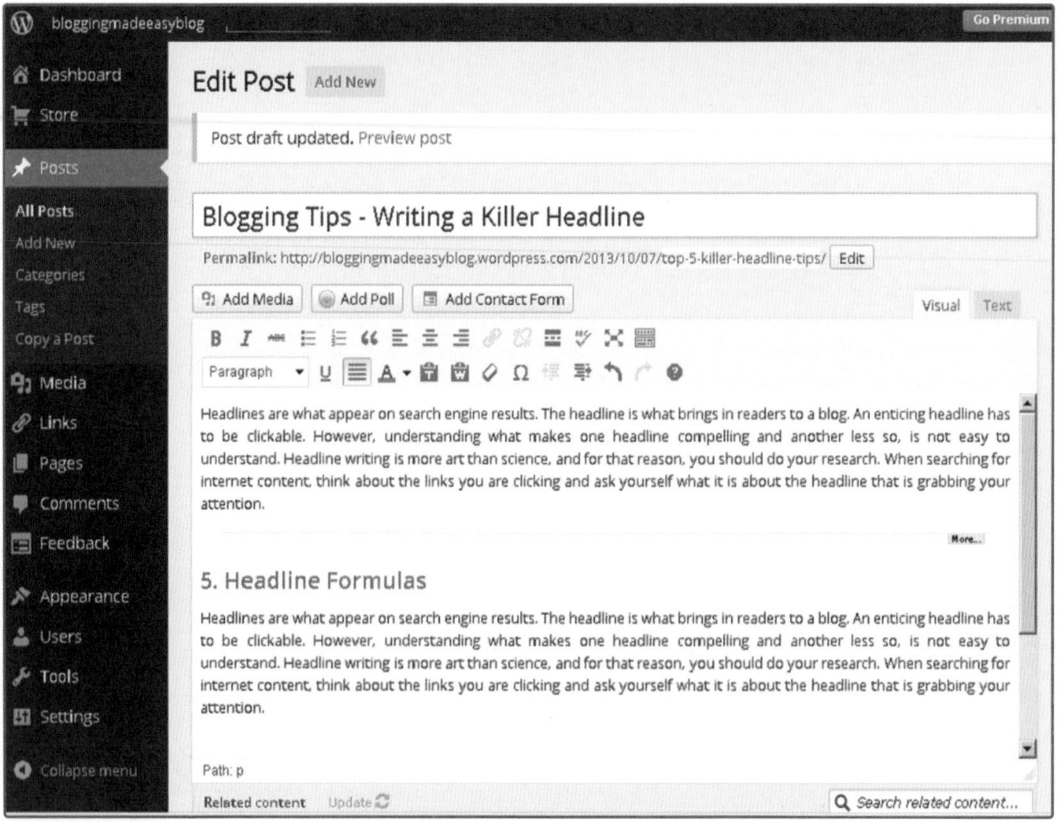
bloggingmadeeasyblog
Go Premium
Dashboard
Store
Posts
All Posts
Add New
Categories
Tags
Copy a Post
Media
Links
Pages
Comments
Feedback
Appearance
Users
Tools
Settings
Collapse menu
Edit Post
Add New
Post draft updated. Preview post
Blogging Tips - Writing a Killer Headline
Permalink: http://bloggingmadeeasyblog.wordpress.com/2013/10/07/top-5-killer-headline-tips/
Edit
Add Media
Add Poll
Add Contact Form
Visual
Text
Paragraph
Headlines are what appear on search engine results. The headline is what brings in readers to a blog. An enticing headline has to be clickable. However, understanding what makes one headline compelling and another less so, is not easy to understand. Headline writing is more art than science, and for that reason, you should do your research. When searching for internet content, think about the links you are clicking and ask yourself what it is about the headline that is grabbing your attention.
More...
5. Headline Formulas
Headlines are what appear on search engine results. The headline is what brings in readers to a blog. An enticing headline has to be clickable. However, understanding what makes one headline compelling and another less so, is not easy to understand. Headline writing is more art than science, and for that reason, you should do your research. When searching for internet content, think about the links you are clicking and ask yourself what it is about the headline that is grabbing your attention.
Path: p
Related content
Update
Search related content...

Above: The dash characters can be used to separate words to add emphasis to part of a sentence.

PROVIDING A BENEFIT

A headline that makes a promise will entice readers searching for information. If you can offer to solve a problem or provide useful information, you are providing a benefit to clicking on your headline and reading the blog post. Try using question words: how, why, what, etc.

Examples of headlines offering a benefit.

- 'How to Cure Writer's Block'
- Why a Killer Headline Is So Important'
- 'What to Do if Your Blog is Losing Visitors'

Ask Questions

Sometimes, readers may not realize they have a problem or that they require information. You can often entice visitors to your blog by posing a question, which will suggest that you have the answer.

BLOGGINGMADEEASYBLOG
This WordPress.com site is the cat's pajamas
UNCATEGORIZED
Blogging Tip: Writing a Killer Headline
NEWBLOGGER1234
LEAVE A COMMENT
EDIT
Headlines are what appear on search engine results. The headline is what brings in readers to a blog. An enticing headline has to be clickable. However, understanding what makes one headline compelling and another less so, is not easy to understand. Headline writing is more art than science, and for that reason, you should do your research. When searching for internet content, think about the links you are clicking and ask yourself what it is about the headline that is grabbing your attention.

Above: Headlines offering a benefit such as solving a problem encourage the reader to click on your blog post.

- Are You Tired of Receiving No Visitors to Your Blog?
- Have You Optimized Your Blog for SEO?'
- Why Are You Reading This and Not Writing Your Blog Post?'

SEARCH ENGINE OPTIMIZATION

Because many of your visitors will use search engines to find information related to your blog, it is important that your headline is search-engine friendly. Search Engine Optimization (SEO) is a complicated and huge subject, and many bloggers pursue all sorts of avenues to make their blog more search-engine friendly. However, you can often do more harm than good. Overly optimizing a blog post or headline can make it clumsy to read for an actual person, but it is worth taking a few steps to make your headline more search-engine friendly.

Google
blogging tips
Web
Images
Maps
Shopping
News
More
Search tools
About 80,300,000 results (0.28 seconds)
Blogging Tips for Your Everyday Blogger - BloggingTips.com
www.bloggingtips.com/
10 hours ago - One of the best ways to succeed as online blogger is by connecting and sharing blogging tips with other well known bloggers and site owners ...
About Blogging Tips - BloggingTips.com Complete ... - Free Wordpress Themes
Top tips for a successful blog | Culture professionals network ...
www.theguardian.com › Professional › Culture professionals network
17 Nov 2011 - Creative Boom: Running a successful blog is no easy task. Here are some top tips on making yours a success.
16 Top Tips from Blogging Experts for Beginners - The Buffer Blog
blog.bufferapp.com/blogging-advice-for-beginners-from-16-ex...
by Belle Beth Cooper
30 Jul 2013 - Blogging advice for beginners (or anyone!) from 16 experts.
Daily Blog Tips
www.dailyblogtips.com/
2 hours ago - Nine Blogging Milestones to Celebrate. For many bloggers, it takes months or even years to build up the traction they hoped for. Instead of ...
25 Blogging Tips for Newbies and Veterans | Goins, Writer
goinswriter.com/blogging-tips/
by Jeff Goins - in 5,640 Google+ circles
We've all seen the lists of regurgitated blogging tips. I'm tired of them. So I put together my own list of tips that I should've been practicing all along.
News for blogging tips

Above: A Google search of keywords relating to a post.

Hot Tip

Think of a question people may ask relating to your blog post's subject and compose a title that answers this question. Blog posts answering a question often appear higher than those including the exact keyword phrase.

Keywords

Keywords are the phrases people use when searching for content. A good way to ensure your blog post gets maximum amounts of visibility is to try to implement these search terms in your headline. Think about the different terms people will use to find the information relating to your blog post. However, the blog title still has to read naturally. Stuffing in search terms just to satisfy a search engine may get you better rankings, but it will not entice readers to click on it.

Think Semantically

Search engines are a lot more sophisticated these days. Keywords no longer have to be exact, as search engines such as Google are able to make semantic links between the different phrases people type in a search box and other keywords. For instance, the phrase 'Blogging Tips' will be linked with the phrases 'Blogging Hints' or 'Blogging Help'.

H Tags

Another way of making a blog post keyword friendly is to implement them in your subheadings. This is because H tags, such as headlines and subheadings, carry more weight when it comes to search-engine rankings. If you are struggling to get a keyword into your actual headline, try to include them in your subheadings.

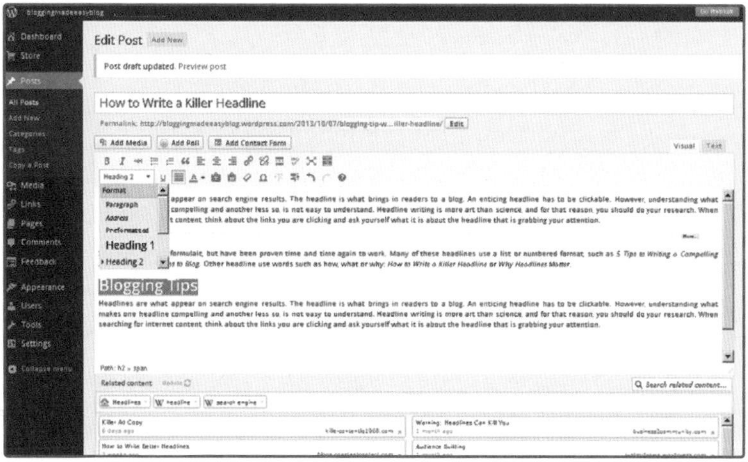

Above: A title that answers a question will appear higher in a list of search-engine results than those including exact key phrases.

Keyword Stuffing

Excessive use of keywords can in some instances be detrimental when it comes to search results. Google and other search engines often penalize blog posts and websites that contain too many keywords. This is to prevent spam results from appearing high up, so avoid putting more than one keyword or phrase in a title.

Headline and URLs

Another consideration when composing headlines is their relationship to the URL of the blog post. Most blogging software automatically assigns the headline as part of the URL. This is another reason to avoid overly long headlines, as long URLs can look awkward in search results. In addition, a long URL can cause problems with linking when using social media platforms such as Twitter, although they can be shortened. This is covered in more detail in Chapter Four.

FINAL CHECK

Before you publish your blog post, always double-check the headline. A mistake in a headline, such as in the spelling or grammar, will not only be embarrassing, but will deter people from visiting your blog.

PROOFING YOUR BLOG

A well-written post will engage your readers and make them come back to your blog, while a badly written post will frustrate readers. Proofing your blog posts is important to ensure you keep people coming back for more.

READING EXPERIENCE

No matter how mind-blowing the content of your blog post, if you don't provide an enjoyable reading experience, you will not encourage visitors to continue reading or view your other blog posts. Ensuring your blog post is easy to read and free from spelling, punctuation and grammar mistakes is key to providing an enjoyable reading experience.

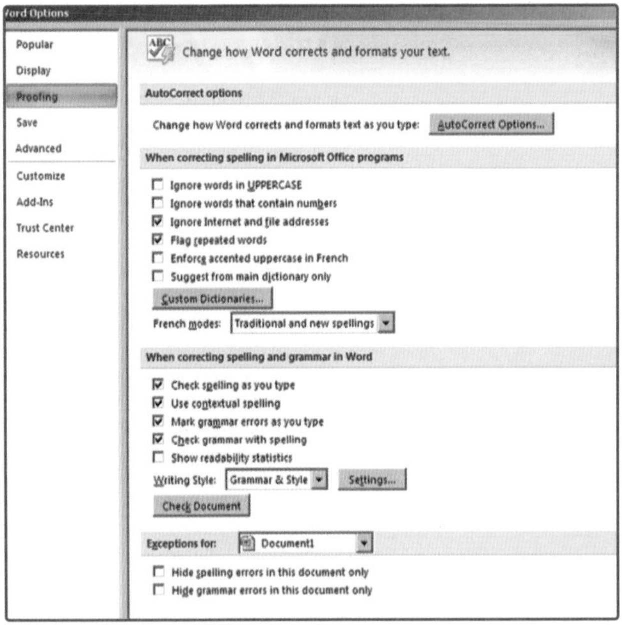

Proofing Software

While blogging software is great for managing your blog posts, it is generally not the best application to compose them in. Some bloggers do write their posts in WordPress and Blogger, but many more prefer to use a word processing program such as Microsoft Word or Open Office. Programs such as these provide a better medium in which to compose your posts, as well as offering many proofing tools to assist in your writing.

Left: Microsoft Word programs provide proofing tools which are great for checking your post prior to publishing.

Using Word Processing Software

Problems can occur when you try to cut and paste from a word processing program such as MS Word directly into WordPress or Blogger. This is because blogging software utilizes HTML, and some of the hidden code behind text written in Word can cause problems. For example, using speech marks and apostrophes can often cause problems in blogs, and it is common to see random symbols inserted into the place where the speech mark or apostrophe once was.

Browsers

While the pasted text may look fine in your internet browser, it may cause problems in another. This is because different internet browsers handle HTML differently. For this reason, it is best to compose your blog post in an HTML-friendly mode. This may prevent you from formatting the post in Word, but it is best to use the blogging software for this and the word processing program for composing the actual words.

Filtered Web Format

Fortunately, you can make MS Word more HTML friendly for writing blog posts by using the Filtered Web format.

1. Open up a new document by either going into the menu and selecting **New** or by pressing **Ctrl + N**.

2. Go into the menu and select **Save As** (alternatively, press **Alt + F + A**).

3. Choose a name for your document and then scroll down the **Save As Type** menu and select **Web Page, Filtered**.

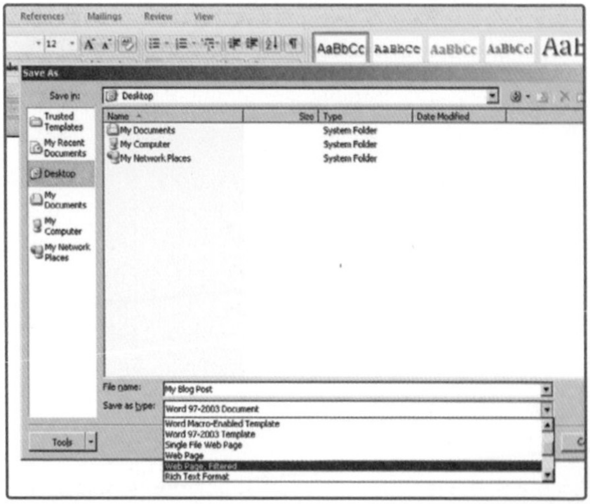

Right: A Filtered Web format on MS Word allows you to not include any unnecessary HTML code in your posts.

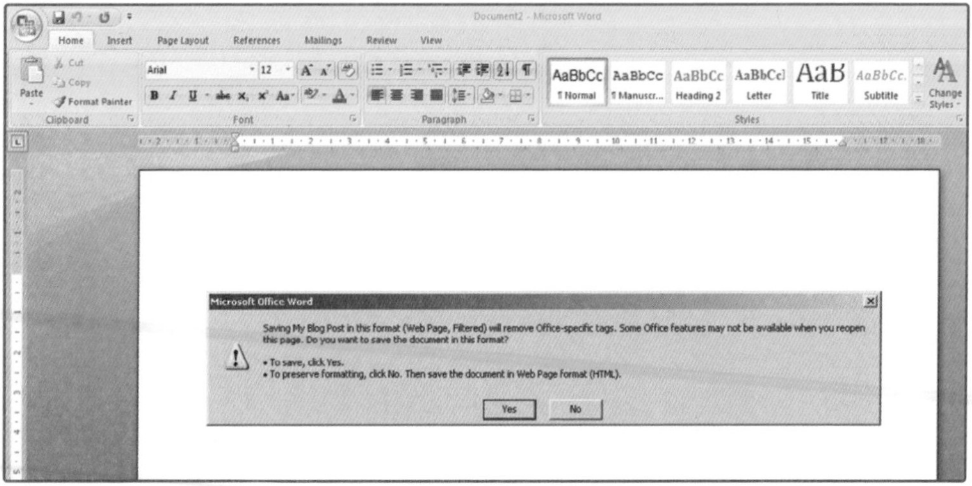
Document2 - Microsoft Word
Home
Insert
Page Layout
References
Mailings
Review
View
Paste
Cut
Copy
Format Painter
Clipboard
Font
Paragraph
Styles
AaBbCc
¶ Normal
¶ Manuscr...
Heading 2
Letter
Title
Subtitle
Change Styles
Microsoft Office Word
Saving My Blog Post in this format (Web Page, Filtered) will remove Office-specific tags. Some Office features may not be available when you reopen this page. Do you want to save the document in this format?
• To save, click Yes.
• To preserve formatting, click No. Then save the document in Web Page format (HTML).
Yes
No

Above: Click Yes when you receive a message telling you that you won't be able to use all of MS Word's formatting features.

4. You will receive a message telling you that you will not be able to use all of Word's formatting features. Click **Yes**.

5. You can now compose your blog post without fear of including unnecessary code.

Hot Tip

Once you have created a Web Filtered document, you can use it as a template to write all your posts. Simply use the Save As function to save each post under a different name.

PROOFING TOOLS

One of the main reasons for composing blog posts in MS Word (or another word processing program) is that you can use the many proofing tools. MS Word has several useful tools to help with proofing.

- **Language**: You can select specific spellings based on language, such as US English or UK English.

- **Spell checker**: MS Word can help you identify misspelled words.

- **Grammar and style checker**: Helps identify grammar errors and poor style choices.

Choosing Your Language

Some bloggers choose to tailor their blog to an international audience, such as a UK blogger opting to write in US English. This is never really a good idea, as there is more to writing in a different English-based language than just spelling. Besides, most people are aware of the UK and US differences, so it is always best to write in your home language. However, it may be a good idea to avoid using certain vernaculars and idioms that some overseas readers may not understand.

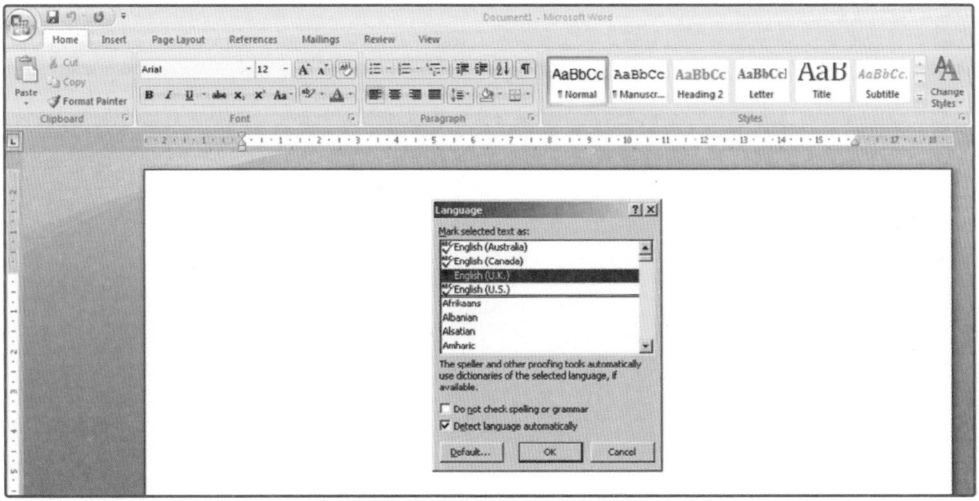

Above: Change your language in MS Word by left-clicking on the language icon and select preferred language from the drop-down menu.

To change your language in Word:

1. Left-click the **Language** icon on the bottom left of the page.

2. Select your preferred language from the drop-down menu.

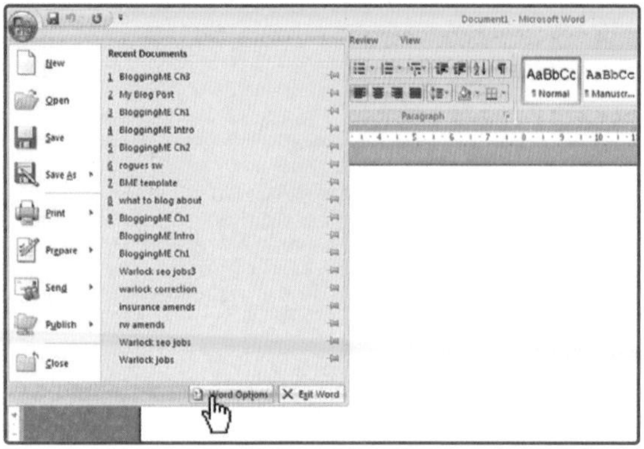

Above: Select Word Options.

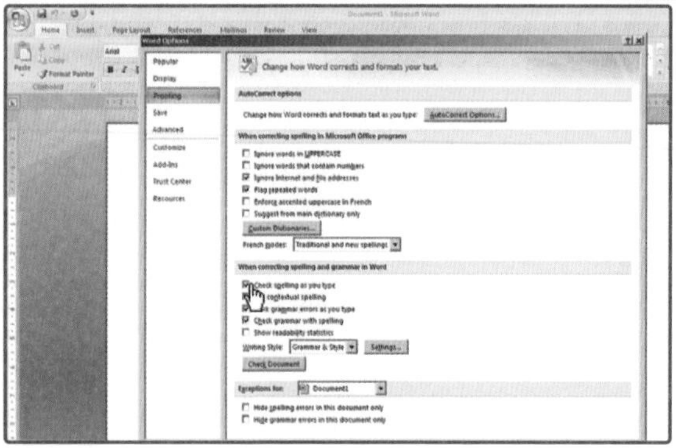

Above: Select Check spelling as you type

Hot Tip

If you have misspelled a word, a red wavy line will appear underneath it. Right-click for a list of spelling choices and choose the correct spelling.

Spell Checking

MS Word will identify misspelled words for you by placing a red wavy line beneath them.

Turning spell checker on:

1. Click the options menu in the top left-hand corner.
2. Select **Word Options** from the drop-down menu.
3. From the options page, select **Proofing**.
4. Tick the box that says **Check spelling as you type**.
5. Click **OK**.

Grammar and Style Checking

Word will check your grammar and style choices as you type, so you can identify passive sentences, overly wordy sentences or poor grammar.

To turn on the grammar and style checker:

1. Go into the **Proofing** menu (see above).
2. Select the **Mark grammar errors as you type** box.

3. Using the drop-down menu, choose whether to have Word check both grammar and style, or grammar only.

4. You can click **Settings** to adjust which style and grammar choices Word should flag up.

5. Click **OK** when finished.

Using the Thesaurus

Word has a built-in thesaurus, which can help you identify alternative words. The thesaurus is activated by highlighting a word, selecting the **Review** menu at the top of the screen and clicking **Thesaurus**.

Limits to Proofing Tools

While MS Word's proofing tools are very useful, they are fallible. In particular, watch out for:

- **Homophone errors**: Words that are pronounced the same but spelled differently, such as bare/bear, made/maid, pause/paws.

- **Contractions**: Be careful with words such as,**you're** (you are) and **your**, **we're** (we are) and **were** and **it's** (it is/has) and **its**.

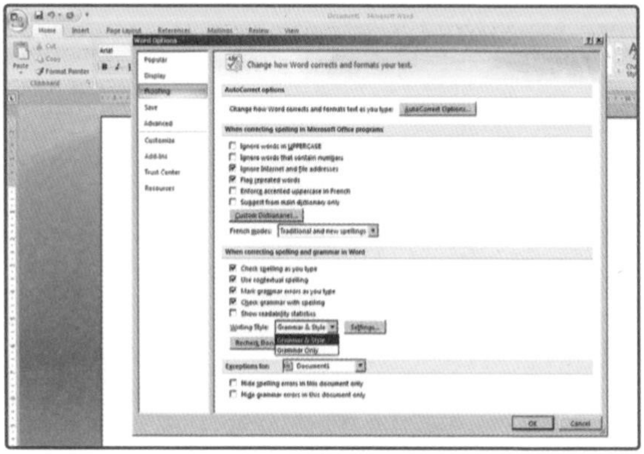

Above: Click Settings to select grammar and style options.

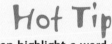

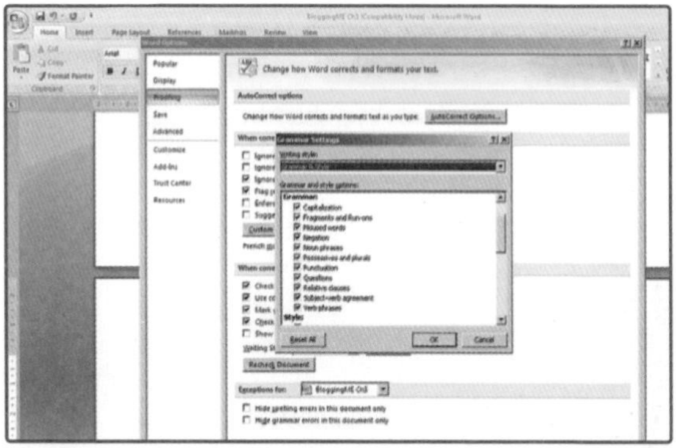

Above: Click OK when you have chosen your preferred styles.

Hot Tip

You can highlight a word and use hot keys to spellcheck a word (F7) or bring up the thesaurus (Shift + F7).

- **Repeated words:** It is easy to miss a word written twice, especially if it is small.

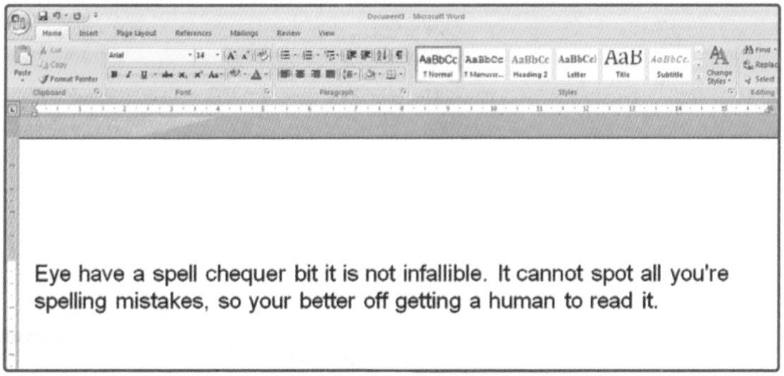

Above: It is always worth getting another person to read through your post, as spell checkers do not always spot all mistakes.

Beta Readers

Because proofing tools are not perfect, and it can be very hard to spot your own mistakes, many bloggers prefer to have a beta reader look over their posts before they publish them. A beta reader does not have to be a professional editor, just a friend or family member with a good grasp of English.

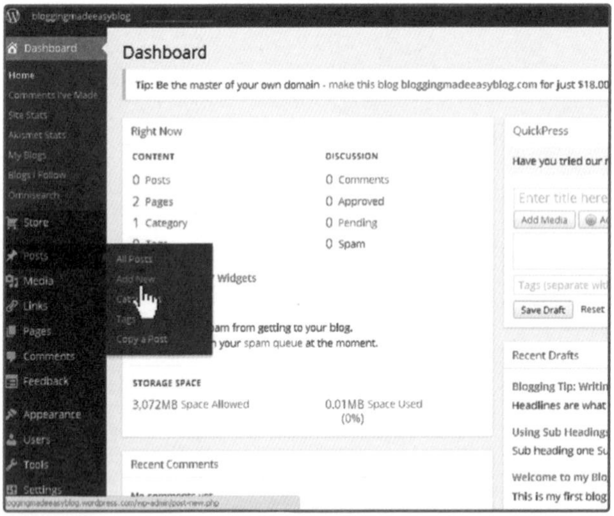

Above: Adding a new post to your blogging platform.

FORMATTING AND LAYOUT

When you have proofed your blog post, it is time to paste it into your blogging software and format it. This is easily done by using the cut-and-paste function.

1. Highlight your blog post's title in MS Word and right-click. Select **Copy**.
2. Go into your blogging platform's dashboard and start a new post.

3. Right-click in the title post and select **Paste**.

4. Highlight the rest of your blog post in MS Word, right click and select **Copy**.

5. In the main blog post window in your blogging software, right-click and select **Paste**.

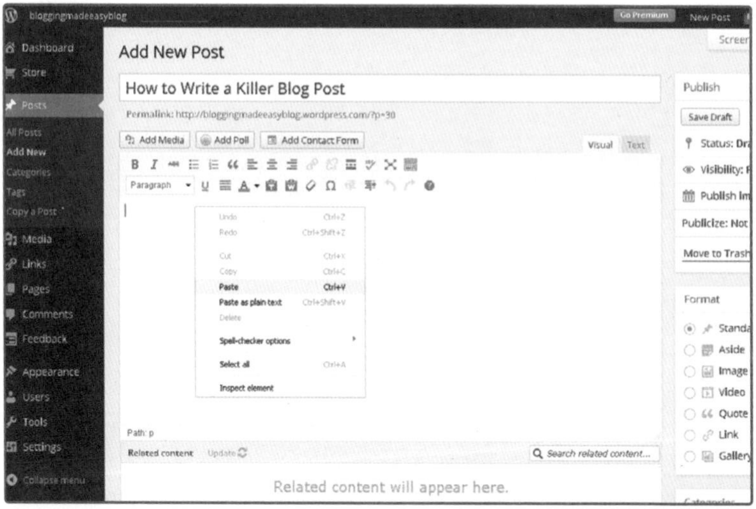

Above: Right-click to paste your blog post into your blogging platform.

Formatting

Once you have pasted your post into your blogging platform, you can begin formatting it to make it look more readable.

Remember:

- **Subheadings**: Include subheadings to break up the text.
- **Bullets and numbers**: Use bullet points or numbers when using lists.
- **Highlight text**: Use bold, italics and underlining to highlight text.
- **Justification**: Align your text to both margins, not just the left.

Hot Tip

Selecting text and pressing Ctrl C will copy text, and Ctrl V will paste it. On a Mac, use Command C and Command V).

Formatting Errors

Even if you have used Web Filtered mode in MS Word, cutting and pasting can still cause some errors in formatting. Before you publish your post, always use the **Preview** button on the right-hand side of your blogging software to see how your post will look.

Common Errors

Blog posts often have formatting errors. Many of the most common problems with blog posts include:

- **No paragraph break**: Your paragraphs do not have a space between them.
- **Bold or italicized text**: Whole sentences have become bold or italicized.
- **Bullets**: Some bullet points are missing or text is bulleted that should not be.
- **White space**: There are large breaks in the text.

UNDERSTANDING HTML

Many formatting errors are caused by problems with HTML. HTML is the code that is used to create and format web pages, including blog posts. It is worth taking a bit of time to understand some of the basic HTML code so you can identify and address formatting errors in your blog posts.

bloggingmadeeasyblog
Go Premium
New Post
Dashboard
Store
Posts
All Posts
Add New
Categories
Tags
Copy a Post
Media
Links
Pages
Comments
Feedback
Appearance
Users
Tools
Edit Post
Add New
Screen Opt
Post draft updated. Preview post
How to Write a Killer Blog Post
Permalink: http://bloggingmadeeasyblog.wordpress.com/2013/10/08/how-to-write-a...ller-blog-post/
Edit
Get Shortlink
Add Media
Add Poll
Add Contact Form
Visual
Text
b
i
link
b-quote
del
ins
img
ul
ol
li
code
more
close tags
proofread
fullscreen
<p>You do not need to be an expert writer to be a good blogger. What you are writing about is far more important than how you write it. However, sloppy writing, riddled with spelling, grammar and punctuation errors could put readers off. In addition, writing well will improve the <strong>reading experience.
</strong></p>
<h2>Concise</h2>
<p>Never use more words than necessary. Making your points simply and concisely will make reading your blog a far easier experience than writing long sentences full of <em>unnecessary words</em>. Remember who your readers are. Not everybody will be as experienced or knowledgeable about your particular topic as you are. Avoid too much jargon and make sure you explain any complicated terms and concepts. At the same time, try not to talk down to your audience. While finding the balance can be difficult, you want your blog posts to be attractive to a wider audience as possible.</p>
For more information...
Publish
Save Draft
Status: Draft
Visibility: Publi
Publish immed
Publicize: Not Con
Move to Trash
Format
Standard
Aside
Image

Above: An HTML view of a blog post in WordPress.

HTML View

You can view your blog post's HTML code by using the HTML VIEW on the main window of your blogging platform (called the **Text** tab in WordPress). HTML code comprises tags that are surrounded by the parenthesis symbols <>.

Basic Tags

- **Bold text**: <strong>
- **Italicized text**: <em>
- **Paragraph**: <p>
- **Line break**:
- **Heading tags**: <h1>, <h2>, <h3>, <h4>
- **Bullet point**: <li>
- **Ordered list (numbered)**: <ol>
- **Unordered list (not numbered)**: <ul>

bloggingmadeeasyblog
Go Premium
Dashboard
Store
Posts
All Posts
Add New
Categories
Tags
Copy a Post
Media
Links
Pages
Comments
Feedback
Appearance
Users
Tools
Settings
How to Write a Killer Blog Post
Permalink: http://bloggingmadeeasyblog.wordpress.com/2013/10/08/how-to-write-a...ller-blog-post/ Edit Get Shortlink
Add Media
Add Poll
Add Contact Form
Visual
Text
b i link b-quote del ins img ul ol li code more close tags proofread fullscreen
You do not need to be an expert writer to be a good blogger. What you are writing about is far more important than how you write it. However, sloppy writing, riddled with spelling, grammar and punctuation errors could put readers off. In addition, writing well will improve the <strong>reading experience.
</strong>
<h2>Concise</h2>
Never use more words than necessary. Making your points simply and concisely will make reading your blog a far easier experience than writing long sentences full of <em>unnecessary words</em>. Remember who your readers are. Not everybody will be as experienced or knowledgeable about your particular topic as you are. Avoid too much jargon and make sure you explain any complicated terms and concepts. At the same time, try not to talk down to your audience. While finding the balance can be difficult, you want your blog posts to be attractive to a wider audience as possible.
Bullet list
<ul>
<li>First bullet</li>
Second bullet</li>
<li>Third bullet</li>
</ul>
Zemanta is inactive!
You need to write your blog post in Rich Text mode for Zemanta to work! Instructions

Above: Make sure when formatting your post that, if you have any errors, you have closed your tags correctly.

Fixing Errors

Missing or extra HTML tags cause the most common formatting errors. All HTML tags have to open and close. A closed tag includes a backslash (/) in the tag parenthesis before the code's letters; for example, a paragraph opens with a <p> tag and closes with a </p> tag, while bold text starts with a <strong> tag and closes with </strong>.

If you have formatting errors in your blog posts, check you have both open and closed tags around the formatted text. For instance, if you have a missing bullet point, check that each section that should start with a bullet opens with <li> and ends with </li>.

REATING YOUR AUDIENCE

BUILDING A COMMUNITY

A successful blog is not just one that brings in a lot of visitors, but one that can nurture a loyal community of people who repeatedly come back to your blog and can help grow your audience for you.

WHAT IS A COMMUNITY?

All successful blogs have a community based around them. This is a group of loyal followers who regularly read and comment on blog posts. A community is made up of like-minded people, and this core audience can help generate further interest in your blog by referring to it on social media platforms and bringing it to the attention of other people with similar interests.

Audience versus Community

There is a difference between an audience and a community. Audiences are passive. They visit a blog to read information, nothing more. A community, however, will actively engage with a blog. People will visit to comment, exchange ideas and debate the subject area. To encourage a community, you need to create an atmosphere that enables interaction, engagement and commentary. Communities also need something on which to focus.

- **A niche topic**: Communities often form around subject topic areas, such as science fiction films, sports teams or hobbies and pastimes.
- **Products and manufacturers**: Blogs centred on products and manufacturers, such as Apple's iPhone, acquire ardent fans of the technology.
- **An idea or belief**: Like-minded people like to have their ideas and beliefs affirmed. Politically based blogs, or those that centre on particular ideas or core beliefs, generate loyal communities.

LEADER OR CONDUIT

When it comes to building a community, you need to decide on what role you as the blogger are playing. Some bloggers thrive on controversy and self-opinion. Their views are what attract people to the blog and the community is very much centred on the blogger. Other bloggers take a different approach. They take more of a back seat, acting as a conduit and presenting the information for others to debate.

Be Yourself

Whatever role you decide on, you need to be yourself. Write directly to your audience and let your personality show in your writing.

Hot Tip

Try to write your blog posts in the same way as you speak. Imagine you are discussing the topic with a friend over a drink to ensure your blog does not sound too formal and your personality is coming across.

STARTING A COMMUNITY

To start a community, you need to encourage interaction. Openly ask for opinions in your blog posts by posing questions in your conclusion. When people make a comment, acknowledge it and thank them for their views. If they have a blog, link to it and promote their comment on social media. Your community can grow from these early commentators, so make sure you cultivate them and encourage them to make further comments.

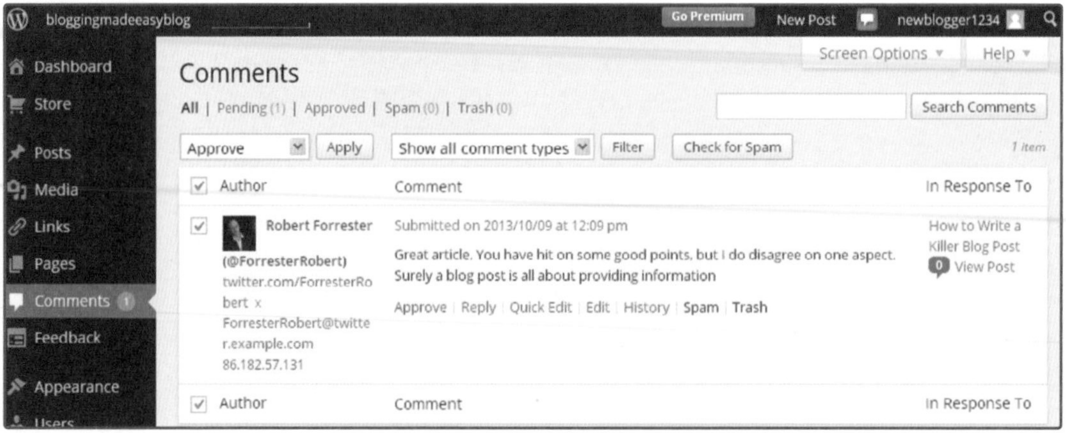

Above: Enabling the comment feature on your blog allows you to communicate with readers directly.

Identify Leaders

When you start getting comments, identify the people who make the most frequent comments, hold strong opinions, sound the most informed or get the most responses from other readers. These people bring value to your blog, so empower them. Ask if they would like to guest blog or to give suggestions for new posts. Consider their views and come up with blog posts that they are likely to comment on.

Write for Your Community

Provide your community with the information they want. Early on, identify those blog posts that are getting the most views and comments. Tailor your posts around these subject areas. Write things that you think the community will appreciate.

Become Part of The Community

You cannot expect a community to suddenly stumble across your blog and form around it. You need to be part of the community you are trying to build in the first place. This means you need to be active in places where the community hangs out.

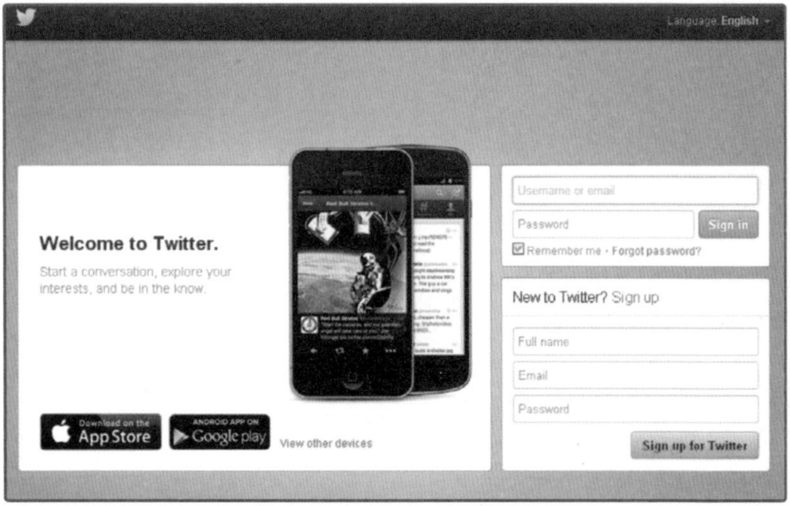

Above: Using Twitter can help you to become part of your online community.

- **Other blogs**: Post regular comments on other blogs and include a link to your own.
- **Forums**: Become an active member of forums related to your topic and make regular contributions.
- **Social media**: Join social media groups relating to your subject area.

> **Hot Tip**
>
> **If you are struggling to get comments, identify people who regularly comment on other blogs and forums. Invite them to comment on one of your posts or ask them to write a guest post.**

Snowball Effect

All communities start small and, once you get one or two readers who regularly comment, you will be surprised at how quickly you can grow your community. However, you need to ensure you are looking after your early community members and providing them with content they want.

NURTURING YOUR COMMUNITY

Once a community has started to form around your blog, you need to nurture it. A blogger can never relax, expecting his or her community to remain loyal. A community needs to be fed and, unless you are providing engaging content that its members can discuss and debate, they will soon go elsewhere. As the community gets bigger, blogging may become more demanding and you may need to find new ways to keep your community engaged.

- **Contact contributors**: Once you have an audience and community behind you, you may be able to convince authoritative sources to contribute to your blog.

- **Share your community**: You are not in competition with other blogs, but part of a wider community, so do not be afraid to link to other bloggers, promote their blog posts and ask for guest contributions.

Don't Forget the Quiet People

Just because people are not commenting on your blog posts does not mean they are not part of the community. You will find that, for every person who regularly comments, dozens more visit your site. While the community members who make regular contributions should be looked after, do not ignore those who do not. You can encourage people who do not like making comments to contribute in other ways.

- **Polls**: Conducting polls makes it easy for people to voice their opinions without having to write comments.

- **Votes**: Like polls, asking for votes can encourage interaction without people having to voice their opinions.

- **Allow anonymity**: Not everybody wants to be known. Allow people to comment anonymously.

Above: Polls allow readers to voice opinions.

Above: Voting is yet another way to engage with readers who shy away from making comments.

Content is King

Above all, to keep a community happy and loyal, you need good content. Make sure you do your research. For your blog to be a valuable resource for a community, you need to be an authority and provide good information that sparks debate and encourages interaction.

SOCIAL MEDIA

No serious blogger can ignore the power of social media. With a social media presence, you can raise the profile of your blog, attract visitors and generate a buzz about your posts.

SOCIAL MEDIA FOR BLOGGERS

Social media has revolutionized the way people communicate. Facebook has over one billion users, while the number of Twitter users has reached the 500 million mark. For bloggers, social media provides a great way to grow an audience, promote your blog and interact with the community.

Promotion

Social media platforms provide an effective method of promoting and marketing your blog. You can post links, share your content and promote the content of others. The great thing about many social media sites is that you can search for people interested in your topic, connect with them and promote your blog directly, rather than broadly promoting your blog to everyone and anyone. Furthermore, if you have built up a community, your audience will do a lot of promoting for you by 'retweeting' and 'liking' your content.

Left: Twitter offers outlets to expand your blog, including retweeting, liking and posting links.

Community Interaction

The other great benefit of social media is that it lets you connect with people in your community. Even if these people do not visit your blog, they may provide useful information and resources that you can use in blog posts. Social media platforms are also great ways to continue the debate away from your blog and further interact with the community.

POPULAR SOCIAL MEDIA PLATFORMS

The number of social media platforms increases all the time. However, few people have the time to use all the platforms available. In addition, some platforms that were popular a few years ago no longer have so many users, but a few dominate the social media landscape and are worth serious consideration for any blogger looking to build an audience.

> **Hot Tip**
>
> **If you are using Google's Blogger, the social media platform Google+ offers easy integration.**

- **Facebook**: By far the world's most popular social media platform. With over a billion users, a Facebook presence is a must for the serious blogger.

- **Twitter**: While not as popular as Facebook, Twitter still has millions of users and makes it easy to share links and information.

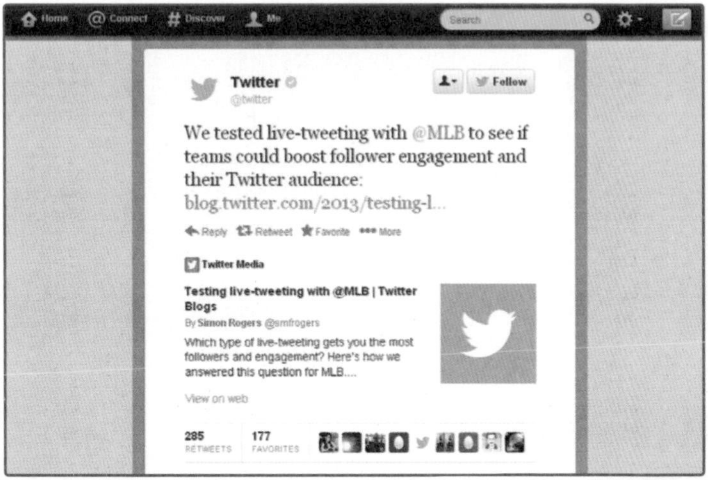

Home
Connect
Discover
Me
Twitter
Follow
We tested live-tweeting with @MLB to see if teams could boost follower engagement and their Twitter audience: blog.twitter.com/2013/testing-l...
Twitter Media
Testing live-tweeting with @MLB | Twitter Blogs
By Simon Rogers @smfrogers
Which type of live-tweeting gets you the most followers and engagement? Here's how we answered this question for MLB....
285 RETWEETS
177 FAVORITES

Above: Twitter is an easy way to share condensed thoughts and links quickly.

- **LinkedIn**: Aimed at professionals and those in the business world, LinkedIn enables corporate bloggers to connect with those in the same industry.

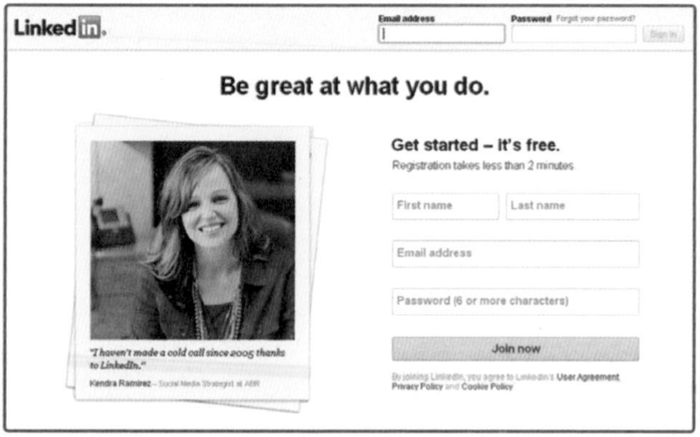

Above: LinkedIn allows individuals in the same industries to communicate with one another.

- **Google+**: Google's social media platform is highly popular and offers some unique features such as the ability to place your connections into groups.

Above: Google+ gives users the opportunity to place their connections into groups.

- **YouTube**: While many people think of YouTube as a video-sharing website, it has a huge community that revolves around video blogging and podcasting.
- **Tumblr**: A microblogging platform similar to Twitter, but with more emphasis on image and picture sharing.

FACEBOOK FOR BLOGGERS

As a blogger, if you are not on Facebook, then you really need to sign up, as no other social media platform is as popular or effective at blog promotion. If you are already on Facebook, you can use your account for promoting your blog.

The great thing about using Facebook is the speed at which content passes from person to person. When you post something, all your Facebook friends see it on their home feed and, if they share it with their network, you can attract hundreds and even thousands of people to your blog.

Fan Pages

If you already have a Facebook page, you may not want it all to be about your blog, as you may bore your existing friends. For this reason, you can set up a fan page.

1. Click the **Create Page** link on the bottom of your Facebook page.

2. Choose the type of new page you want. For a blog fan page, choose **Cause or Community**, unless you are corporate blogging, in which case choose **Company, Organization or Institution**.

3. Choose a name for your fan page and enter the details. Remember to include a link to your blog.

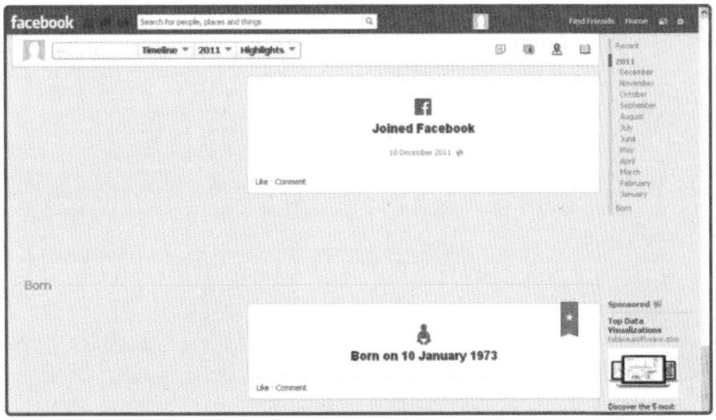

Above: Facebook gives you the option to create a blog fan page.

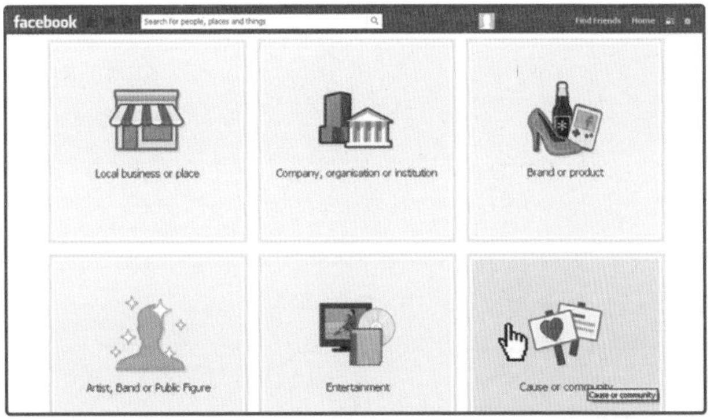

Above: Select Cause or Community to begin a blog fan page.

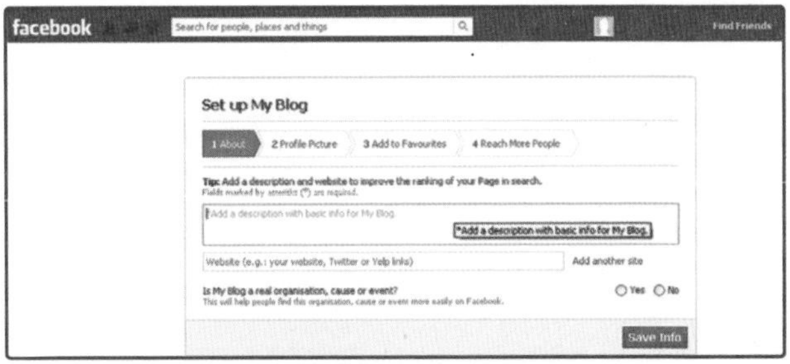

Above: Be sure to enter your fan page's details, as well as a link to your blog.

Once you have set up your fan page, you can even import your blog posts directly into it using your blog feed. (More on this in the next section: Interfacing With Your Audience).

TWITTER FOR BLOGGERS

Twitter is one of the simplest ways of spreading the word about your blog and announcing new blog posts to like-minded people. Twitter works in a different way to Facebook. Essentially, Twitter is a microblogging site, in which you can post content up to 140 characters long, such as a link to your latest blog post.

Following

What makes Twitter so useful for bloggers is that, rather than having friends, you have 'followers' and, in turn, those you follow. This enables you to follow all those people in your community or those with an interest related to your blog's topic. When you follow people, quite often they will reciprocate, especially if your profile includes details of your chosen topic, which may interest them.

Tweeting About Your Posts

Twitter is great for sending links and details about your latest blog posts.

1. Click in the compose box and write your message. Include the title of your post in the compose window and insert a link to your blog in a message. Do not worry if the link is too large, as Twitter will shorten it.

2. Include a relevant hashtag.

3. Press **Tweet**.

Hot Tip

Twitter uses 'hashtags' that people include in their posts to make it easier for others to find relevant content, for example #blogging or #fishing.

Above: Hashtags on Twitter allow followers to access information through keywords that appeal to them.

Retweets

What makes Twitter so effective for getting the word out to a wide community is the 'retweet' function. When followers like one of your posts, they can forward it on to all their followers. This makes it possible for one of your tweets to reach a large number of people, no matter how many followers you have yourself. Make sure you retweet other people's posts too, as this helps affirm your position in the community.

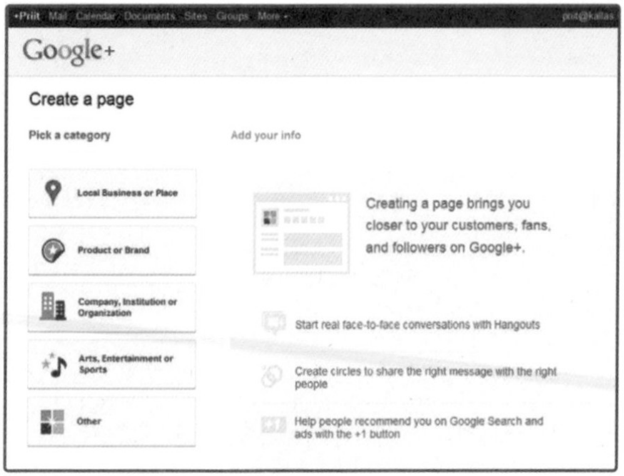
Google+
Create a page
Pick a category
Add your info
Local Business or Place
Product or Brand
Company, Institution or Organization
Arts, Entertainment or Sports
Other
Creating a page brings you closer to your customers, fans, and followers on Google+.
Start real face-to-face conversations with Hangouts
Create circles to share the right message with the right people
Help people recommend you on Google Search and ads with the +1 button

Above: Creating a page on Google+ may mean a boost in Google's search-engine rankings.

Best of YouTube
Popular on YouTube - Unit...

Above: If you are interested in 'vlogging,' you may want to set up a YouTube channel.

Hot Tip

Bloggers who post regular and consistent content on Google+ often find they get a boost in Google's search-engine rankings.

OTHER SOCIAL MEDIA PLATFORMS

While Facebook and Twitter are the two most widely used social media platforms, there are others. Whether or not you wish to take advantage of other social networking sites will depend on how much time you have and the type of blog you are using.

LinkedIn

Aimed at those in the business world, LinkedIn is a useful platform for connecting with others in the same industry as you. If you have a corporate blog, announcing new posts on LinkedIn to your connections can be an effective way of boosting your audience.

Google+

A fairly new social media platform, Google+ does have a fairly substantial number of users. If you are using Blogger, you will find it is easy to interact with Google+. You can also create a group for all those people in your community.

YouTube

Many bloggers now implement podcasts and videos in their blog, and YouTube is a great platform for getting these seen and heard. Creating a short video is a great way to keep your community engaged and keep your blog interesting and fresh. You can create your own YouTube channel for all your videos.

Tumblr

Tumblr works in a similar way to Twitter and, for those with an image-based blog, such as photographers or artists, it is a great way to share pictures and spread the word about your blog. Tumblr is also great for posting videos and audio clips.

Above: Tumblr is a great way to display images, videos and audioclips.

PITFALLS OF SOCIAL MEDIA

There is no doubt that social media can be useful for growing an audience. However, it is only effective if it is used properly. Many bloggers make the same two mistakes when employing social media, and then wonder why it is not working for them.

- **Self-promotion**: Social media is great at promoting your blog, but not if that is all you do. If the only updates you post are promotions for your blog, your friends and followers will soon get tired of you.

- **Time consumption**: Spending too much time on social media can cut into the time you should be using for writing and researching blog posts. Schedule a set number of hours for social media promotion each week.

MAKING YOUR BLOG SOCIAL-MEDIA FRIENDLY

The great thing about social media is that you can leave a lot of your promotion to your audience. However, to ensure this, you need to make it easy for your audience to share your blog posts on their social media platforms, and for this you will need to include social media buttons on your blog.

Social Media Buttons

Adding social media buttons to a blog used to be unnecessarily difficult and involved searching for icons and embedding code into your blog. However, due to the prevalence of social media platforms, including social media buttons is now pretty straightforward, especially on WordPress.

Above: Adding social media buttons gives readers direct access to the content you post outside of your blog.

1. At the bottom of your blog post, check the two boxes under **Likes and Shares**.

2. When you publish your blog post, your social media buttons will appear on the bottom of the blog.

Hot Tip

To add social media buttons on Blogger, use the Add Gadget function in Layout. You will find social media buttons called Share It in the More Gadgets menu.

INTERFACING WITH YOUR AUDIENCE

Once you start getting visitors to your blog, you need to make sure they keep coming back for more. Interacting and interfacing with your audience is an important part of making your blog an engaging and interesting place to be.

KEEPING YOUR VISITORS HAPPY

Keeping your visitors happy is the surest way of growing an audience. This means not only providing regular content that they want, but also providing it in an easy-to-access manner.

Categories and Tags

Finding information easily is essential. If your visitors cannot find what they are looking for quickly, they will look elsewhere. You should think of your blog as one large filing cabinet, where things are properly ordered and labelled. Your blogging platform provides two ways of labelling your blog posts.

- **Categories:** Label a post so it falls under a particular category. This enables a visitor to find all posts related to the same theme or topic.
- **Tags:** These are words that sum up different aspects of the blog post, usually relating to a subject, product or item mentioned.

Hot Tip

WordPress will recommend tags based on words in your blog post that are used by other bloggers.

Adding Tags and Categories to Your Posts

You will find the category and tag tools beside your main post window. When you have written your posts, think about the central themes. Your categories should reflect this. Is it opinion? News? Practical information?

When it comes to tags, look for names and things that you have mentioned in other posts.

Above: Categories and tags allow readers to find what they are looking for quickly and without hassle.

Above: A user is notified whenever you post a new blog entry.

Above: Click Full to activate your feed in Blogger.

BLOG FEEDS

Rather than rely on your visitors coming to you, you can notify your visitors whenever you have a new blog post by using a live feed. WordPress automatically includes a blog feed as a small tab labelled **Follow** at the bottom right-hand corner of each blog post, which users can click to insert their email address.

Activating Feeds in Blogger

To activate feeds on a Blogger blog:

1. Go into the **Settings** menu and click **Other**.

2. Where it says **Allow Blog Feeds**, change from **None** to **Full**.

ENCOURAGING COMMENTS

To build a community, you need to encourage debate and discussion. This means you need to encourage your audience to leave comments and contribute to the blog, and you can do this in a number of ways.

CONTRIBUTION

Even if your blog is getting plenty of visitors, you are not going to be able to build a community unless people are leaving comments. Comments are the single most powerful tool for enabling interaction and contribution. Some of the most popular blogs often have hundreds of comments after each post, so how do they do it?

Start the Ball Rolling

People do not like to be the first to raise their head above the parapet, especially on a new blog. So the first step to encouraging comments is to get the ball rolling. Some bloggers resort to using sock puppets (logging in under a fake name to post fake comments), but this is not recommended, as there is a chance you will be found out. So how do you encourage those first comments?

- **Be opinionated:** Nobody is going to comment on a blog post if you are presenting straightforward, unchallenging information. Voice your opinions about the topic and be passionate.

Above: Encourage comments and interaction with readers by being opinionated and provoking questions.

- **Be contrarian:** Nothing starts debate more quickly than playing devil's advocate. Present your blog posts from contrarian viewpoints to provide a catalyst for discussion.

- **Call to action:** Do not just leave it up to your audience to make a comment; prompt them.

Hot Tip

People are more likely to comment if people know who you are. Make sure your name is on your post and, if need be, use an author's bio or an About Me page so people know they are interacting with a real person.

YOUR CALL TO ACTION

Utilizing a call to action in your post can prompt your audience to comment. A simple way is to round off your blog post with a question, such as 'What do you think?' However, you can also centre your entire post on a question. Use headlines such as: 'Is This the Best/Worst ... You Have Ever Seen?'

Keep the Conversation Going

When you get your first comment, try to keep the conversation going. Offer an open-ended response or pose an alternative question to allow the commentator to come back with a response. However, do not pressure people to respond. Keep your blog welcoming and friendly.

Be Interested

Many people think the key to successful blogging is to provide interesting content. While this is essential, interest goes both ways. If your audience feels you are not interested in their views or anything they say, you will start to lose them. When people start commenting on your blog, engage positively with them, even if you do not hold with their views and opinions. Rather than just saying thank you for their comment, discuss what you agree and disagree with, but make sure you remain friendly and, whatever you do, never get into an argument. Always make sure people feel you appreciate that they have taken the time to make a comment and you value what they have to say.

Admitting When You Are Wrong

Most of us find it hard to admit it when we are wrong, but failing to do so can make us appear arrogant and obnoxious. If your views and opinions have generated a large number of opposing views, do not be afraid to backtrack and concede you could have been wrong.

COMMENT SETTINGS

You can control the comment settings in your blogging platform's control panel. In WordPress, this is under the submenu **Discussion**; in Blogger, it is under **Posts and comments**. Usually, you have several options.

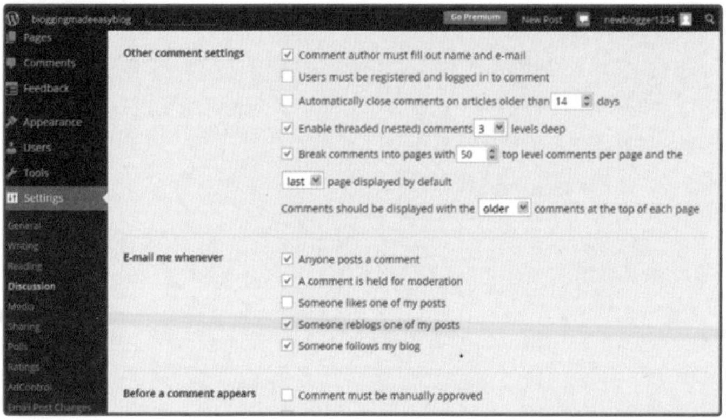

Above: Comment settings in WordPress can be found under the submenu 'Discussion.

Above: Modify your comment settings on Blogger to fit your needs.

- **Comments on or off**: You should only turn off comments for a good reason, such as on older posts or if the topic may lead to discussions with legal ramifications.

- **Moderation**: Enables you to view a comment before you post it or allow a comment to go live as soon as the poster presses submit. You can also control whether you permit links in people's comments.

- **Anonymous commenting**: You can choose to allow anonymous comments or only people who have included an email address or logged in with social media account details.

Hot Tip

Set your comment settings to accept pingbacks. These are notifications when another blog links to yours and can help you identify other bloggers and audiences relevant to your subject area.

TO MODERATE OR NOT TO MODERATE

Choosing not to moderate comments has its advantages. When people post a comment, they like to see it appear straightaway, which enables others to comment and discussions to begin that are close to real time. Having to wait several hours or days to see a reply to a comment can frustrate your audience. However, not moderating comments can also cause problems.

Offensive Comments

Not moderating comments can mean that people may post something offensive. These can be personal attacks against you or somebody else or the comment may include bad language or content you would rather not have attached to your blog.

Spam

Another problem in not moderating comments is that you may find your blog becomes attractive to spammers. While some blogging platforms such as WordPress have antispam software to block spam, these are never 100 per cent effective.

Retrospective Moderation

To encourage comments but prevent the negative aspects that can result in not moderating comments, many bloggers choose to moderate comments retrospectively. This means taking the time each day to look at the comments on your blog and deleting or censoring comments.

Comment Policy

Make sure your audience knows what is permitted on your blog and what is not. The best way to do this is to draft a comments policy and post it on your blog. This should include all those things you do not want to see on your blog.

- **Legal**: Ensure your audience knows you do not want to see anything that breaches somebody else's copyright or breaches the law in any way.
- **Obscenity**: Make sure your audience knows that you will not tolerate obscene or offensive comments, including abuse and harassment.

About
Message from Dr. Noseworthy
Mission & Values
Addresses & Phone Numbers
Facts & Statistics
Annual Report
Governance
Newsroom
In The News
News Releases
Medical Edge
Blogs
RSS Web Feeds
Social Media
Podcasts
Resources
Contact
Destination Medical Center (DMC)
Publications
Share on:
Comment Policy
We encourage your comments on Mayo Clinic's various blogs, and hope you will join the discussions. We can't respond to every comment, particularly those that deal with individual medical cases and issues. We review comments before they're posted, and those that are off-topic or clearly promoting a commercial product generally won't make the cut. We also expect a basic level of civility; disagreements are fine, but mutual respect is a must, and profanity or abusive language are out-of-bounds.
That's the plain English version. Here it is in legal language:
By posting any comments, posts or other material on Mayo-sponsored blogs, you give Mayo Foundation for Medical Education and Research ("Mayo") the irrevocable right to reproduce, distribute, publish, display, edit, modify, create derivative works from, and otherwise use your submission for any purpose in any form and on any media. You also agree that you will not:
1. Post material that infringes on the rights of any third party, including intellectual property, privacy or publicity rights.
2. Post material that is unlawful, obscene, defamatory, threatening, harassing, abusive, slanderous, hateful, or

Above: Specify the kind of commentary you're encouraging, so as to avoid legal conflict and obscenity.

- **Advertisements and spam:** It is your blog, not somebody else's platform to sell their goods and services.

- **Content:** Make sure your audience knows the type of content you permit. If you do not like bad language, ensure your audience knows it.

Moderating Comments In WordPress

You can moderate comments in WordPress using the **Comments** menu on the dashboard. Here you can see who sent a comment, their email and IP addresses.

bloggingmadeeasyblog
Go Premium
New Post
Dashboard
Store
Posts
Media
Links
Pages
Comments
Feedback
Appearance
Users
Tools
Settings
Collapse menu
Comments
Screen Options
All | Pending (0) | Approved | Spam (0) | Trash (0)
Bulk Actions
Apply
Show all comment types
Filter
Check for Spam
Author
Comment
A Newbie's Guide to Blogging | oldienewbies
oldienewbies.wordpress.com/2013/10/09/a-newbies-g...
192.0.82.86
Submitted on 2013/10/09 at 2:49 pm
[...] How to Write a Killer Blog Post (bloggingmadeeasyblog.wordpress.com) [...]
Robert Forrester (@ForresterRobert)
twitter.com/ForresterRobert
ForresterRobert@twitter.example.com
86.182.57.131
Submitted on 2013/10/09 at 12:09 pm
Great article. You have hit on some good points, but I do disagree on one aspect. Surely a blog post is all about providing information
Author
Comment

Above: Moderating comments allows you to filter out anything you deem inappropriate.

1. To permit a comment, tick the box and click **Approve**.

2. To remove a comment already posted, click **Unapprove**.

3. To edit a comment's content, tick the box and click **Edit**.

4. To delete or mark a comment as spam, tick the box and click either **Trash** or **Spam**.

Above: Editing a comment can be useful in removing obscenities, while still allowing posters to voice opinions.

Blacklisting and Auto-moderation

WordPress also allows you to set up a blacklist that holds certain content in moderation but allows other posts to appear immediately. This is useful for stopping people with certain IP and email addresses from making comments on your blog.

1. In **Discussion** settings, scroll down to **Comment Moderation** and **Comment Blacklist**.

Hot Tip

If you edit somebody's post to take out bad language or anything that contravenes your comments policy, ensure you let the person know what you have done and why.

2. Enter which words, email address or IP numbers you want to block for moderation or blacklisting.

FREEDOM OF SPEECH

You have to be careful when moderating comments not to exert too much censorship. Some bloggers make the mistake of only permitting comments that reinforce their arguments. However, if your audience feels that you are censoring what they say or do not permit contrarian views, they will stop commenting and possibly stop visiting your blog altogether. Only censor those things that may cause offence or contravene your comments policy.

Anonymous Comments

Some people do not like to post under their name. This may be for good reasons, such as if they hold a position in an industry and want to share their experiences without jeopardizing their job, or they may feel vulnerable to being bullied or harassed because of their views. However, some people use anonymity to post offensive comments, as well as bullying and harassing other people. This has become commonly known as 'trolling'. For this reason, if you permit anonymous comments, ensure you moderate your comments regularly to avoid trolls from harassing and bullying your visitors.

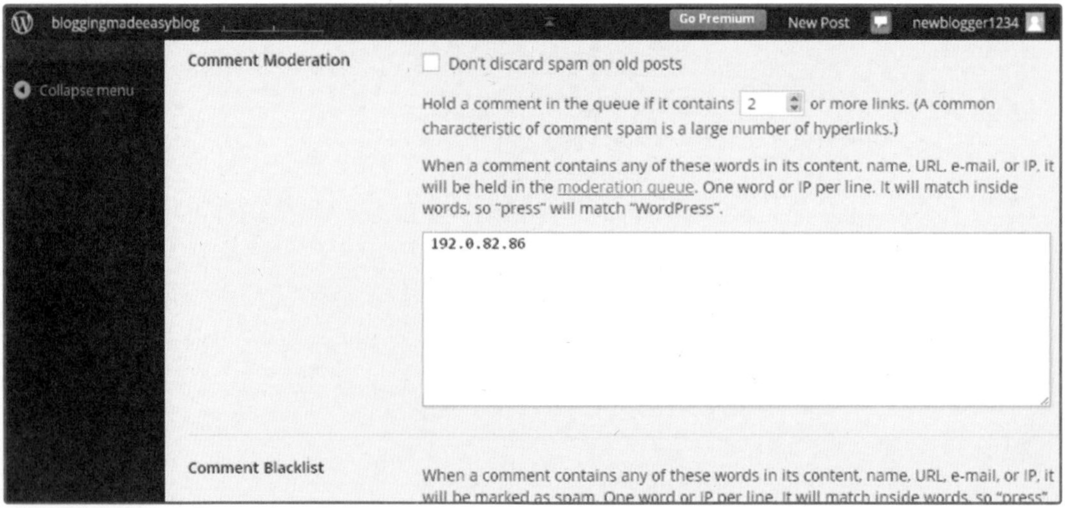

bloggingmadeeasyblog
Go Premium
New Post
newblogger1234
Collapse menu
Comment Moderation
Don't discard spam on old posts
Hold a comment in the queue if it contains 2 or more links. (A common characteristic of comment spam is a large number of hyperlinks.)
When a comment contains any of these words in its content, name, URL, e-mail, or IP, it will be held in the moderation queue. One word or IP per line. It will match inside words, so "press" will match "WordPress".
192.0.82.86
Comment Blacklist
When a comment contains any of these words in its content, name, URL, e-mail, or IP, it

Above: Blacklisting enables you to stop the owners of certain IP and email addresses from commenting on your blog.

SETTING THE TONE

Some blogs are light-hearted, while others are more serious. Setting the tone of your blog will depend on your subject matter and the type of person you are, but it is not always easy to get right.

DEFINING THE TONE

The right tone can make or break a blog. The tone is what gets a reader's attention and is often the reason they keep coming back for more. Even if you are publishing similar posts to other bloggers, you can become unique by setting a different tone to everybody else.

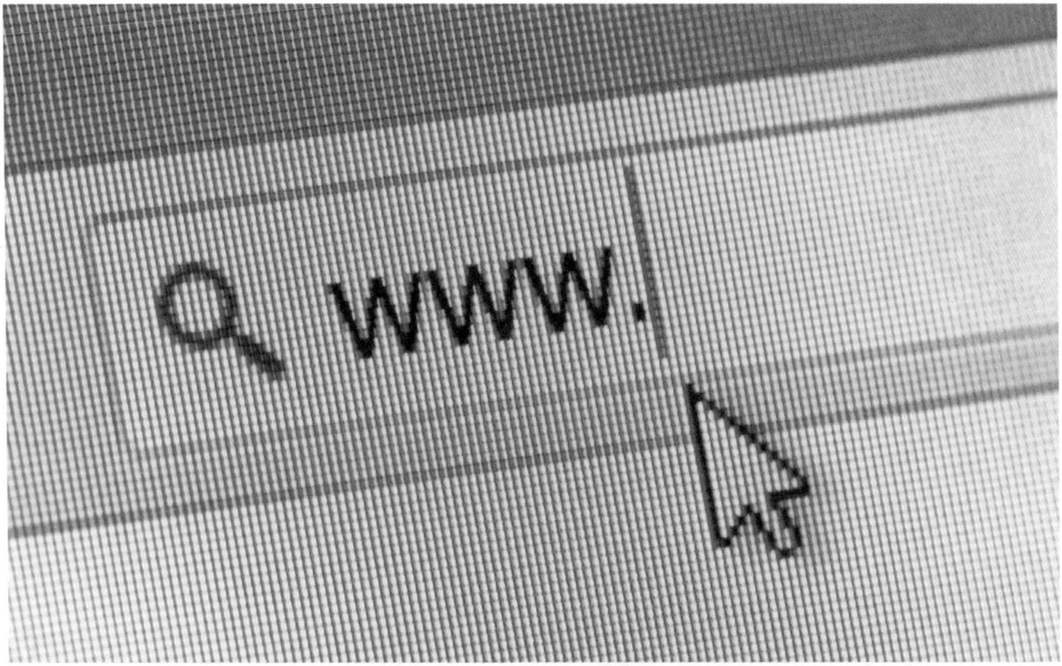

Attributes

The tone of your blog will be based on several factors.

- **Your voice**: This is your unique author's voice. Your voice is how you communicate, the way you use words, together with your humour and wit that comes across in your writing.
- **Content**: Blogging on a serious subject may require a serious tone, while light-hearted topics suit a more jocular tone.
- **Audience:** Knowing what sort of tone your audience prefers is often the hardest aspect of setting the tone of your blog.

About Us
With over 20 years of quick and easy recipes we have thousands of dishes for the beginner and the enthusiastic!
The Complete Step-by-Step Baking Cookbook
The Quick and Easy Recipe Blog
Current Articles | RSS Feed
Top 10 Simple Recipes for Students #7: Jacket Potatoes and Chilli
Posted by Esme Chapman
Like 1
Tweet 0
8+1 0
Share 2
Submit
I don't know about you, but one of my favourite things about winter has to be cosying up in warm, wooly jumpers accompanied by good friends and a plateful of homemade food hot from the oven. Things may be a little more draughty away from home, so being at uni is even more reason to indulge in warming feasts. If you are looking for a filling and healthy winter warmer, look no further than this Chilli Con Carne with Crispy Jacket Potato – another one to add to the list of fantastically simple recipes!
A perfect balance of comforting carbs and tasty meat, this easy recipe is great for the bank balance as it is pretty much wholly comprised of cheap and easily available ingredients. If you are vegetarian, don't stop reading!
Free Download
FREE Recipe book here
Download a digital Recipe book, a special edition Party Cakes.
Step-by-Step, Practical Recipes
party cakes
Follow Me

Above: In this cookery blog, the author is matching her tone with the recipe she is including: her language is cosy, comforting and inviting, making you want to read on.

VOICE

When discussing writers, people often refer to the author's voice. Voice is simply the way an author writes and is what makes them unique. All sorts of things determine an author's voice, such as their sense of humour, word choice and the way they use different writing techniques such as metaphors or similes to get their points across.

Determining Your Voice

Many writers struggle to identify their voice. However, you will probably find that, if you let your personality show in your writing, you will develop your own unique style. Try not to be contrived when you write. Aspects of your personality, such as humour, cannot be forced, so be yourself and allow your voice to come through naturally.

Language

One of the key factors in developing your voice is in the way you use language. Some bloggers enjoy using colourful words while others take a more restrained approach.

> **Hot Tip**
>
> **To inject some personality into your blog, think of the many phrases you use in everyday life and include them in your writing.**

Content

The type of content you are writing about will also affect the tone of your blog. Do not make light of serious subject matter, as you may cause offence. However, this does not mean you cannot inject humour and wit into even the gravest of topics, as long as you handle it properly and do so with empathy and consideration for other people's feelings.

Ever feel angry with your children? Here are 10 coping strategies to help you defuse

I don't know about you, but sometimes I get a bit angry and shouty with my children. It's usually because they're not listening, or they're squabbling or faffing about while I'm trying to get their hair and teeth brushed before it's time to leave for school. Sometimes it's simply the level of noise – a house with three kids is lived at top volume, and it can make my head spin. Sometimes, however, I shout because I'm dead tired and ready for the day to end. And of course, they're still not listening.

But I don't like myself much when I lose control with my kids, so recently I signed up for a course on understanding anger for parents run by the British Association of Anger Management (BAAM).

Here are the top 10 things I learned:

1. It's not them, it's you. Think about the last time you were angry with your children. 'A parent doesn't get angry because of what a child says or does,' says Mike Fisher, director of BAAM. 'Instead you get angry because of a sense of momentary inadequacy – for that moment, you felt like a failure as a parent because you had no control over your child.' He says that when your child pushes back against your rules, you feel you then have justification for getting angry.
2. Listen carefully to your child. Many parents don't listen properly, according to Mike. Ask your child what he needs, and hear what he has to say. Accept that it's okay to have a different opinion.
3. We all have unmet needs – yes, parents too. Everyone has primary needs which must be met in order for us to feel content as human beings. For example, we need attention, praise, love, reward, affection, fairness, justice, to be listened to, valued, understood, trusted, supported and heard.Problems start when parents expect to receive these primary needs from their children. For example, you become angry if your child doesn't listen to you (a primary need) when it's time for his bath.'It's important that you meet your own primary needs if you're also going to meet your children's,' says Mike. Take time to think about what you would like out of life too. Consider taking up a new interest, and strengthening your friendships or relationship so you feel more fulfilled in daily life.

Above: By blogging about something that is familiar to you, you will be well placed to offer advice to your audience based on your own experience, as in this parenting blog.

Passion

If you write about subjects that you are passionate about, you will find it much easier to develop your voice. Choose topics that really interest you and express your opinions and views. If you can write passionately, you can invoke a similar response from your readers. Make sure you are being honest and genuine to yourself and your audience. Faking enthusiasm rarely works.

Outspoken Bloggers

Some bloggers thrive on being outspoken and controversial. Of course, you can take this too far and risk offending and alienating your audience, but it is better to be passionate about a subject than to come across as being flat and uninteresting.

AUDIENCE

Ensure you know the type of people who are likely to read your blog. If you are writing for a young audience, your blog will have a much different tone than a blog aimed at serious professionals. In many respects, your audience will help define the tone of your blog. Even if you lack humour in your writing, you may find many of the people who comment will bring a degree of light-heartedness to your blog.

Control the Tone

Many bloggers start to lose their audience when they lose control of the tone. Allowing the community to take over and control the tone of your blog can create a negative atmosphere. Never allow people to be intimidated or alienated on your blog by another's comments. Make sure everybody knows the rules and that everybody has the right to their opinion.

Hot Tip

Maintain a regular presence in the comments on your blog. People are less likely to break the rules if they know you are there. If you think things are getting out of control, step in.

Be Welcoming

Above all else, the tone of your blog should be welcoming. This means setting an atmosphere that ensures people feel comfortable in commenting and engaging in discussions. Make sure everybody who visits your blog feels important and welcome. When you get people who comment regularly on your blog posts, it can be very easy to concentrate on their views and opinions, but do not forget the rest of your audience.

Be Personal

Address people by name. When it is the first time somebody comments, welcome them to the community and encourage them to take part in more discussions.

Niger River Project
4 countries, 3 months, 2 guys, 1 canoe...
SEARCH
« Leaving Timbuktu | Home | Journey from Hell, part 1 , or El Dorado »
LOGIN
Pink sand
Gao is the former capital of the once great Songhai empire that ruled this part of West Africa several hundred years ago. Today, it's not all that much to look at, a typical Sahara/Sahel town with wide sandy streets, flat-topped mud buildings and the innevitable piles of filth.
I get the overnight bus from Mopti to Gao, arriving at about six in the morning. Emerging tired and bleary, I'm immediately set upon by the innevitable tout who takes advantage of my state and whisks me off to some dismal looking campement south of the town.
Actually, it turns out to be a gem of a place - cheap, relaxed with friendly staff and other guests, though from first glance it looks a total flea-pit.
I meet up with a young Tamashek speaking local, who introduces himself as Small Guy. I never find out his real name, but he's a handy fellow and helps me arrange my onward trip to Niger.
The thing I immediately notice about Gao is actually apparent from its absence: here, the children aren't yelling 'toubab' at me every step I take as they do in other parts of Mali. And they aren't demanding 'cadeaux' - the presents that kids in Mali's touristy areas seem to expect from whites.
Recently Posted
» Endings
» Metropolis
» Oil on troubled waters
» Capital of Nigeria
» Echoes from the past
» Journey from hell, part 2: into the fire
» Dash
Categories
» Travel (55)
Mungo Park
» BBC Radio 4
» Overview
» Project Primate
» Undiscovered Scotland
My Links
» Charity
» Map
» Roger McCarey
» Travel Blog Support
Travel Links
» Cheap Air Tickets
» Travel Insurance
» Travel Blogs
» Travel Deals
» Last Minute Adventures

Above: Blog about something you love; if it enthuses you, it will enthuse your audience, as with this travelogue.

Enjoy Yourself

One sure way of maintaining a positive and welcoming tone on your blog is if you are enjoying it. If you are finding that blogging is becoming a chore or an irritation, it may be time to take a break. Ask somebody to guest blog for you and take over the moderation for a while. That way, you can come back refreshed, which will ensure you maintain your enthusiasm.

USING MULTIMEDIA IN YOUR BLOG

USING PHOTOS AND IMAGES

They say a picture is worth a thousand words and, in blogging, this is certainly the case. Using images and photographs is crucial for capturing people's attention, but using them comes with plenty of pitfalls.

WHY USE IMAGES?

As with other forms of publishing, images serve various purposes on blog posts:

- **To catch the eye**: An image can draw attention to a blog post and entice a visitor to read more.

UNVEILING...
L'OREAL
NEW PERFECTLY INVISIBLE FOUNDATION
OUR IDEAL NUDE.
The Wicked Girls - a riveting and intelligent psychological thriller
Mark Frauenfelder at 9:17 am Mon, Oct 7, 2013
THE WICKED GIRLS
In 1986 two girls, Bel and Jade, achieved international infamy at age eleven for murdering a four-year-old girl. Twenty five years later, the now-grown up and rehabilitated women are back in society, living under new identities given to them by the British government. They haven't seen each other since their trials, and in fact are forbidden from
— FEATURED —
FEATURE
BOOK REVIEW
BOOK REVIEW

Above: Using images can be a useful way to structure your blog.

- **To break up text**: Long blocks of text can be off-putting to readers, but images can improve the appearance of a blog post and make it look more palatable.

- **To provide explanation**: An image can help describe what the post is about, or help emphasize a particular point.

- **To set the tone**: The right images can help set the tone of a blog post.

- **To boost visibility**: People search for information in various ways on the internet, including using image searches. Having images on your blog increases the number of ways people can find you.

SELECTING YOUR IMAGES

You have to be selective when including images in your blog post. An image has to be relevant to what you are writing about, as well as reflecting the tone of the post. For instance, if you are writing about a serious subject, you do not want to use a humorous image or cartoon, but for light-hearted posts, you will want a frivolous image. The best images to use are those that tell a story or clearly explain what your blog post is about.

> **Hot Tip**
>
> **Images of people pulling different facial expressions, such as shock, anger or happiness, are a great way to set the tone of your blog post.**

Searching for Images

These days, finding appropriate images for blog posts could not be easier. Tools such as Google Image search, Flickr and Photobucket mean that, with just a few keywords, you can find an image for almost anything. However, while finding images on the internet could not be easier, using them is fraught with problems, especially when it comes to copyright and licences.

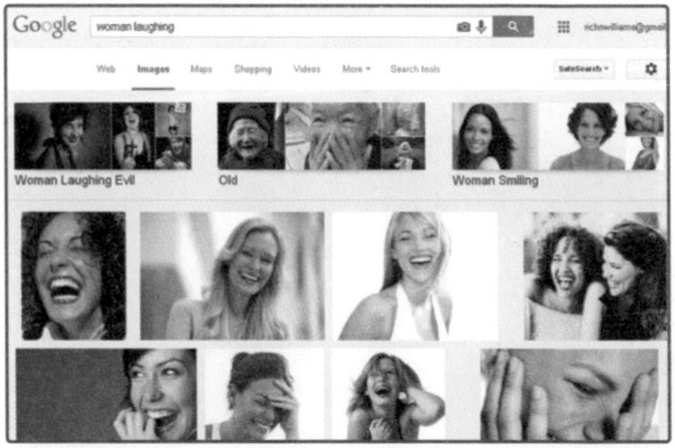

Above: Results from a Google Image search.

LEGAL ISSUES

Just because the internet makes it easy to find images, this does not mean you can use anything you find. Images are subject to copyright. This means that, unless you get permission from the rights holder, using an image could result in legal ramifications. The internet is full of horror stories of how bloggers have been sued

Above: Google Image search is a quick way to find images that are relevant to your text.

for copyright infringement, so it is important to understand copyright rules and know what you can and cannot publish on your blog.

Copyright Myths

Many people fail to understand copyright law and many myths have developed about using images on blogs and websites.

- **An image is on another blog, so I can use it:** This is simply not true. An image is protected by copyright, no matter where it is published.

- **Only images with a copyright symbol (©) are protected:** Again, not true. All intellectual property, including images, are automatically copyrighted when they are created. Just because you do not see a copyright symbol does not mean you can use the image.

- **You can use an image if you attribute it:** Some bloggers think by referencing where they got an image, it makes it okay. Not the case; you may still be infringing copyright.

Seeking Permission

Before you can use an image, you need permission from the rights holder. This is not an easy process. It may not be clear who the rights holder is. If it is a photograph, normally the photographer owns the copyright for the image. However, as it is possible to sell and license rights to other people, you may have to follow a long chain until you find the owner of the image.

Hot Tip

If you see an image on the internet that you want to use on your blog, contact the blog or website where you found it and ask who owns the rights.

IMAGE RESOURCES

There are easier ways of finding images for your blog. Not all images are subject to copyright, and there are numerous ways of using images on your blog posts without falling foul of the law.

Taking Your Own Photos

The simplest way to avoid the headache of copyright is to take your own photos for your blog. These days, you do not need an expensive camera to take a good-quality picture, as most phones have decent digital cameras on them. In addition to providing you with images to use, taking your own photos means your blog will be more original than those that use stock images from an image library.

Stock Images

Above: Shutterstock's picture library provides a wide variety of images to subscribers.

Stock images are those from an image library. Often, these are called royalty-free images. However, this does not mean the image is free. A royalty-free image simply means you pay a one-off fee, which entitles you to use the image for multiple purposes without having to pay royalties to the rights holder. When using royalty-free images, it is important to read the terms and conditions carefully, as some pictures may be subject to specific stipulations of usage, such as how often they can be reproduced or whether they can be used for commercial purposes.

Some of the most popular stock image libraries include:

- **iStockphoto**: One of the largest image libraries on the internet, iStock has millions of images. Users purchase credits, which they can trade for images, many of which work out at less than a dollar (60–70 pence).

- **Shutterstock**: A huge library of images available to users who purchase a subscription or image-on-demand package, which vary from £29–£139 ($45–$220) depending on the size and quantity of images required.

- **Getty Images**: A little more expensive than other stock libraries, Getty Images is aimed more at businesses and corporate websites and blogs.

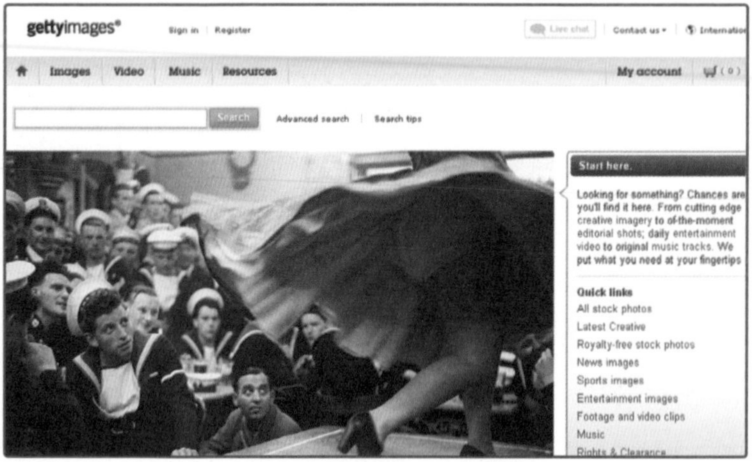

Above: If you are blogging for a business or corporation, Getty Images may be an option.

Free Image Resources

Not all image libraries charge. If you do not have the budget to buy stock images, you can find numerous places on the internet where images are free to use on your blog.

Hot Tip

Many companies include images with their press releases. If you are blogging about a company, product or service, visit their, website as you may find images in their media department or press office.

Creative Commons

Creative Commons is a nonprofit organization that licenses creative works, such as images, free of charge for the public to use. Some of the top Creative Commons image resources include:

- **Wikicommons**: Contains free-to-use images and other media files, many of which are used by the online encyclopedia Wikipedia.

- **Flickr**: An image-hosting website where users can upload images under the Creative Commons licence.

- **Photobucket**: Another image-hosting website full of free-to-use Creative Commons licensed images.

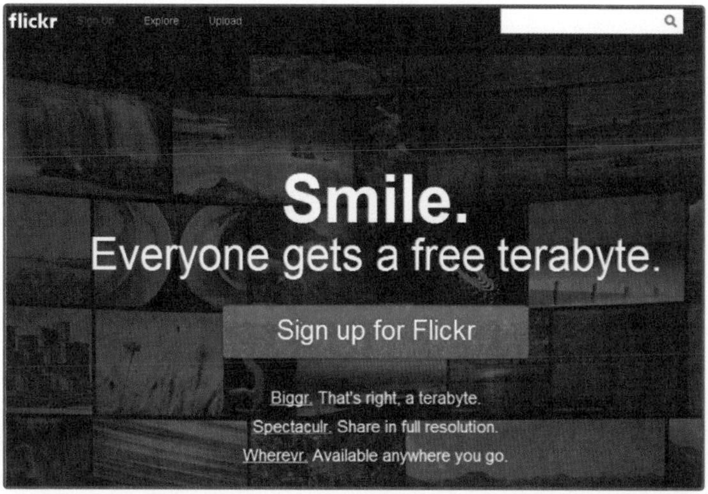

Above: Flickr allows users to upload images under the Creative Commons licence.

Creative Commons Licence

Not all images on the above websites are free from restrictions. Some images are marked 'All Rights Reserved', which means you still need permission from the rights holders. Other images may fall under one of four licences:

- **Attribution generic:** You can use the image in any way you like, as long as you credit the rights holder.

- **Attribution noncommercial generic:** As above, but you cannot use the image for commercial purposes.

- **Attribution no derivative works generic:** Means you must credit the rights holder but cannot alter the image in any way, such as by cropping.

- **Attribution noncommercial no derivative works generic:** As above, but you cannot use the image for commercial purposes.

MANIPULATING IMAGES

When you find an image for your blog, you may wish to make some changes so that it looks and fits better. While there may be restrictions on making alterations on a licensed image, in many cases, you are permitted to crop and resize an image. However, for this, you will need some image-editing software.

Image-editing Software

Image-editing software varies from the very basic, useful for simple tasks such as cropping and resizing images, to the more complicated that can make all sorts of manipulations and alterations to an image. Image-editing software can be expensive, but you can also download free programs that can do many of the basic tasks required by bloggers.

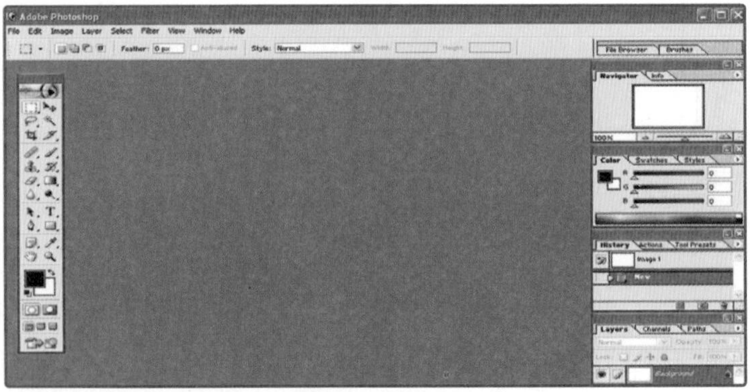

Above: If you are looking to run a photo-based blog, you may want to consider using Photoshop.

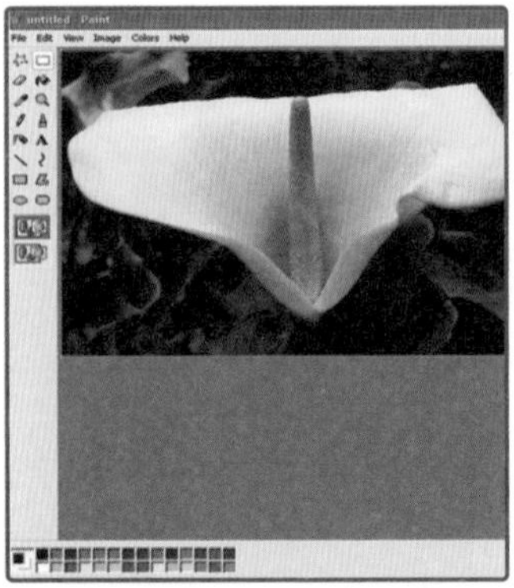

Above: Microsoft Paint, available to most PC users, enables access to basic level image editing.

- **Photoshop**: Industry-standard image-editing software that is used by professional photographers and graphic designers. Probably too sophisticated for most bloggers, but is worth considering for anybody with a photo-based blog.

A free-to-download imagemanipulation program that can do many of the same tasks as Photoshop.

- **Microsoft Paint**: Installed on most Windows PCs, Paint provides very basic image-editing functions.

- **Paint.net**: Another free image-editing program that has functionality somewhere in the middle between MS Paint and Photoshop.

Hot Tip

Many digital cameras come with basic image-editing software that enables you to do some simple manipulations such as cropping, resizing and touching up your pictures.

Cropping an Image

It is often necessary to crop to improve composition, zoom in on a particular aspect of the picture or to change the shape of the picture (orientation). There are multiple ways to crop an image in image-editing software. Some programs have specific crop tools, while others need you to cut out the part of the image you need, which is simple to do.

1. Remember to save a copy of the image, as cropping pictures will change the original image.
2. Open up the image in your editing software.
3. Choose the **Select** tool. This often resembles a rectangle.
4. Select the area you want to keep by drawing a rectangle around it.
5. Go into the edit menu and select **Copy** (or press **Ctrl C/Command C**).
6. Go into the file menu and select **New** (Or press **Ctrl N/Command N**).
7. Paste the image into the new window by using **Paste** in the edit menu (or **Ctrl V/Command V**).
8. Save the new file under a different name.

Above: Cropping in Microsoft Paint allows you to manipulate photos to best suit your needs.

Above: Select the area, then copy it.

Above: Paste the image into a new file.

INSERTING IMAGES INTO YOUR POSTS

Once you have cropped your image, it is time to include it in your blog post. Different blogging platforms handle the insertion and manipulation of images slightly differently, but in most cases, you can upload straight from your computer.

Uploading Images To WordPress

1. Choose the point in your blog post where you want your image to be included and click **Add Media**.

2. Choose the image to upload from the **Insert Media** menu; alternatively, choose an image from your WordPress library by selecting **Media Library**.

3. Click **Insert to Post**.

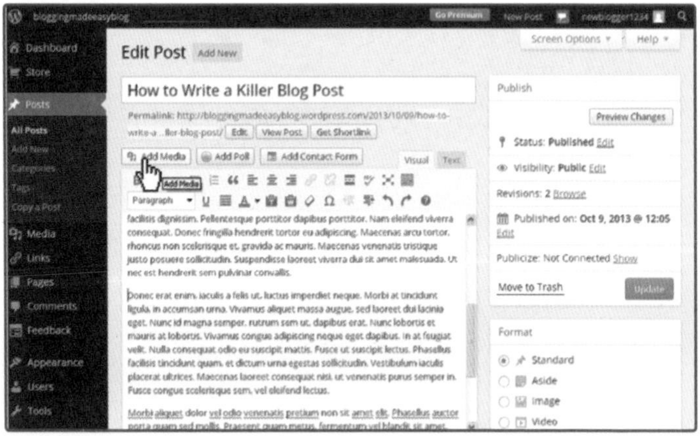

Above: Select Add Media once you have determined where you want your image to appear.

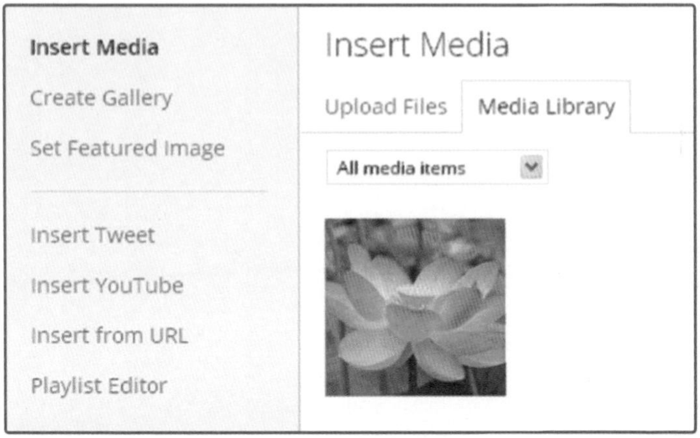

Above: Choose the image that you would like to display from your image library.

Hot Tip

If you are using an image from the internet, simply use the Insert from URL option. This saves space in your image library.

Uploading Images To Blogger

1. Choose the point in your blog post where you want your image to be included and click the picture symbol.

2. Select the location of the image you want to upload.

3. Click **Add Selected**.

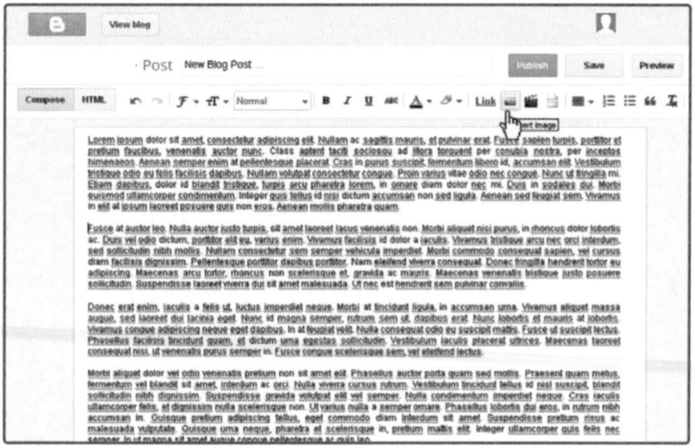

Above: Select the picture icon in Blogger to begin the uploading process.

Repositioning And Resizing

Once you have inserted the image into your blog post, you can make further changes by clicking on your image, which brings up various editing options (in WordPress, you have to click the picture icon).

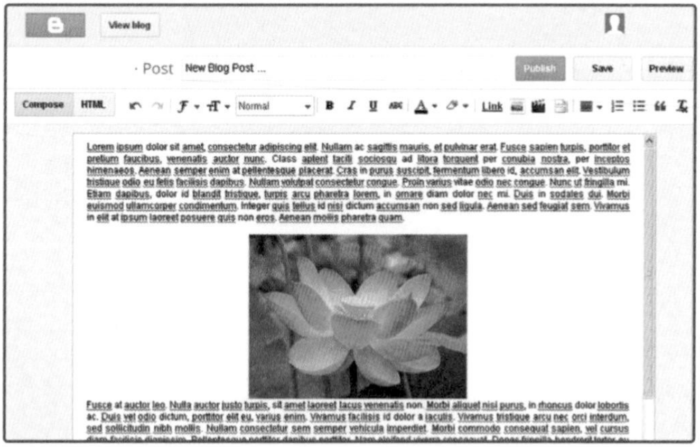

Above: Your image will appear in your post and is ready to be repositioned and resized.

- **Resizing**: Allows you to enlarge or shrink your image so it fits better on the page.

- **Position**: Allows you to determine whether you want the image on the left, right or centre of the page, and whether you want the text to wrap around the image.

- **Caption**: Lets you add text under your image. Important if you need to add an attribution.

Consistency

Just as the tone of your blog requires consistency, so does your use of images. Use the same justification and positioning for all your images, and try to keep all images of a similar size.

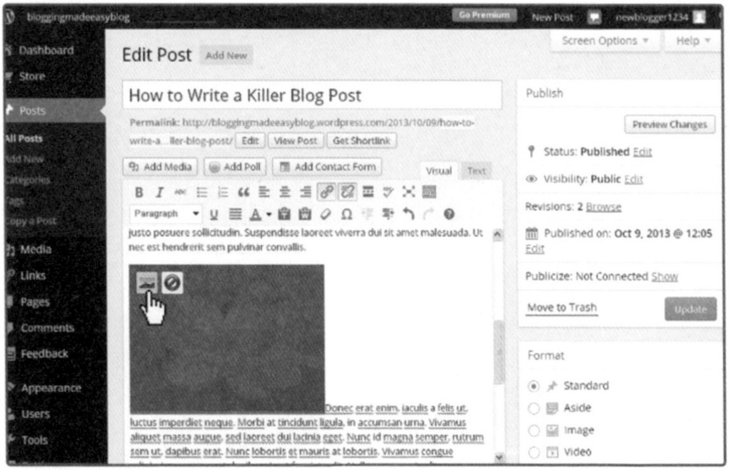

Above: WordPress allows you to edit your image so that it fits exactly to your liking.

CAPTIONING YOUR IMAGE

Not all images you post on your blog will need captions. Images used to set tone or catch the eye may be self-explanatory. However, in some instances, captions can help explain the relevance and context of an image. Because of this, captions need to do more than just label an image.

- **Explanation**: A good caption needs to clearly and concisely explain what is going on in an image.
- **Tone**: A caption should reflect the tone of your blog post.
- **New information**: Avoid just regurgitating copy from your blog post. Provide new information on your caption.
- **Credits**: A caption should include the image attribution.

Hot Tip

Use a different font or italicize your image attribution to separate it from the rest of the caption.

PODCASTING

Instead of writing your blog posts, you can record them. Podcasting is a great way to reach a wider audience and provides an alternative method for getting your views and opinions heard.

WHAT IS PODCASTING?

Essentially, podcasting is blogging with sound. Instead of writing your blog posts, you record them. Podcasting enables people to listen to what you have to say on their computer, MP3 player or mobile phone. A podcast is not hard to make and it can make a nice change for your audience from all those written posts. Some people podcast instead of blogging, others use a combination of the two.

Hot Tip

You can record all your blog posts after you have published them to provide both a written and audio version of your blog post.

Podcasting Hosts

While you can simply upload your podcast to your blog, to reach a wider audience, you may want to upload it to a podcasting service. This enables people to subscribe to your podcast and receive notification when you have a new download available.

GETTING STARTED

Podcasting does not require any expensive equipment. All you need to make a podcast is a microphone connected to your PC and some audio-recording software.

> **Hot Tip**
>
> **If you use Audacity as your audio-recording software, make sure you download the LAME MP3 encoder so that you can save your recordings as MP3 files.**

Audacity

While there are many recording and editing software packages around, Audacity is by far the most popular for podcasting. Audacity is an easy-to-use platform that has all the tools you need to record and edit your podcasts. It is also free to download and install.

Recording Your Podcast

1. Plug your microphone into your PC or Mac. If you have a built-in microphone, ensure it is activated.
2. Run Audacity or other recording software.
3. Click, record, (the big red circle) and read aloud your blog post into the microphone.
4. When you have finished, click, stop, and save the podcast using the **File** menu.

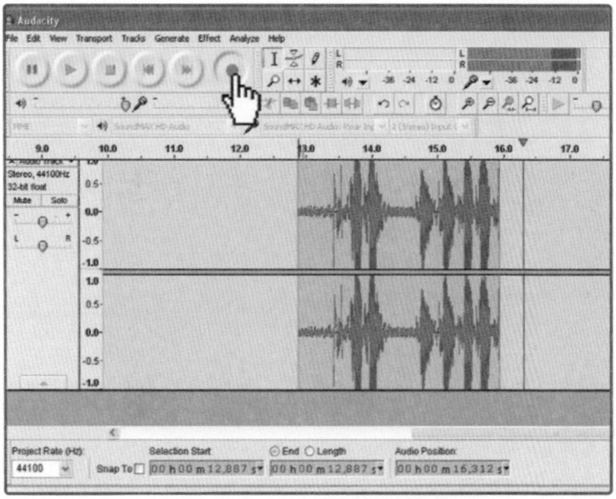

Above: Audacity allows you to record and edit podcasts to include on your blog.

Editing Your Podcast

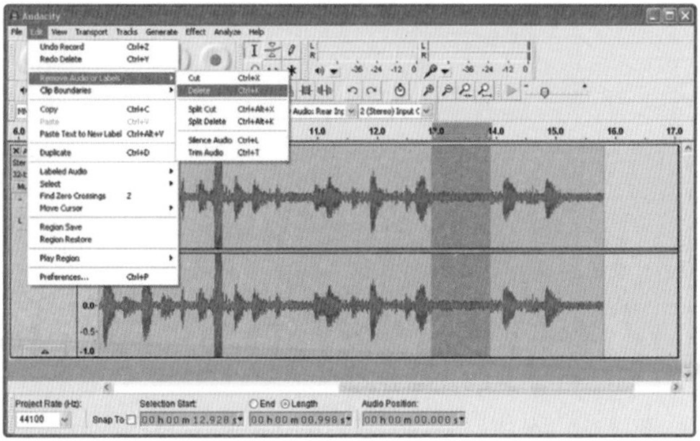

Above: Audacity allows you to cut, copy and paste recordings, as well as remove any mistakes you may have made.

When you record your podcast, you want to ensure the levels are as close to zero as possible. These are the bars at the top that move back and forth as you speak. Peaks in sound can cause distortion. If you have left long pauses, repeated yourself or made mistakes, you can easily edit them out. Simply play back your recording (click the triangle symbol) and use the mouse to select areas on the recording graph, which you can cut, copy and paste.

Exporting to MP3 Format

Once you have edited your recording, you need to export it to MP3 format.

1. Open your recording and, in the **File** menu, select, export.

2. Name your file, choose a location to save your podcast and select **MP3 Files** in the drop-down menu.

3. Fill in the fields in the description box if required. Click **OK**.

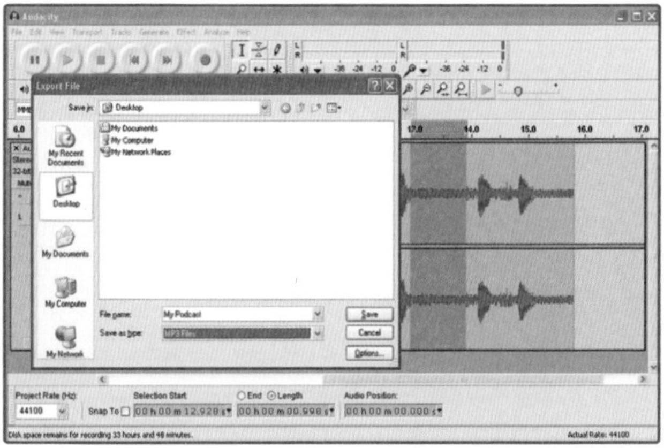

Above: It is important to export your audio recording in MP3 format.

Checking Your Podcast

After exporting your podcast to MP3, play the file to ensure it sounds okay. Try playing it on various media players to ensure it works on different platforms.

PODCASTING SERVICES

To ensure maximum availability, you should upload your podcast to a hosting service. You can find numerous podcasting hosts on the internet. The main benefit of using a hosting service is that an audience can use podcast aggregator software, known as podcatchers, to find and download your latest podcast. Some hosting services charge a small fee, while others provide free hosting. Some of the most popular podcast hosts include:

- **Libsyn**: The most popular podcasting hosting service, Libsyn (Liberated Syndication) provides hosting from $5 (£3) a month and offers unlimited bandwidth.
- **HipCast**: Formerly called audioblog.com, Hipcast has four different plans, with prices starting at $10 (£7) a month.
- **Archive.org**: Free Creative Commons hosting for all types of multimedia.
- **Odeo Studio**: Free podcast hosting, with a 50 MB limit on file size, although short commercials accompany each podcast.

Hot Tip

Do not be tempted to add music to your podcasts unless you have the rights to do so. Using music can be a breach of copyright.

RSS Feeds

An RSS feed (Really Simple Syndication) enables websites and blogs to host your podcast, as well as ensuring podcatching software can find and download it. Depending on your hosting service, you may already have an RSS feed on the page that is hosting your podcast. This is normally a link called EMBED, which provides you with a piece of code. If you do not have this link, you can create one in a feed service, such as Feedity (www.feedity.com) or Google Feedburner (www.feedburner.google.com).

ADDING PODCASTS TO YOUR BLOG

You can include the link to your podcast in your posts, but you can also embed the podcast's RSS feed to enable your visitors to listen to it from your blog.

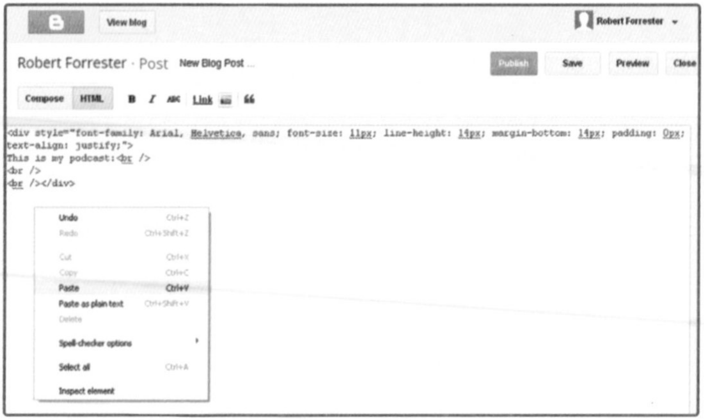

Above: Paste your RSS code into HTML in Blogger.

Above: After pasting the code, an embedded media player bar will appear.

Embedding a Podcast in Blogger

1. In your blog post, find a place where you want to include your podcast.

2. Click **HTML** in the control bar.

3. Paste in your RSS code.

4. Click, save, and, when you preview the blog post, you will see a media player bar where you entered the code.

Podcasting In WordPress

By far the simplest way to include a podcast on your WordPress blog is to upload it directly. For a hosted WordPress blog, you will have to pay for a space upgrade to upload MP3 files. Just go into **Store** on your dashboard and choose the size of your upgrade.

1. Once you have upgraded, go into the post you want to upload your podcast to, and click **Add Media**.

2. Select **Insert Media** and either drag and drop your file into the pane, or click **Select Files**.

3. Choose the file to upload.

Embedding a Podcast in WordPress

Embedding a podcast into WordPress can be more complicated, as it can depend on the browser a person is using and your podcasting host. If WordPress cannot embed your podcast, it will provide a link to it instead.

1. Find the place you want to include your podcast.

2. Click **Add Media**.

3. Select **Insert from URL**.

4. Enter the web address for your podcast.

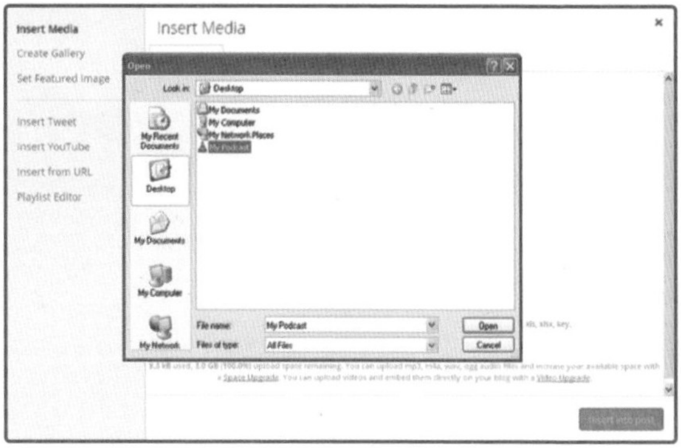

Above: Uploading a podcast directly onto your WordPress blog is the easiest way to ensure its accessibility.

Above: Entering your URL into WordPress.

PROMOTING YOUR PODCAST

Once you have created a podcast, you may wish to promote it to maximize your audience.

iTunes

iTunes is the world's most popular media store. Millions of people rely on iTunes to download MP3 files, so by submitting your podcast, you can tap into a potentially huge audience. To submit to Apple's iTunes store, you will need:

- **An iTunes account**: Anyone can sign up for an iTunes account. It only takes a moment, but you will need to download the iTunes software, which is free.
- **An iTunes-acceptable RSS feed**: This is an RSS feed with specific iTunes extensions and tags.

Editing RSS Feed for iTunes

In order to upload to iTunes, you will have to edit your feed. Software such as FeedForAll (www.feedforall.com) or Google FeedBurner can edit your feed automatically so it is acceptable to iTunes.

Hot Tip

List your podcast on websites such as The Podcast Directory (www.podcastdirectory.com), iPodder (www.ipodder.org) and Podcast Alley (www.podcastalley.com), as these have millions of subscribers between them.

Submitting to iTunes

1. Once you have edited your RSS feed, you can submit to iTunes by running your iTunes program and clicking the iTunes Store button in the navigation bar.

2. Click **Podcasts** to go to the podcasts page.

3. Below the Podcast Quick Links header, click **Submit a Podcast**.

4. Follow the instructions on screen to add your RSS feed link.

5. After your podcast feed has been accepted, you will receive a link to your podcast on the iTunes store.

Above: After editing your RSS feed, you have the option to submit your work to iTunes.

IMPROVING YOUR PODCASTS

As with blogging, it takes time and experience to master the art of podcasting and the same rules apply.

- **Passion:** Try to sound enthusiastic about the subjects you are talking about. Inject some energy into your performance.

- **Wording:** What works in written form may not work so well when spoken. Practise reading your blog posts aloud and make necessary changes to make them sound better.

- **Practise:** Rehearse your podcasts before recording them to avoid stumbling and to ensure a smooth delivery.

VIDEOS

Adding videos is a great way to enhance your blog and provide interesting content for your audience, but vlogging, as it has become known, can be pretty daunting for the inexperienced.

VLOGGING

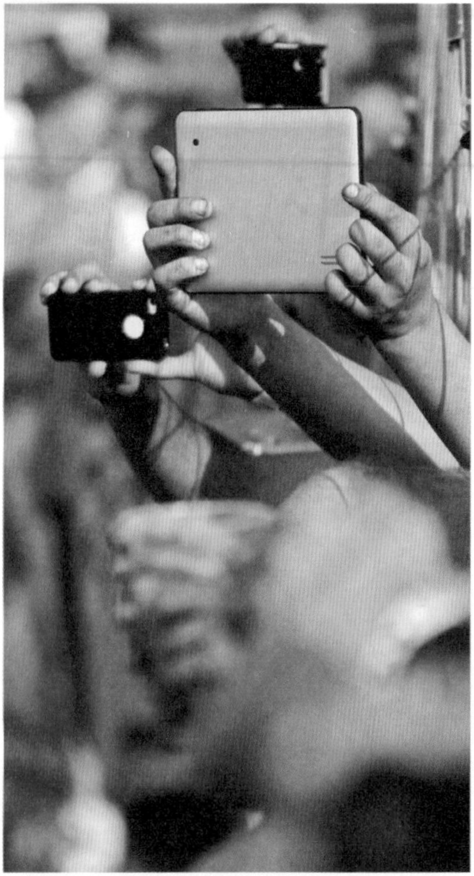

Video blogging (vlogging) can help you connect with many more people than simply writing blog posts. Given a choice, people prefer to see content on video. Just think of how many hours people spend watching TV compared to reading. Yet there is more to vlogging than just expanding your audience.

Reasons to Video Blog

- **Be different**: While videos have been around on the internet for many years, vlogging is still new to most bloggers. By providing videos on your blog, you can really stand out from the crowd.

- **Connect**: Videos help you to better connect with your audience. Being able to see and hear somebody makes a video blog much more personal than a standard written blog.

- **Be detailed**: You can demonstrate and explain things so much better by video, especially if you are trying to provide complicated information.

Challenges of Vlogging

Of course, posting videos on to your blog is not as easy as regular blogging. Vlogging comes with many challenges.

- **Time**: A video requires preparation and planning. A five-minute video may take several days to prepare, shoot and edit, compared to an hour or so for a blog post.

- **Requirements**: You do need equipment, although webcams and smartphones have made shooting videos easier than ever before, and editing software is widely available.

- **Content**: Coming up with ideas for a video is not easy, and video is not suitable for all topics.

- **Visibility**: Search engines rely on keywords and written content, so are not that effective at discovering video content.

> **Hot Tip**
>
> **If you have a how-to information blog, embed videos of people doing tasks in your topic area.**

HOSTING VIDEOS

The simplest way to begin vlogging is to host content from third parties. The best way to do this is to embed them directly from websites such as YouTube, Vimeo and Blip.tv.

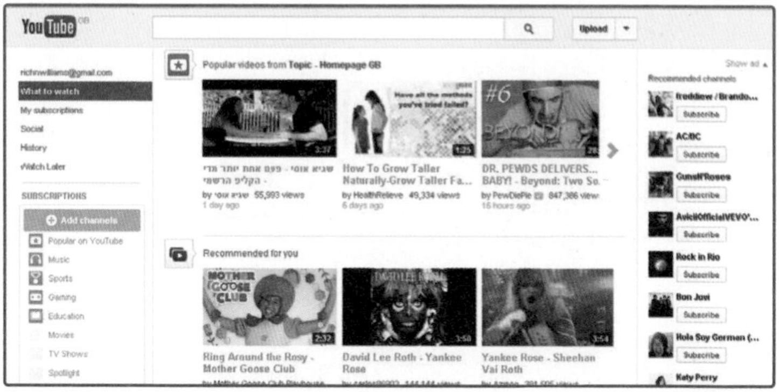

Above: YouTube is a popular website for embedding videos directly.

Copyright

Court rulings have declared that bloggers who embed videos cannot be held liable for copyright infringements. This is because, by embedding a video, you are merely creating a portal to a third-party website, not hosting the video yourself.

Above: Make sure to copy the website's URL.

Above: Insert the URL of the video, then add a customized title.

Above: Copy the embed code.

Embedding a Video in WordPress

Embedding videos on a WordPress blog is extremely simple.

1. Find the video you want to embed on websites such YouTube or Vimeo.

2. Copy the website's URL.

3. Select the area in your blog post where you want to insert the video and click **Add Media**.

4. Select **Insert from URL**, paste in the URL of the video and add a title to your video.

5. Click **Insert to Post**.

Embedding a Video in Blogger

Blogger also makes embedding videos simple.

1. Find the video you want to use and right-click on it.

2. Select **Copy Embed Code**.

3. Select where you want to place the video, then choose HTML mode.

4. Paste the code.

Above: Finally, paste in the code.

Hot Tip

If you are embedding a video from YouTube, both Blogger and WordPress allow you to search and select YouTube videos automatically from their video menus.

CREATING YOUR OWN VIDEOS

While embedding other people's videos on your blog is a great way to provide interesting content, to expand your audience, you may want to create your own.

Requirements

Creating videos has never been easier. While you can use expensive video cameras, some vloggers use nothing more than a smartphone or webcam. You do not even need expensive video-editing software, as you can edit videos when you upload them to websites such as YouTube.

Planning Your Video

Before you shoot any video, you need to plan it out. For this, you may need:

- **Script:** Rehearse your script well to ensure a smooth, faultless delivery.

- **Storyboard**: If you are planning action shots, such as in a how-to video, you might want to create a storyboard so you know which scenes to shoot.

- **Location**: You may not be able to afford to hire a studio, but you want somewhere with decent lighting and perhaps a neutral background.

Content

Knowing what makes a good video is not easy. Some types of content translate really well into video, others less so. In addition, some people can be quite natural in front of the camera, while others may come across as awkward. As with other aspects of blogging, if you can demonstrate your enthusiasm for your subject, it will help to engage your audience. There are other ways to grab people's attention too.

- **Get to the point**: Avoid long, rambling introductions. Get to the point straightaway and keep the momentum going.
- **Length**: Just as people do not want to read extremely long blog posts, you want to keep your video short. Try not to exceed 3–5 minutes unless your content is really gripping.
- **Production values**: No matter how you are shooting your video, make sure it looks as professional as possible. Pay particular attention to how it sounds, as muffled or mumbled voices will soon lose an audience. This also includes how you look. Dress suitably for your audience and topic.

SHOOTING YOUR VIDEO

While it is quite possible to shoot a video on your own, if you are new to it, it might be a good idea to enlist the help of a friend. There is a lot to do when recording a video, and an extra pair of hands can be quite useful. In addition, it is always difficult to judge your own performance, so a third party may be able to tell how you are coming across.

> **Hot Tip**
>
> **Record several takes of your video and choose the best one or edit together different scenes in post-production.**

Lighting

Before you begin shooting, make sure you have good lighting. Good lighting can make a huge difference in picture quality. Some vloggers invest in proper video lighting, which is worth the

investment if you intend to shoot a lot of videos. If not, take advantage of natural light, as this contributes to a much better image than indoor lighting. Most important of all is to make sure the source of the lighting is behind the camera.

Audio

Just as important as the images you are shooting is the sound. Even if your video shoot is unsuccessful, if you have good sound quality, you can turn your video into a podcast. While most cameras will have an in-built microphone, think about using an external one to ensure good sound levels. You can even shoot without sound and add a voiceover later.

POST-PRODUCTION

While websites such as YouTube now offer some editing facilities when you upload a video, post-production software can help you create really stylish and professional-looking videos. With editing software, you can add music and credits, and introduce stylized cuts and fades.

Editing Software

Editing software varies from easy-to-use free software to more complicated professional editing suites. Some of the most popular include:

- **iMovie**: Comes installed on most Apple computers and is incredibly easy to use.

- **Movie Maker**: Another simple-to-use video editor that is installed on most Windows PCs.

- **Final Cut Pro**: Industry-standard professional editing software, worth the investment for serious vloggers.

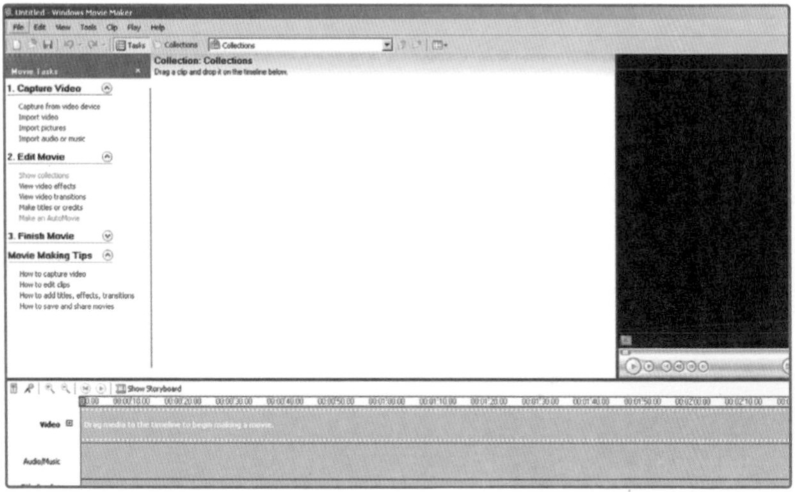

Above: Windows Movie Maker allows you to add all sorts of exciting features to your video post-production.

Making Basic Edits to Your Video

1. Run your video-editing software and select **Import Video** to load your video file.

2. Drop your video file into the video timeline. Repeat the process and drop the file into the audio timeline, unless you have a separate audio file.

3. Play the timeline by using either the menu or right-clicking. Then make edits by selecting sections of the timeline and cutting, copying or pasting. You can slide the audio and video timelines to synchronize pictures and sound.

4. Add effects, fades and overlay titles by using the **Tools** or **Effects** menu.

5. Save or export your movie file.

DISTRIBUTING YOUR VIDEO

While you can simply upload your video straight to a blog post, you will want more than just your blog's audience to see it. You can reach a larger audience by uploading to video-sharing platforms.

YouTube

When it comes to video sharing, YouTube is the world's number-one website. Some videos on YouTube have accumulated millions of unique views. YouTube lets you tag your videos and share them easily with other sites, such as Twitter and Facebook. It is also easy to embed videos from YouTube on to your blog. To take full advantage of YouTube's many features, it is worth setting up your own YouTube channel.

1. Set up a YouTube account by clicking the **Create Account** link at the top right-hand corner. If you already have a Google account, you can use this instead.

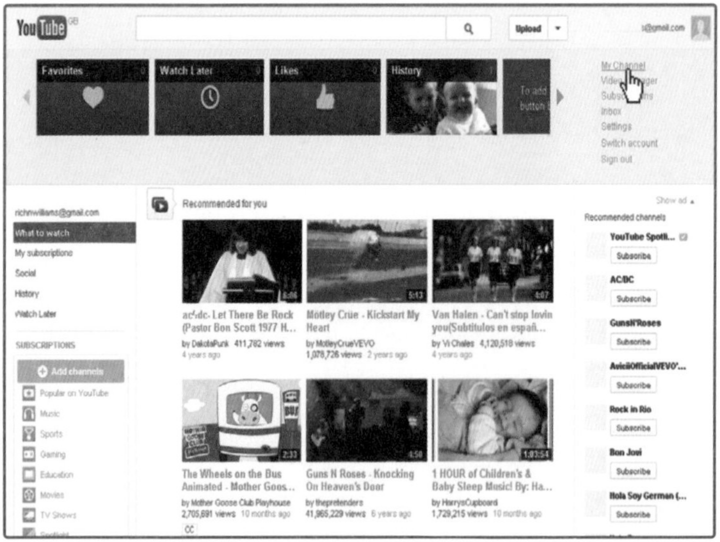

Above: Select My Channel to begin the process of setting up a channel of your own.

2. Click the menu under your profile and select **My Channel**.

3. Enter your profile name, age and sex.

4. Click the **About** tab and add your channel description and include a link to your blog. You can also add links to your social media pages, as well as, uploading an image for your channel.

5. Click **Done** when finished, then use the **Videos** tab to upload your first video.

Other Video Distribution Services

While YouTube is the most popular video-sharing website, it is not the only one. For maximum exposure, you should upload your video to as many sites as possible. Other popular platforms include:

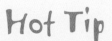

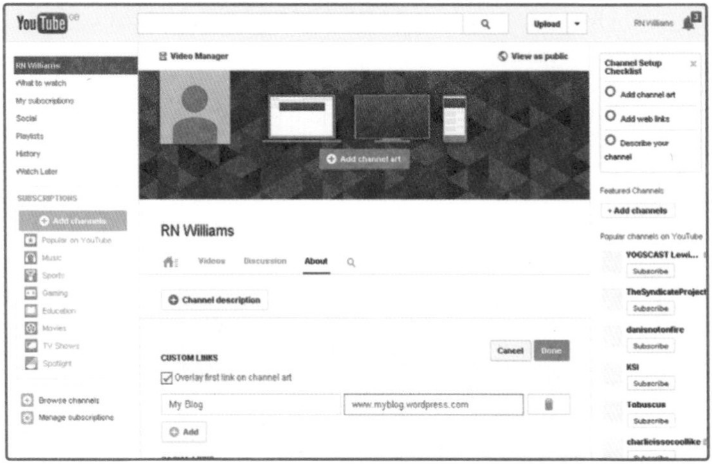

Above: Once you have set up your YouTube channel, you can add your own preferences.

- **Vimeo**: With over three million members, Vimeo is a popular platform, although it does not accept commercial content.

- **Blip.tv**: With a focus on episodic content, Blip.tv also provides a distribution service to websites such as YouTube and Vimeo.

- **Viddler**: For monetizing your videos, Viddler provides a revenue-sharing option for advertisements.

Hot Tip

Embed your video into your blog from YouTube. This will save you from having to store the file on your server or having to pay for additional storage.

Promotion

Promotion is just as important for vlogging as it is for blogging. Once you have uploaded your video to your blog and the popular channels, do not forget to promote it on social media. You can embed your video in Facebook pages, as well as sending links to your YouTube channel via Twitter.

FUNDING YOUR BLOG

ADVERTISEMENTS

The most obvious and easiest way to generate income from blogging is through advertising. Blog advertising comes in many forms and the amount you can earn depends on many factors.

MONETIZING YOUR BLOG

Blogging takes up a lot of time. In addition, you may have to spend money hosting and building your blog. While many bloggers are happy just to have a platform for their views, many others want a return on their investment. Some bloggers are even able to generate a good living from their blog. Earning money from your blog is not only possible, but thanks to the many forms of advertising programmes available to bloggers, fairly easy to do. As with most advertising, revenue is reliant on audience size, so the more people visit your blog, the more money you can make.

Hot Tip

It is best to start advertising on your blog at the very beginning, because if you build up a community on a blog and then start monetizing it, your audience may take exception to suddenly seeing adverts.

Expectations

It is important to be realistic at the beginning. If you only have a handful of visitors to your blog, you may not earn very much, if anything. However, as your audience grows, the money will start to trickle in, and even a small amount of income from your blog can be a great motivator.

TYPES OF BLOG ADVERTISING

Blog advertising comes in three different types:

- **Sponsored ads**: These are delivered by advertising networks such as Google Adsense and appear in various forms.
- **Direct sponsorship**: Bloggers with a large audience can contact advertisers and companies for sponsorship, where adverts appear as large banners on the blog.
- **Affiliate marketing**: These adverts provide links to products, and bloggers are paid a commission every time somebody clicks a link and purchases the advertised product.

SPONSORED ADS

You can run sponsored ads on your blog page as soon as you start blogging. These vary in type.

- **Contextual ads**: These adverts are usually at the side of your blog posts and have some relevance to the content on your blog. Often, these are based on keywords that users search to reach your blog.

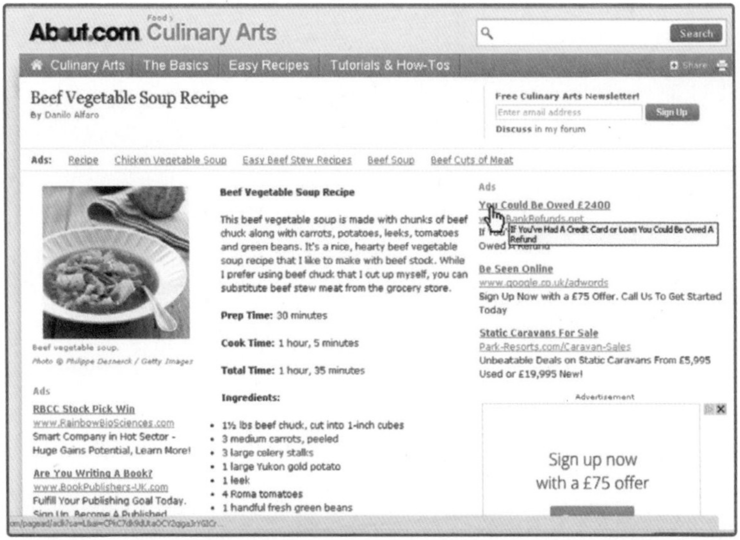

About.com Culinary Arts
Search
Culinary Arts
The Basics
Easy Recipes
Tutorials & How-Tos
Beef Vegetable Soup Recipe
By Danilo Alfaro
Free Culinary Arts Newsletter!
Sign Up
Ads: Recipe Chicken Vegetable Soup Easy Beef Stew Recipes Beef Soup Beef Cuts of Meat
Beef Vegetable Soup Recipe
This beef vegetable soup is made with chunks of beef chuck along with carrots, potatoes, leeks, tomatoes and green beans. It's a nice, hearty beef vegetable soup recipe that I like to make with beef stock. While I prefer using beef chuck that I cut up myself, you can substitute beef stew meat from the grocery store.
Prep Time: 30 minutes
Cook Time: 1 hour, 5 minutes
Total Time: 1 hour, 35 minutes
Ingredients:
1½ lbs beef chuck, cut into 1-inch cubes
3 medium carrots, peeled
3 large celery stalks
1 large Yukon gold potato
1 leek
4 Roma tomatoes
1 handful fresh green beans
Ads
You Could Be Owed £2400
If You've Had A Credit Card or Loan You Could Be Owed A Refund
Be Seen Online
www.google.co.uk/adwords
Sign Up Now with a £75 Offer. Call Us To Get Started Today
Static Caravans For Sale
Park-Resorts.com/Caravan-Sales
Unbeatable Deals on Static Caravans From £5,995 Used or £19,995 New!
Advertisement
Sign up now
with a £75 offer
Ads
RBCC Stock Pick Win
www.RainbowBioSciences.com
Smart Company in Hot Sector - Huge Gains Potential, Learn More!
Are You Writing A Book?
www.BookPublishers-UK.com
Fulfil Your Publishing Goal Today.

Right: Running sponsored ads, like these shown on this About.com cookery page, are a good way to generate income.

- **Text-link ads**: While not contextual, these ads appear as underlined links in specific text in your blog posts, such as the name of a product or service.

SPACE.com
TECH SPACEFLIGHT SCIENCE & ASTRONOMY SEARCH FOR LIFE SKYWATCHING ENTERTAINMENT SHOP
Cheap Alaska Cruises
SEO Services UK
The End Of Britain
On Mars, Spirit is slowly making its way toward a rock target dubbed "Home Plate" at its Gusev Crater landing site. Its robotic twin Opportunity, meanwhile, is exploring a crater named Erebus on the plains of Meridiani Planum. While the stars of Roving Mars are the rovers themselves, the film includes comments rover scientists such as Steve Squyres, the mission's leader at Cornell University.
AdChoices
MORE QUALITY OUTPUT, LESS OUTLAY
High Productivity
Quality and Precision
LEARN MORE
EPSON
EXCEED YOUR VISION

Above: Text-link ads appear as underlined links within the text of your blog.

- **Impression-based ads**: A more direct form of sponsored ads, where you host an advertisement on your blog and are paid depending on the number of impressions you receive. You are often paid for every thousand visitors to a page, known as CPM (Cost Per Mille [in Latin, *mille* means 'thousand']).

Pay-per-click

Some sponsored ads work on a pay-per-click, or PPC, basis. This means you earn money whenever somebody clicks the advertising link on your page. Obviously, the more visitors you get on your page, the more people will click on a link.

Google AdSense

Google AdSense is the undisputed king of PPC. Google has more advertisers than any other online advertiser, which makes it more likely you will find adverts that are both relevant to your blog and financially worthwhile.

Using AdSense

Advertisers do not pay a set fee to advertise with Google AdSense. Instead, they bid on different keywords. This means when somebody clicks an advert on your blog, you can be paid anything from a few cents to over a hundred dollars, depending on the competitiveness of the keyword in question.

Hot Tip

With Google AdSense, you can specify which type of advertisements to run on your blog and which type to exclude.

To use AdSense, you need:

- **Space**: Enough space alongside your posts to run advertisements.
- **Compliance**: You have to comply with certain conditions, such as not having adult content on your page.

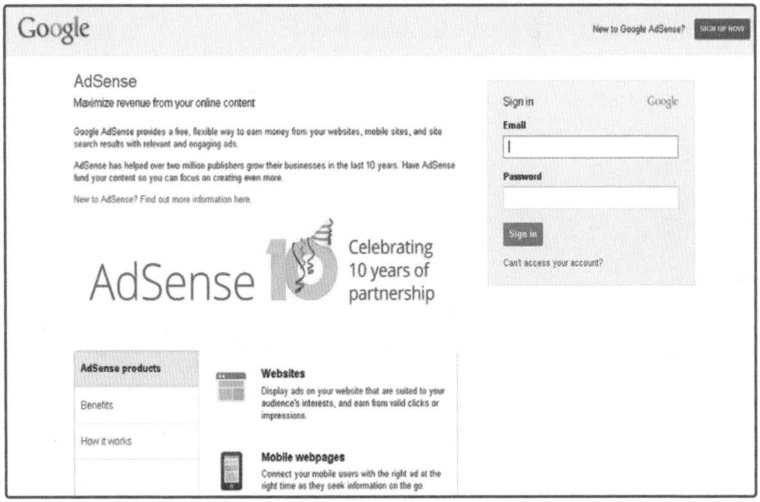
Google
New to Google AdSense?
SIGN UP NOW
AdSense
Maximize revenue from your online content
Google AdSense provides a free, flexible way to earn money from your websites, mobile sites, and site search results with relevant and engaging ads.
AdSense has helped over two million publishers grow their businesses in the last 10 years. Have AdSense fund your content so you can focus on creating even more.
New to AdSense? Find out more information here.
AdSense
Celebrating 10 years of partnership
Sign in
Google
Email
Password
Sign in
Can't access your account?
AdSense products
Benefits
How it works
Websites
Display ads on your website that are suited to your audience's interests, and earn from valid clicks or impressions.
Mobile webpages
Connect your mobile users with the right ad at the right time as they seek information on the go.

Above: Google AdSense is an effective way to run adverts of your choosing on your blog.

- **To be indexed**: Your blog has to have been indexed by Google, so if you have just created your blog, you may have to wait a week or so to apply.

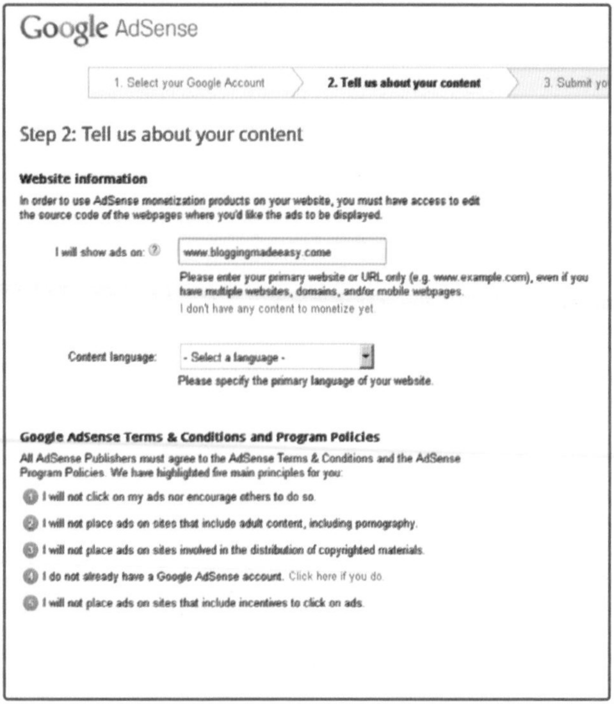
Google AdSense
1. Select your Google Account
2. Tell us about your content
3. Submit yo
Step 2: Tell us about your content
Website information
In order to use AdSense monetization products on your website, you must have access to edit the source code of the webpages where you'd like the ads to be displayed.
I will show ads on:
www.bloggingmadeeasy.come
Please enter your primary website or URL only (e.g. www.example.com), even if you have multiple websites, domains, and/or mobile webpages.
I don't have any content to monetize yet.
Content language:
- Select a language -
Please specify the primary language of your website.
Google AdSense Terms & Conditions and Program Policies
All AdSense Publishers must agree to the AdSense Terms & Conditions and the AdSense Program Policies. We have highlighted five main principles for you:
I will not click on my ads nor encourage others to do so.
I will not place ads on sites that include adult content, including pornography.
I will not place ads on sites involved in the distribution of copyrighted materials.
I do not already have a Google AdSense account. Click here if you do.
I will not place ads on sites that include incentives to click on ads.

Above: AdSense takes you through the process of setting up an account.

Signing up to AdSense

1. Go to the AdSense homepage (www.google.com/adsense). If you already have a Google account, sign in; if not, click on the **Sign Up Now** button.

2. Enter the address of the blog that you wish to run adverts on and specify its language.

3. Read the rules governing AdSense, and press **Continue** if you agree.

4. Select your account type and enter your personal information.

5. Click **Submit My Application**.

Running AdSense

It can take several days for Google to review your blog, but after this you will then be able to use Google AdSense and start earning money. Once you are approved, you will have access to reports that can show how much money your blog is generating. However, you only receive payment once you have earned over $100 (£65). Your money is then transferred straight to your bank account.

Hot Tip

Never try to boost your payments by clicking on your advertising links yourself or asking others to do so, as Google is very quick to close accounts it suspects of click fraud.

Other Sponsored Ad Networks

While AdSense is the leading sponsored ad network on the internet, it is by no means the only one. Many bloggers opt to use more than one advertising network to prevent being reliant on one company for their revenue stream. However, some companies, such as Google, will not permit other advertising on a blog.

- **Media Net**: Very similar to Google's AdSense, Yahoo and Bing's Media Net (www.media.net) offers the same sort of PPC advertising, as well as having similar facilities and tools to track the effectiveness of running adverts.

- **Chitika**: Not only can you use Chitika (www.chitika.com) alongside other advertising networks, but also their threshold for payment is lower than Google's, as you only need to generate $50 (£35) before they make a payment.

- **Infolinks**: Text-link advertisements from Infolinks (www.infolinks.com) only appear when visitors hover their mouse pointers over the link, making them one of the most unobtrusive forms of blog advertising.

- **Bidvertiser**: You can earn money on both clicks and when visitors make purchases on the link destination, which maximizes the amount of money you can make from one advert (bidvertiser.com).

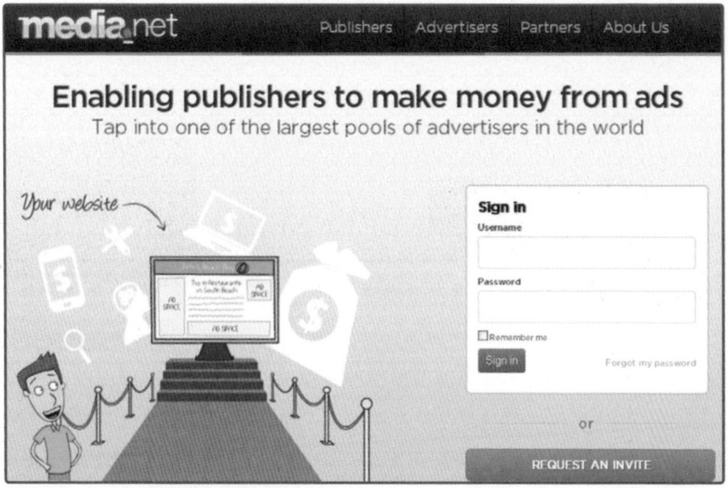

Right: Yahoo and Bing's Media Net provides PPC advertising that is very similar in style to Google's AdSense.

GETTING SPONSORSHIP

Once you have built up a large enough audience, you may be able to attract sponsors to advertise on your blog. You can earn far more money from direct sponsorship than any other form of internet advertising, but it is not without its problems.

DIRECT ADVERTISEMENTS

If you can attract sponsors to your blog, you can sell them advertising space. Often called direct ads, these normally come in the guise of banners or boxes, similar to the types of advertisements you see in print publications. The number of people you attract to your blog will greatly affect the value of your advertising space, and your audience needs to be relevant to what your sponsors sell.

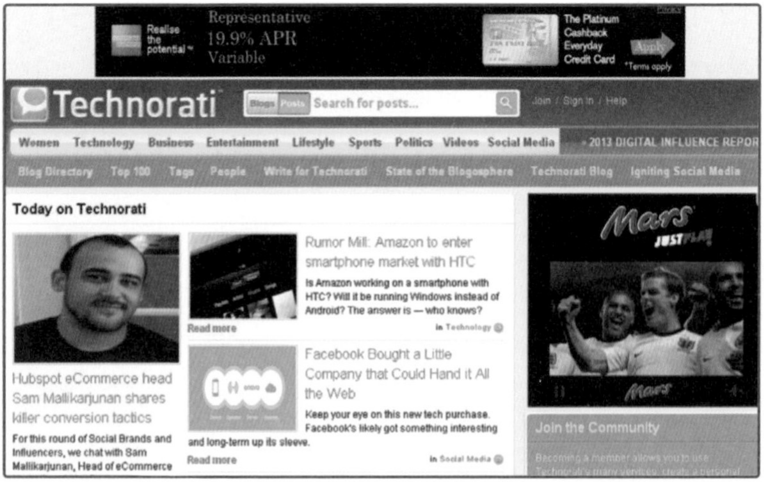

Representative
19.9% APR
Variable
The Platinum
Cashback
Everyday
Credit Card
Technorati
Search for posts...
Women Technology Business Entertainment Lifestyle Sports Politics Videos Social Media
Today on Technorati
Rumor Mill: Amazon to enter smartphone market with HTC
Is Amazon working on a smartphone with HTC? Will it be running Windows instead of Android? The answer is — who knows?
Read more
Facebook Bought a Little Company that Could Hand it All the Web
Keep your eye on this new tech purchase. Facebook's likely got something interesting and long-term up its sleeve.
Hubspot eCommerce head Sam Mallikarjunan shares killer conversion tactics
For this round of Social Brands and Influencers, we chat with Sam Mallikarjunan, Head of eCommerce
Mars
Join the Community

Above: When your blog has obtained a large audience, you may begin to display advertisements from sponsors, as seen on Technorati.

Visitors

How many visitors you need to attract sponsors can vary. A blog in a specific niche may be able to attract sponsors with just a few thousand visitors a week. In other instances, advertisers may not be interested unless you receive tens of thousands of unique visitors.

ATTRACTING SPONSORS

Many bloggers find that they do not have to seek out advertisers, as sponsors come to them. Advertisers often approach bloggers with high levels of traffic if they have a blog with a relevant readership. However, to increase your chances of getting sponsors, you need to make sure your blog looks as attractive to advertisers as possible.

Authority

As with other aspects of blogging, in order to attract sponsors, you need good content. However, providing blog posts that people want to read is only the first step, as you also need to have generated some level of authority with your audience. If your readers trust your views and opinions on a topic, then they will trust your endorsements. While you need a high level of traffic to attract sponsors, having influence over your visitors is just as necessary.

> **Hot Tip**
>
> **Sponsors are unlikely to want their adverts to appear on messy, cluttered websites. Make sure your blog is well designed, well organized and easy to navigate.**

Making it Easy for Sponsors

If sponsors cannot find your contact details or the information they need to decide whether your blog is a good fit for their advertisements, you are going to deter them from approaching you. In order to attract sponsors, you need to make it easy for them.

Sponsorship Page

A clear 'Contact' or 'About Us' page makes it easy for sponsors to get hold of you. However, in order to make it even easier, you can include a sponsorship page. On this, you can detail all the information relevant to advertisers, such as the demographics of your audience, readership numbers, prices for advertising space and payment methods.

Advertising Space

If you have a lot going on in your sidebars and banners, sponsors may wonder where you will be able to fit in their advertisements. Even if you do not have current sponsors, ensure you have space on your blog for adverts. You can leave placeholders with text saying: 'You advert here' or 'Advertise with us'.

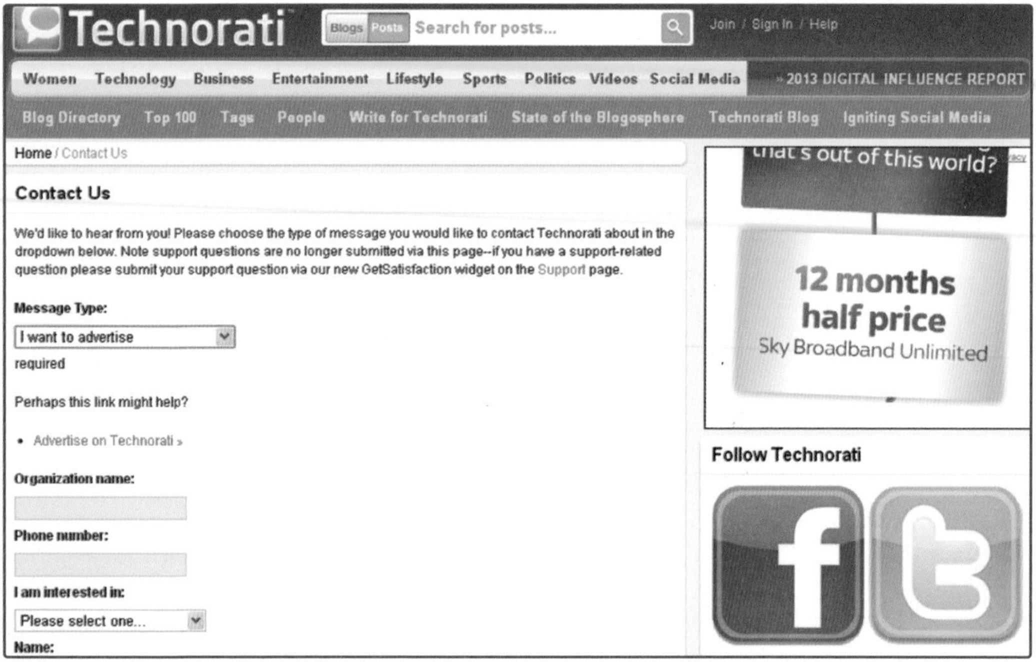

Above: Including a Contact Us or Sponsorship page on your blog gives sponsors an easy way to set up correspondence with you.

SEEKING SPONSORS

Not all bloggers find that sponsors come to them. In addition, if your blog is new, you may have to seek out advertisers. Finding sponsors means doing a bit of research to find relevant companies in your subject area. You can find sponsors in all sorts of places.

- **Personal contacts**: If you have friends or family in a business related to your topic, ask if they would like to sponsor your blog.

- **Industry figures**: Think about organizations or businesses you have blogged about and ask yourself who would benefit from advertising on your blog.

- **Websites/Magazines/Blogs**: Read industry magazines, websites and other blogs. See who is paying for advertising space and contact the companies directly.

- **Search engines**: Use industry-related keywords to find companies on search engines. Pay particular attention to those businesses that advertise on AdSense.

Hot Tip

Write a blog post explaining that you are looking for advertisers. If sponsors are already reading your blog, it may prompt them to get in touch.

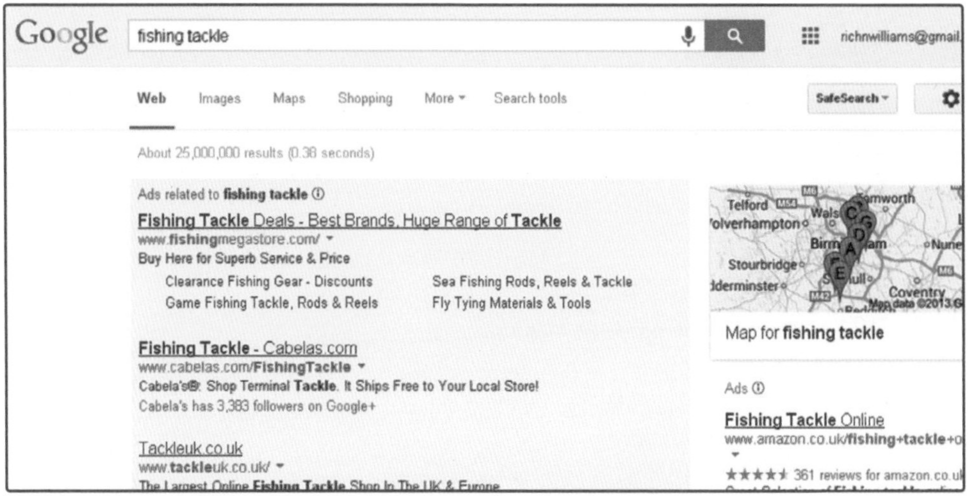

Above: Sponsored ads on Google provide an idea about which companies are worth approaching.

Approaching Sponsors

Once you have found potential advertisers, you need to contact them to enquire if they would be interested in sponsoring your blog. You can do this by letter or email. The most important thing is to be as professional as possible. To write a query, you need to ensure you include all the relevant information relating to your blog.

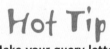

Advertising Opportunity with BloggingMadeEasyBlog.com
johnsmith@blogger.com
Advertising Opportunity with BloggingMadeEasyBlog.com
Dear Mr Smith
I am writing to introduce myself and my blog www.bloggingmadeeasyblog.com, which I think might offer a good advertising opportunity for you company. My blog receives 50,000 unique visitors each

Above: When composing a query letter, be formal and professional. Include all of the relevant details relating to your blog.

1. Introduce yourself and explain your interest and expertise in the subject area relating to their business.

2. Describe your blog. Mention how long it has been going and explain what topics you cover. Do not forget to include a link.

3. Include information relating to your traffic and visitor numbers. Make this as detailed as possible and include information such as a breakdown of your audience's location and demographics.

4. Detail your fees for advertising space.

Hot Tip

Make your query letter unique to each company you approach. Do your research on their business and address your query to an individual person, and explain why your blog would be a good fit for their company.

SETTING FEES

One of the biggest quandaries bloggers have when seeking sponsorship is knowing how much to charge. It is important to be competitive. However, setting prices that are too cheap may put potential sponsors off, as it may suggest your blog has little value.

Things to take into account when setting fees are:

- **Audience size**: The more unique visitors you have, the more you can charge.
- **Sponsors**: If you have multiple advertisers, you may have to charge less compared to what you might charge an advertiser that wants to be your sole sponsor.
- **Size of adverts**: How large your sponsor's or sponsors' adverts are should also be reflected in the price.

Pricing Example

While different bloggers charge different rates, a good formula to stick to is $1.25 (or £0.80) for every thousand unique visitors a month for an average-sized advertisement or banner from a sole sponsor. Therefore, if you have 200,000 visitors each

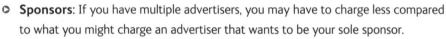

month, charge $250 (£170) a month. If you have several advertisers on the same page, reduce the formula amount by 25 cents (15 pence) for every advertiser you have.

LOOKING AFTER YOUR SPONSORS

Just as you have to nurture your audience, you need to look after your sponsors. It may be worth writing an occasional blog post thanking them for their sponsorship. In addition, you could write an advertorial on one of their new products or services. You should arrange this with your sponsors in advance, but ensure your audience knows it is an advertorial. It can be a fine balance between keeping your sponsors happy and ensuring you are being true to yourself and your audience. These tips may help.

- **Endorsement**: Do not accept sponsorship from companies you dislike, and never endorse products or services you are not happy with.

- **Bias**: If you are writing a critical article about your sponsors, such as a negative review, tell them first.

- **Audience**: Never put your sponsors before your audience. Refusing to be critical or falsely suggesting their products or services are better than others will cost you visitors; and, when your audience goes, so will your sponsors.

THE GRAY REPORT
BEST BLOGGER/ONLINE WINE WRITER (IN THE WORLD!) · ROEDERER AWARD 2011
My advertorial and sponsored post policy
An advertorial is a post paid for by the advertiser.
A sponsored post is a post in which somebody pays me to cover a topic.
I will write either -- I'm a professional writer, that means writing for money.
In either case, the post will be clearly labeled as either a sponsored post or an advertorial.
The distinction is this. With an advertorial, the advertiser gets content approval (For this blog, I insist on joint approval; we both must be happy with it.) With a sponsored post, the sponsor does not get content approval; the sponsor sees it for the first time when it goes live. This is cheaper.
Either one always raises a question: Would you praise this item/event/concept if you weren't being paid?
My advertorial/sponsored post policy here is simple.
I will not write an advertorial about something I oppose. And I will try not to write a sponsored post any differently than an unsponsored post.
BLOG ARCHIVE
► 2013 (111)
▼ 2012 (185)
► December (15)
▼ November (15)

Above: Advertorial policy blog posts are a good way to identify sponsors and a respectful way to say 'thank you' for their sponsorship.

AFFILIATE MARKETING

Linking to third-party products through your blog can be a great way to make money. Affiliate marketing pays you a commission every time somebody makes a purchase from your blog .

AFFILIATE PROGRAMS

Unlike pay-per-click (PPC) sponsored ads, affiliate advertising pays on cost per action (CPA). This means somebody has to click on your affiliate link, go to another website and either make a purchase or sign up to register for something before you get paid. For a blogger, affiliate programs offer some significant benefits over other forms of advertising.

- **Control**: You get to choose exactly the types of products or services you want to promote through your blog.
- **Income**: The commission for CPA advertisements is much higher than for PPC sponsored ads.
- **Association**: Having links to big brands and companies on your website can boost your reputation.

How It Works

Affiliate marketing has a reputation of being a little complicated to implement, but it really is quite simple.

1. Sign up to an affiliate program that is suitable for you and your blog. Many of the big online vendors offer such programs to websites and bloggers.

Hot Tip

CPA is not reliant on the number of pageviews your blog receives, more the audience type, and whether they are interested in the products advertised.

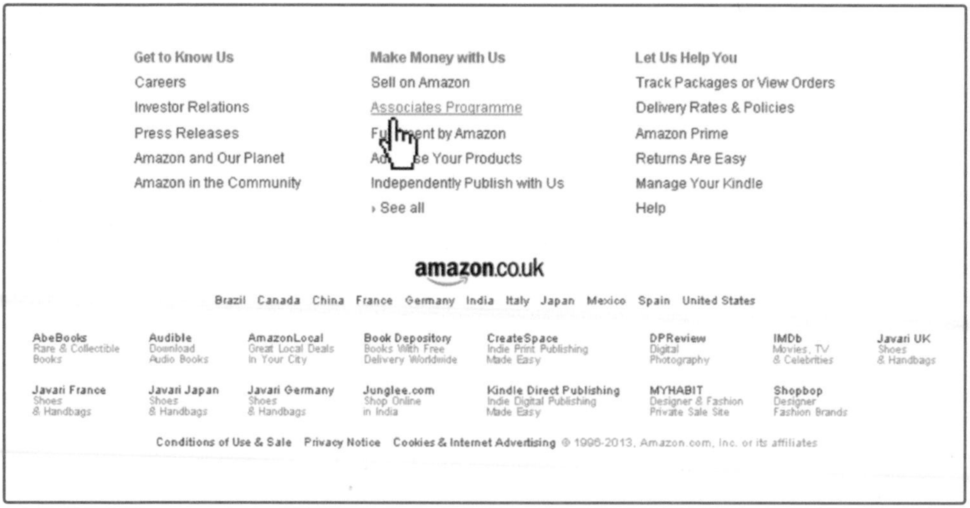

Above: Amazon offers an associates program that helps you to make money with them.

2. Search for products you want to feature. You should choose items that are representative of the content of your blog.

3. Create links to the products and place them on your blog.

Cookies

Affiliate links use cookies to help track your visitors and ensure you are paid if they make a purchase. Cookies are simply little bits of code. Tracking cookies does not store any of your visitors' personal information.

Commission Rates

Commission rates for affiliate programs vary from vendor to vendor and even product to product. Some vendors pay a sliding scale of commission depending on how many customers you have sent to their website. Expect to earn between five to 10 per cent on low-cost items, such as books and DVDs.

Costs

An important thing to note about affiliate marketing is that your blog visitors pay no more through one of your affiliate links than they would by going direct to the vendor. In addition, advertisers do not have to pay you anything if your visitors click on an affiliate link but do not make a purchase.

CONTENT AND LINKS

The more relevant the ad is to your content, the higher the likelihood visitors will click on the ad and make a purchase. Because of this, many bloggers in affiliate programs choose products to complement their blog content. You can also tailor the type of blog articles to suit your affiliations, such as writing product reviews or doing top-10 lists of products.

Placing Links

You can place affiliate links anywhere on your blog, either in the copy or down the sidebars. However, they are best used in the same way as other links. Think of them as resources. If you mention a product or service, use an affiliate link to the vendor.

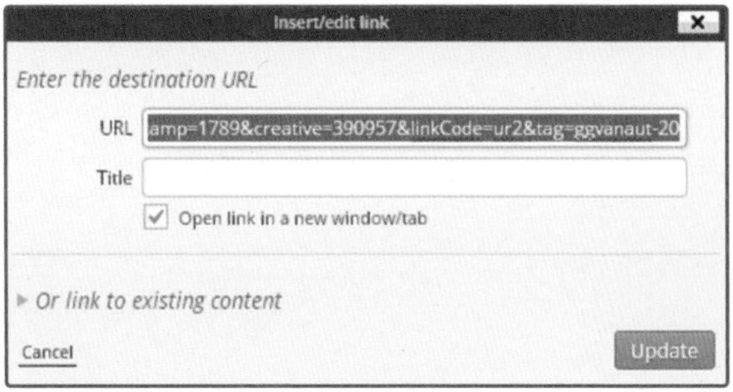

Above: Insert affiliate blog resources into your posts.

Disclaimer

Affiliate links have a specific URL unique to you, which helps the vendor identify where a customer has come from. If you implement affiliate links on your blog, you have to tell your audience that you are paid if they click it. This is a requirement of many affiliate programs and is now law in many countries.

Hot Tip

Place a disclaimer on a sidebar with such wording as: 'Some links in this post are affiliate links. I may earn a small commission if you purchase something after clicking it.'

AFFILIATE NETWORKS

Bloggers who cover a diverse range of topics may find sticking to specific products and vendors too restrictive. Rather than sign up to dozens of different vendors individually, it is possible to join an affiliate network. These services have access to hundreds and even thousands of different affiliate programs, so you can earn commission on links without having to sign up to the individual vendors.

Above: LinkShare, one of the most popular affiliate networks, lets you manage your own program.

Popular Affiliate Networks

Some of the most popular affiliate networks can handle all aspects of your affiliate marketing while providing tracking and reporting capabilities, helping you determine the best products or services to link to.

- **LinkShare (www.linkshare.com):** You can choose from 2,500 affiliate programs and manage your own program or have LinkShare handle everything.
- **Viglink (www.viglink.com):** With over 30,000 vendors on their program, Viglink has one of the largest affiliate programs on the internet.
- **Commission Junction (www.cj.com):** Another large network that also offers commission on leads as well as sales.
- **ShareASale (www.shareasale.com):** A highly popular affiliate network that is trusted by a lot of bloggers.

Hot Tip

Some affiliate networks can even identify links in your copy and insert relevant products to suit, helping you to maximize revenue potential.

Amazon Associates

By far the most popular affiliate program is Amazon Associates. Commission ranges from four to 15 per cent. This may not seem like a lot, but when you consider that Amazon sells everything from books and CDs to TVs, cameras and tablet computers, you can earn some decent money.

Above: Commission Junction offers sales and commission on leads.

Signing Up to Amazon Associates

1. Visit Amazon.com or Amazon.co.uk and scroll down to the links at the bottom of the homepage.
2. Click on **Associates Program**.
3. Read the associates homepage and, if you are happy to sign up, click **Join Now For Free**.
4. Create an Amazon account. If you already have one, simply sign in.

Above: Join Amazon Associates today.

5. Enter the details of your blog, including the URL and a brief description.

6. Fill in all the required details, including your subject area and the type of products you want to advertise. Click, next, and then follow the instructions to verify your identification.

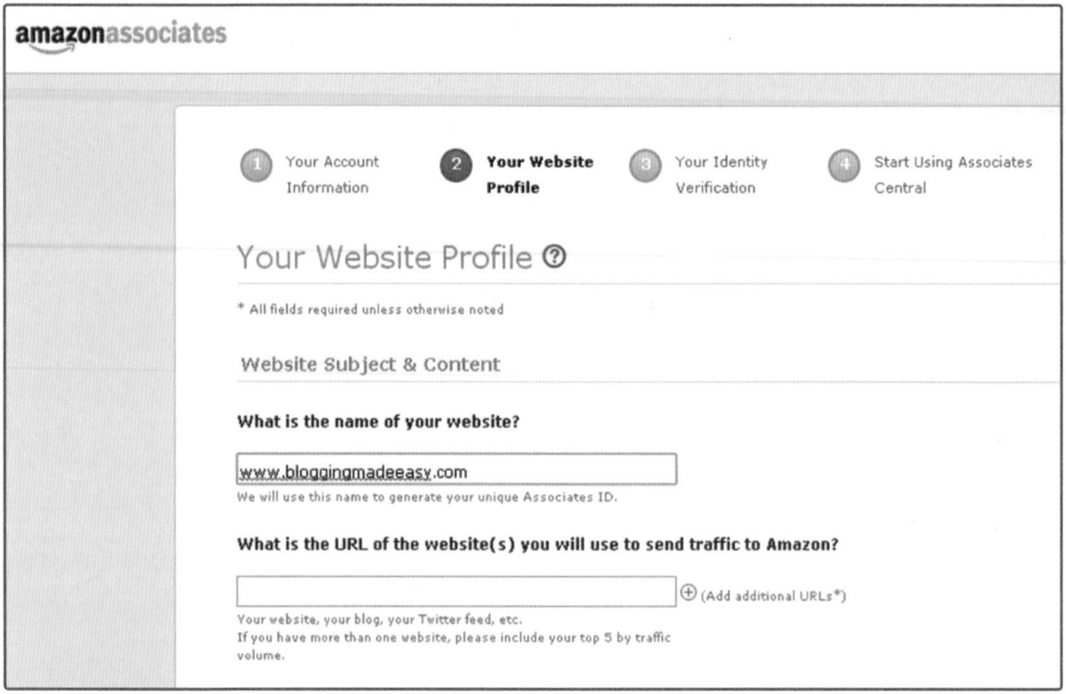
amazonassociates
1 Your Account Information
2 Your Website Profile
3 Your Identity Verification
4 Start Using Associates Central
Your Website Profile
* All fields required unless otherwise noted
Website Subject & Content
What is the name of your website?
www.bloggingmadeeasy.com
We will use this name to generate your unique Associates ID.
What is the URL of the website(s) you will use to send traffic to Amazon?
(Add additional URLs*)
Your website, your blog, your Twitter feed, etc.
If you have more than one website, please include your top 5 by traffic volume.

Above: Amazon Associates, the most popular affiliate program is easy to join.

Using Amazon Associates

The main strength of Amazon Associates is its simplicity. When somebody clicks on one of your Amazon links and makes a purchase, you receive your commission. Once you have been accepted, you are given access to **Associates Central**, where you can control the products and links you wish to use, as well as viewing how much money you are making.

MERCHANDISING

The most direct way to make money from blogging is to sell your own products and services. Even if you have nothing to sell, plenty of companies can help you produce merchandise for your blog.

SELLING

While selling advertising space and earning commission for other people's products are effective ways of generating an income from blogging, nothing is more direct or straightforward than selling your own goods to your audience. Selling your own products means you do not have to pay anybody else a commission, but while merchandising is a great way to fund your blog, you have to be careful you do not drive away your audience.

Blogging Versus Selling

People usually visit blogs for information, opinion and debate. People rarely visit a blog because they want to be sold something. A blog is not a sales platform, but that does not mean you cannot sell merchandise on your blog, just as long as you retain your quality content and refrain from pushing products at people.

WHAT TO SELL

If your blog is related to what you do, knowing what to sell becomes pretty obvious. Those in the creative industry, such as writers, artists and musicians, find blogging a good platform to discuss their work. Consequently, providing the facility for your audience to buy your books, music and art somewhere on the blog makes sense. In addition, if you are a fitness coach and blog about health, your blog provides a good place to advertise your services. However, what if you do not have something related to your blog topic to sell?

Merchandise

All sorts of merchandise can be customized to reflect your blog or blog topic.

- **T-shirts**: T-shirts with a slogan on the front prove to be highly popular, especially if they are light-hearted or jokey.

- **Mugs**: Also highly popular, you can have almost any message you want printed on mugs.

- **Stationery**: Low-cost items such as pens and pencils often sell in large numbers.

Merchandising Services

If you wish to sell merchandise on your blog, you need to find a supplier. Various companies are around that will provide products for you to sell and customize them for you.

Some of the top merchandising companies include:

- **CafePress (www.cafepress.com)**: A popular site among bloggers, you can buy a wide range of merchandise customized to your own designs or you can have CafePress design them for you. In addition, the company can handle payment and shipping for you.

Hot Tip

Many merchandising companies offer print on demand services, which means you do not have to buy in bulk as they will print and despatch your items as and when people order them.

- **Zazzle (www.zazzle.com)**: Another popular merchandising site, Zazzle offers volume discounts and can handle all aspects of customer service, including shipping, returns and payment processing.

- **Printfection (www.printfection.com)**: Free to join, Printfection has set costs for all items that you can price as you like on your blog. They can also handle all aspects of delivery and payment.

Above: Zazzle is a useful website for selling merchandise through your blog. They handle shipping, return, and payment processing.

HANDLING PAYMENT AND SHIPPING

The great advantage of using a merchandising service is that the company will handle all aspects of the order process, from accepting payment to delivery. However, if you are selling your own products and services through your blog, you will need to set up a payment and shipping system. This may sound daunting, but you can get plug-ins and gadgets to add to your blog that makes the process simple.

Hot Tip

If you have a Blogger blog, you can add Google Checkout simply by signing up to the service and using the, add gadget, feature to install the Google Checkout button.

Payment Services

While some bloggers choose to install their own online payment system that accepts credit and debit cards, these require monthly subscriptions, can be difficult to set up and you have to be careful about security. A far simpler solution is to use a third-party payment service.

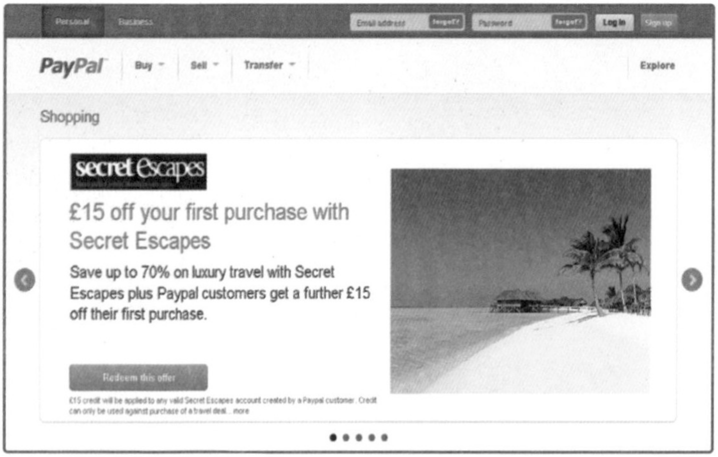

PayPal
Buy
Sell
Transfer
Explore
Shopping
secret Escapes
£15 off your first purchase with Secret Escapes
Save up to 70% on luxury travel with Secret Escapes plus Paypal customers get a further £15 off their first purchase.

Above: Websites such as PayPal will handle all aspects of payment for you.

- **PayPal**: PayPal will handle all aspects of payment for you, but you will need to sign up to a business account in order to accept credit and debit cards.
- **Google Checkout**: Similar to PayPal, but being a Google product, it is much easier to implement on a Blogger blog.

Adding a PayPal Button

Adding a PayPal button to accept payments on your blog is relatively straightforward.

1. Sign up to PayPal (www.paypal.com). You may have to wait a few days for PayPal to verify your bank account.

2. Login to your PayPal account and click the **Merchant Services** tab.

3. Select **Create payment buttons for your website**.

4. Choose the button you want to include on your blog, such as a shopping cart, and click the relevant link.

5. Fill in the details of your button, such as price and payment methods and any custom features you require. Make sure you check the box that requests your customer's shipping address. Click **Create**.

6. You will then be offered the code required to insert your button into your blog. Select and copy this code.

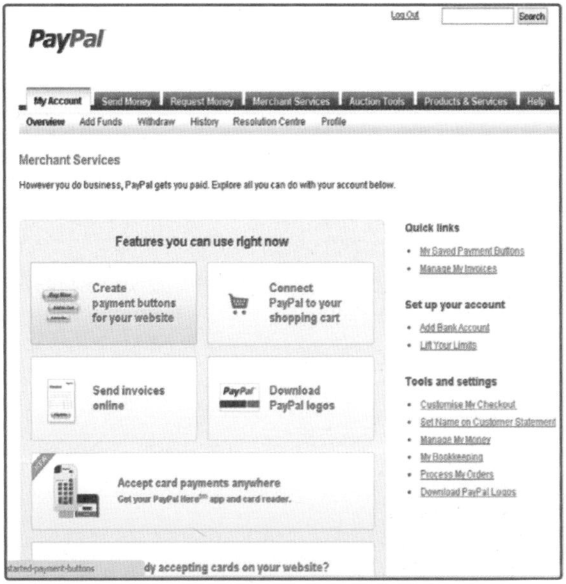

Log Out
Search
PayPal
My Account
Send Money
Request Money
Merchant Services
Auction Tools
Products & Services
Help
Overview
Add Funds
Withdraw
History
Resolution Centre
Profile
Merchant Services
However you do business, PayPal gets you paid. Explore all you can do with your account below.
Features you can use right now
Create payment buttons for your website
Connect PayPal to your shopping cart
Send invoices online
Download PayPal logos
Accept card payments anywhere
Quick links
My Saved Payment Buttons
Manage My Invoices
Set up your account
Add Bank Account
Lift Your Limits
Tools and settings
Customise My Checkout
Set Name on Customer Statement
Manage My Money
My Bookkeeping
Process My Orders
Download PayPal Logos

Above: Select 'Create Payment Buttons' on PayPal as you set up your account.

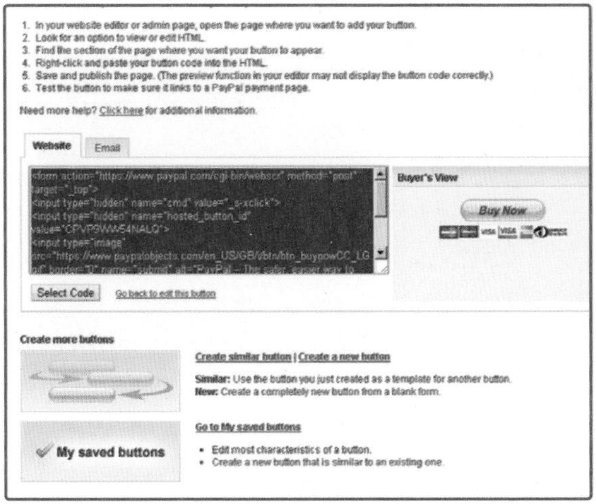

1. In your website editor or admin page, open the page where you want to add your button.
2. Look for an option to view or edit HTML.
3. Find the section of the page where you want your button to appear.
4. Right-click and paste your button code into the HTML.
5. Save and publish the page. (The preview function in your editor may not display the button code correctly.)
6. Test the button to make sure it links to a PayPal payment page.
Need more help? Click here for additional information.
Website
Email
Buyer's View
Buy Now
Select Code
Go back to edit this button
Create more buttons
Create similar button | Create a new button
Similar: Use the button you just created as a template for another button.
New: Create a completely new button from a blank form.
Go to My saved buttons
My saved buttons
Edit most characteristics of a button.
Create a new button that is similar to an existing one.

Above: Copy the button code given to you that will enable you to insert your button into your blog.

7. Log into your blog's dashboard and open the post or page where you want your button to appear. Use the, edit HTML, mode and paste in the code.

8. Your button will now appear on your blog. When users click it, they can enter their payment and shipping details. Funds will be transferred to your PayPal account while PayPal will email you the shipping address.

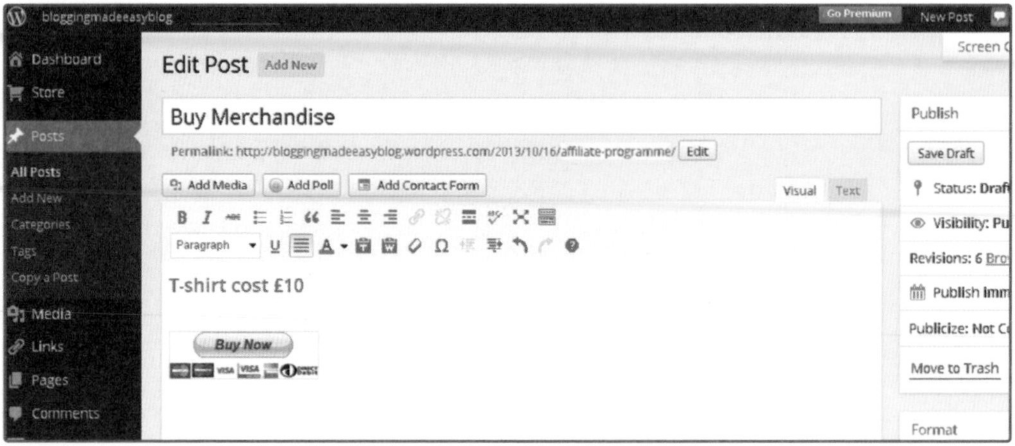

Above: The PayPal button will now appear on your blog.

PROMOTING YOUR PRODUCTS

Because visitors come to your blog for information and not to be sold something, you have to be careful how you promote your products. Merchandise is best offered on the sidebars of your blog or on a separate page. Of course, this does not mean you cannot promote your products to your readers.
It is fine to occasionally blog about your products and merchandise, as long as it is not too often.

Hot Tip

You can use your merchandise to actually promote your blog. Giving away these products in contests and competitions is a great way to keep your audience engaged.

PROBLEMS

If you require funding to keep your blog going, when you run into trouble, it can mean the end of your blogging days. However, funding problems can be rectified, and there are always other avenues you can follow to keep your blog alive.

BLOGGING AS A BUSINESS

If you wish to earn money from blogging, or provide enough of an income to pay for your blog-hosting and other costs, you need to approach blogging as you would approach any other business. When people set up businesses, they first identify a need that can be fulfilled with their product or service. Ideally, if you want your blog to earn money, you should identify a subject area that will earn enough interest that you can earn money from it. Of course, most bloggers start their blog because they want to write about their interests and passions and they think about making money afterwards. When funding problems occur, you need to address the cause.

Profit and Loss

As with any business, it is important to maintain a record of your expenditure and income. By tracking your profit and loss, you can identify funding problems before they become too serious.

AUDIENCE EQUALS INCOME

All income streams available to bloggers are reliant on audience. The more people visit your blog, the more money you can make from advertising, sponsors, affiliate links and merchandising. If your audience dwindles, so will your income stream. Sponsors will lose interest, while income from PPC and affiliate links will slow to a trickle. When audience numbers decrease or fail to grow, it is normally due to multiple reasons.

- **Staleness**: Producing the same old content week after week will soon lose an audience. When your blog stops being fresh, it is time to have a rethink.

- **Competition**: Other blogs arriving on the scene can easily steal away your audience.

- **Peaked**: Some blog audiences are finite. You may have reached as many people as you ever will and have exhausted the number of monetization opportunities from these people.

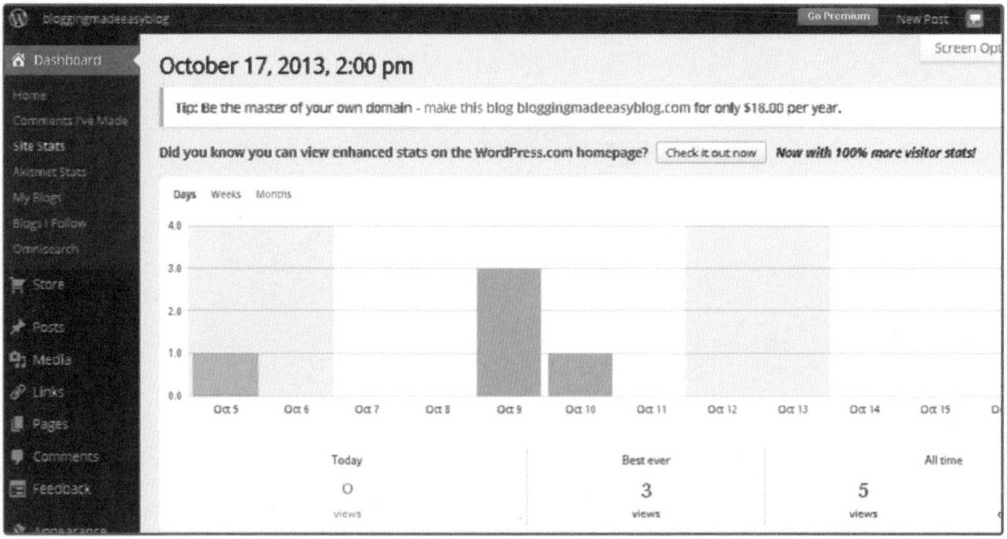

Dashboard
October 17, 2013, 2:00 pm
Tip: Be the master of your own domain - make this blog bloggingmadeeasyblog.com for only $18.00 per year.
Did you know you can view enhanced stats on the WordPress.com homepage?
Check it out now
Now with 100% more visitor stats!
Days
Weeks
Months
Today
0
views
Best ever
3
views
All time
5
views

Above: Maintaining an audience is a crucial part of your income stream. If audience numbers are falling, identify the problem immediately and work towards repairing it.

Hot Tip

Monitor your audience numbers regularly. If you start to notice a decline in the number of visitors, take action before the rot sets in.

Recapturing Your Audience

If your audience starts dwindling, you need to recapture them as soon as possible. You can employ various methods to breathe new life into your blog and reignite your audience's enthusiasm.

- **Revamp**: Completely redo your blog. Revamp both your blog's appearance and the type of content you are delivering. Think about using different types of content, such as videos and podcasts.

- **Research**: If your field is becoming more competitive, make sure you remain on top by researching your posts thoroughly and providing information your audience cannot get elsewhere.

- **Expand your niche**: Perhaps your subject area is too narrow. Bring in new visitors by broadening your subject area.

- **Guest blog**: Offer to guest blog on other blogs in a bid to promote your own and attract new visitors.

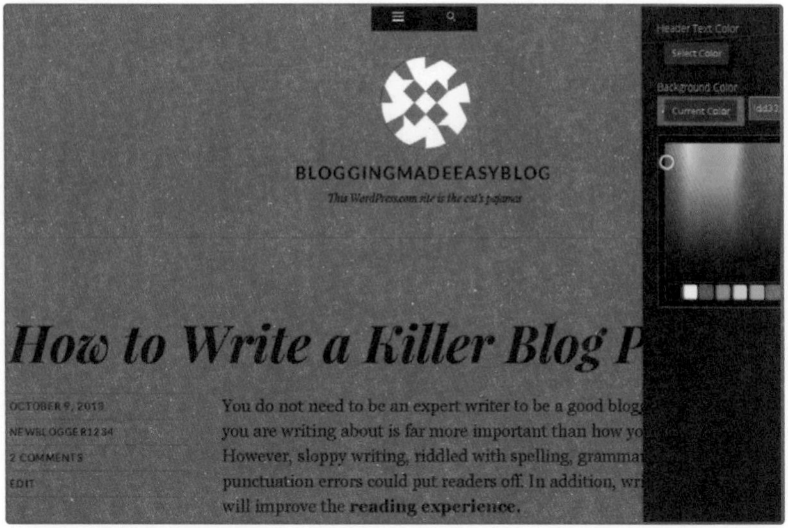

Above: Remodelling your blog is one way to re-engage with audience members. Give them something fresh by delivering new kinds of content.

ADVERTISING PROBLEMS

Audience numbers are not always the cause of funding problems, and many bloggers run into trouble because they have lost a sponsor or been excluded from certain advertising programs, such as AdSense. If this happens, approach new sponsors and sign up to other PPC networks and affiliate services as soon as possible to replace your lost income.

SAVING MONEY

As with any business, if you cannot generate enough income, you can always look at your expenditure to make savings. Various methods of saving cash are available to help keep your blog going.

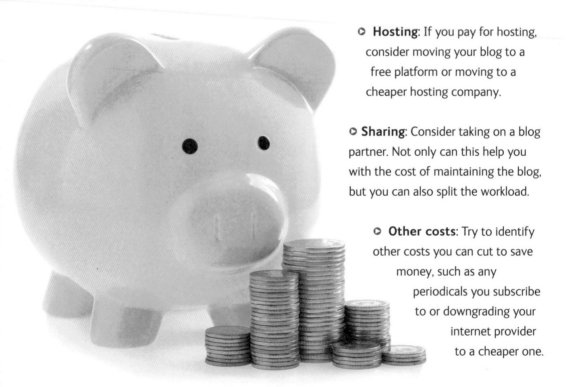

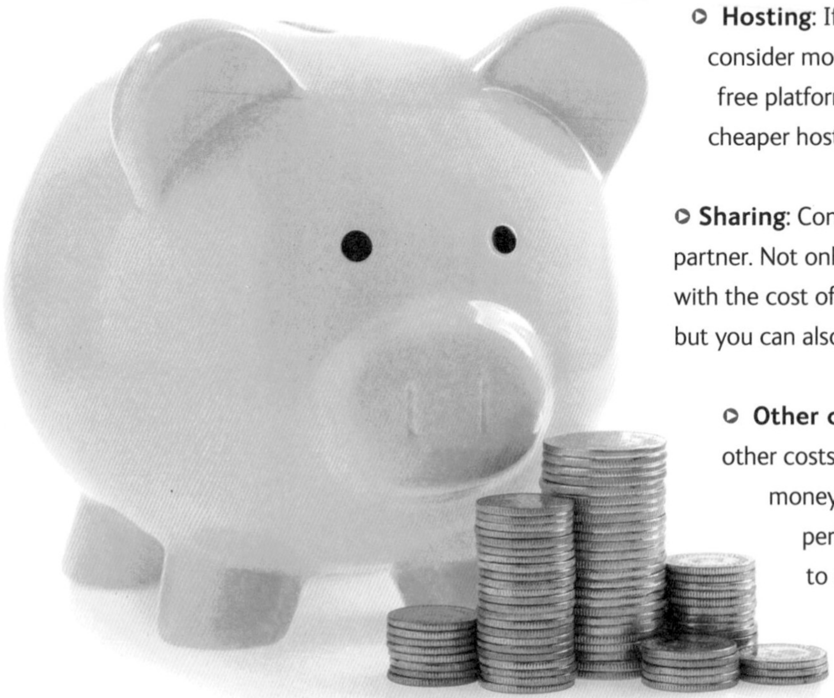

- **Hosting**: If you pay for hosting, consider moving your blog to a free platform or moving to a cheaper hosting company.
- **Sharing**: Consider taking on a blog partner. Not only can this help you with the cost of maintaining the blog, but you can also split the workload.
- **Other costs**: Try to identify other costs you can cut to save money, such as any periodicals you subscribe to or downgrading your internet provider to a cheaper one.

ALTERNATIVE MEANS OF FUNDING

If all else fails, you can always appeal to your readers for help. Many bloggers manage to pay for their blog by asking for donations from their audience. You will be surprised at how generous your readers might be, especially if they value the content you are providing.

> **Hot Tip**
>
> **If you are having problems with one aspect of your funding, look to different funding methods. If you have not tried approaching sponsors or selling merchandise, give it a go.**

Donations

You can insert a donation button on to your blog in a similar way to inserting a shopping cart or payment button. Most payment services, such as PayPal, will have the relevant code for a donation button (see previous section for instructions on setting up a payment button o0n your blog). Once you have placed the button in your blog, write a short piece of text to go with it to help encourage people to donate, such as: 'If you wish to help maintain this blog, please make a donation.'

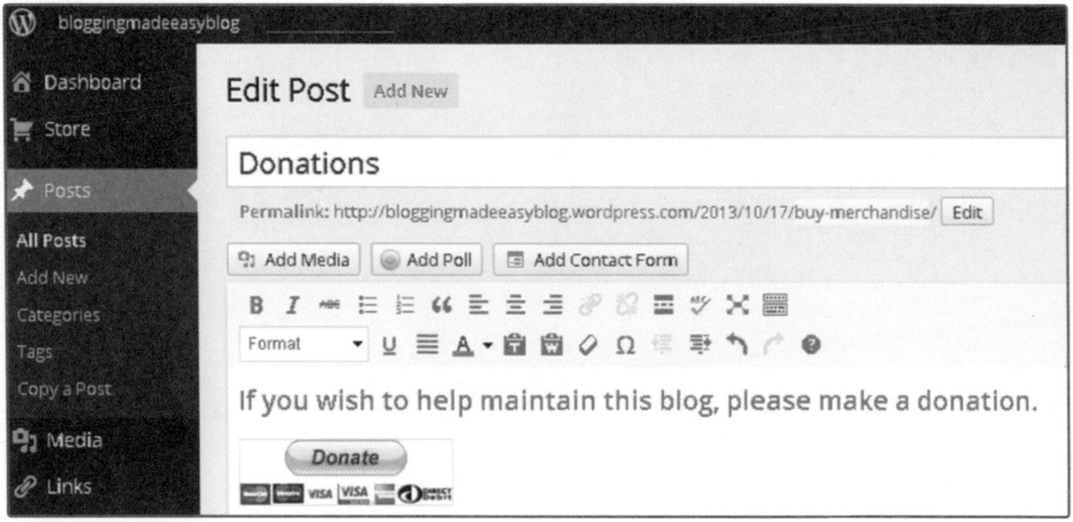

Above: Donations are a good way to help maintain your blog.

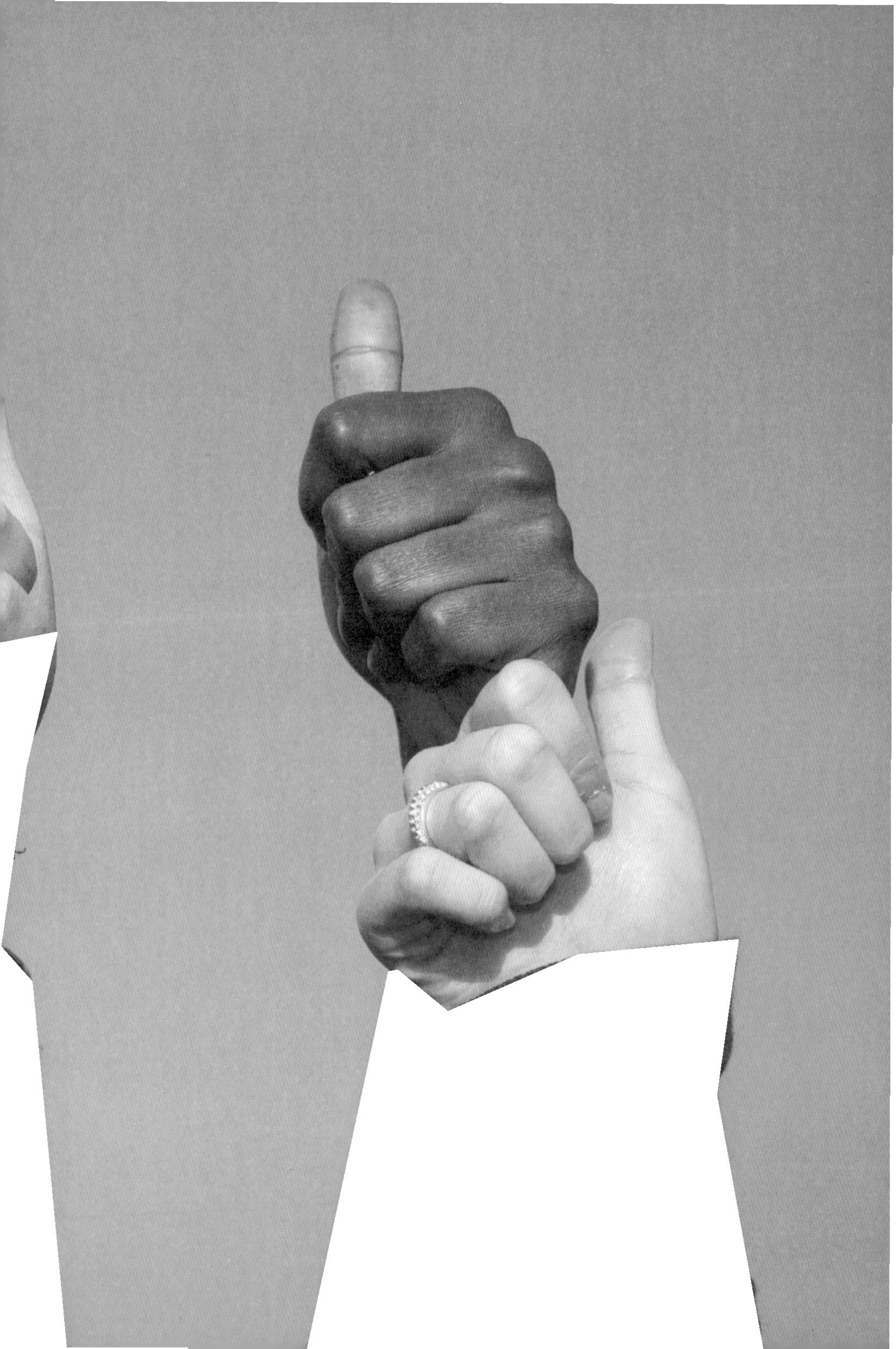

ESTABLISHED BLOGS

After you have been blogging a while, you may find that you have developed a loyal readership. However, once your blog is established, there is still no time to relax. You need to keep hold of your audience and keep your blog fresh.

REACHING THE TOP

Established blogs are those that everybody interested in the topic has heard of. These blogs become authorities on the topic and a trusted source of information for many people. Some bloggers find it takes months, even years, to establish their blog, develop a loyal audience and become a dependable bank of information.

Success Indicators

Just because your blog has been going a while does not been it is now established in the Blogosphere and you have become an authority in your subject area. All sorts of things can suggest how well you are doing, and spotting these indicators will gain you some insight as to what you are doing that is working and what you are doing that is not.

Indicators of Success

- **Audience**: Your audience will have grown from nothing to hundreds or even thousands of readers. At this point, most established bloggers find their audience plateaus.
- **Interaction**: Established blogs will have numerous comments on each blog post, as well as having their blog posts shared on social media.
- **Subscriptions**: When people start subscribing to your blog, it is a good sign you are building a loyal following.
- **Money**: If you have monetized your blog, the more you become established, the more money you will start to make.
- **Authority**: Are other bloggers sending links to your posts, mentioning your posts or asking to guest blog?

KEEPING THE MOMENTUM GOING

Once you have become established, in many ways, things get harder. Building up a loyal audience is one thing; keeping it is another. The more established a blog, the more difficult it is to keep the momentum going, keep everything fresh and continue at the same pace.

Above: Blog stats can help identify how established you are.

Blogging More Efficiently

One way established bloggers keep up their momentum is to learn how to blog in a more efficient manner. For many new bloggers, they blog on their home computer at set times during the week. However, the more experienced blogger learns to write posts on the go or whenever an idea takes seed. These days, blogging is easily done on mobile phones, tablet computers and laptops. All you need is a blogging app, and most blogging platforms provide a mobile version, although some are better at blogging on the go than others.

- **Blogger**: A very mobile-friendly blogging platform that even lets you create a blog on a smartphone. You can also send posts by email to your blog.
- **WordPress Mobile Admin Plug-in**: Only available for self-hosted installs, but you can enter posts directly to your blog. Best used on iPhone and iPads, as other devices can experience problems.

Hot Tip

You can write your blog posts on your mobile device, save them to draft and then revise and publish your posts from your home computer.

Microblogging

If you find it difficult to blog on the go, you can help keep your audience invested in your blog by providing regular posts on microblogging websites. Twitter is by far the best platform for microblogging, and it is available to use on any mobile device. Twitter enables you to provide regular commentary on a topic, whenever thoughts occur to you. However, you first need to ensure your readers are following you, and for that, you will need a Twitter button on your blog.

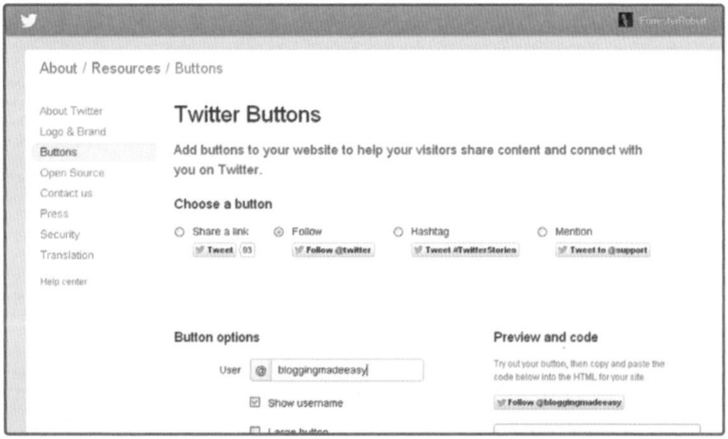

Above: Twitter serves as an outlet to express smaller thoughts, keeping your blog readers engaged.

1. Go to Twitter.com and click the **About** link (alternatively, type in the URL www.twitter.com/about/) and then click **Buttons**.

2. Select the type of 'follow' button you want on your blog.

3. Copy and paste the button code in the box under where it says **Preview and Code**.

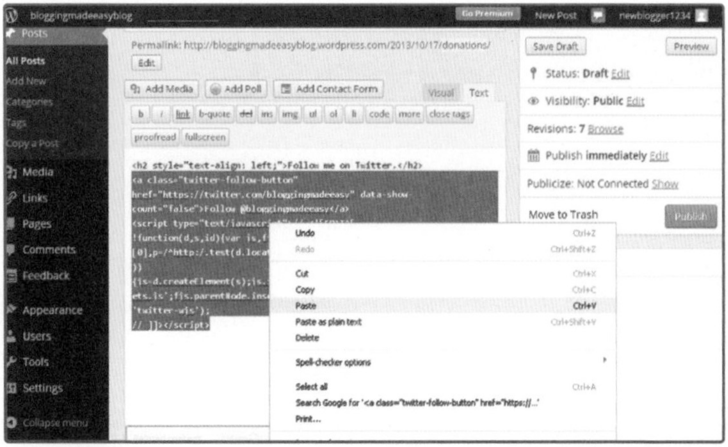

Above: Pasting your Twitter code into your blog creates a link between your Twitter account page and your blog.

4. Paste the code into your blog using HTML mode.

Hot Tip

Use hashtags in your posts to denote particular keywords and categories. These will help those who do not follow you to find your posts.

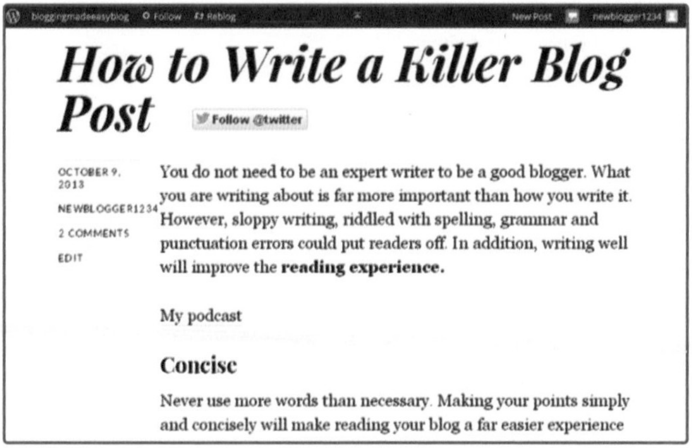

bloggingmadeeasyblog
Follow
Reblog
New Post
newblogger1234
How to Write a Killer Blog Post
Follow @twitter
OCTOBER 9, 2013
NEWBLOGGER1234
2 COMMENTS
EDIT
You do not need to be an expert writer to be a good blogger. What you are writing about is far more important than how you write it. However, sloppy writing, riddled with spelling, grammar and punctuation errors could put readers off. In addition, writing well will improve the reading experience.
My podcast
Concise
Never use more words than necessary. Making your points simply and concisely will make reading your blog a far easier experience

Above: The Twitter button added to your page appears at the heading of your post, making it accessible to readers.

KEEPING CONTENT FRESH

One of the biggest challenges for established bloggers is continuing to come up with fresh, informative content. Established bloggers employ all sorts of techniques to help come up with new blog posts and keep their blog fresh.

- **Post updates:** Expand, update and revisit subjects you have covered earlier on in your blog. Many newer readers will not have seen these posts, while your established audience will not mind you revisiting subjects as long as you can add something new to the post.

- **Develop discussions:** Some posts elicit lots of responses. Many of the comments on these posts can be used as a basis for new posts by expanding the topic in a different direction.

- **Planning:** Having an editorial schedule in which you plan when you are going to make certain posts can help you establish the direction you are taking the blog and come up with ideas to suit.

- **Mixing content**: If you mainly write tips or informative pieces, try including some opinion in your blog, and vice versa. This can help keep the blog fresh by taking it in different directions.

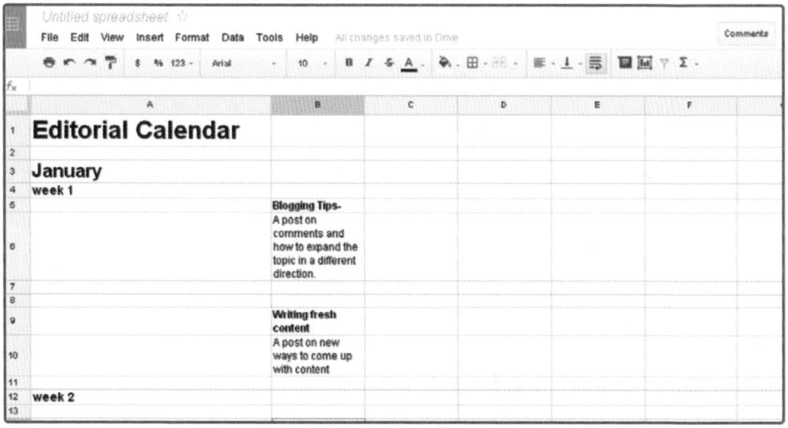

Above: An editorial calendar organizes your thoughts, determining where you want to take them.

Identifying Your Strengths

One way to ensure you continue to engage your audience is to identify what you are good at. Some posts will be better received than others, and identifying these can help you develop better content that is more suited to your audience. Look at your statistics and draw up a list of posts that have had the most traffic, comments and links from outside sources, then ask yourself what these posts have in common.

- **Topic**: Are some topics generating more interest than others?
- **Style**: Do your opinion pieces generate more interest than your information articles?
- **Looks**: Do posts with more images receive more visits? What about the titles you use?
- **Length**: Are you writing posts that are too long? How long are your most popular posts?

Hot Tip

Concentrate on writing blog posts according to what your readers want. Come up with a formula that governs style, looks and length, and write within it.

DEALING WITH SUCCESS

Some bloggers hit it big and receive tens of thousands of visitors a week. There are even bloggers who earn a good living from their blog. But when you've got your audience and perhaps even exceeded your goals, what comes next and how do you capitalize on this success?

ACHIEVING YOUR GOALS

Success means different things to different people. Some bloggers start out just wanting to reach a decent number of people and voice their opinions about their subject area. For others, success is monetary, and some bloggers want to earn enough money to blog full time.

Secrets of Success

Whatever your goals, three things are essential.

- **Sense of realism**: Hoping to become rich and famous through blogging is unrealistic and unlikely, although it can happen. Successful bloggers have more achievable goals.

- **Perseverance**: Most bloggers fail because they simply give up. Keep at it and you have a good chance of achieving what you want.
- **Experimentation**: Do not be afraid to try different things. If something is not working, try something else.

WHAT NEXT?

Once you have achieved your goals, you may wonder what your options are. Some people are happy continuing as they are, maintaining their blog as they always have, while others want to expand and take their blog to the next level.

Finding New Goals

Once you have achieved success in blogging, it can be a springboard to many new things. Some people who have achieved success in blogging have found themselves careers in the mainstream media; other bloggers have developed their own brand and expanded their blog into online magazines; others decide to sell their blog and go and do something else.

YOUR BRAND

When you have built up a successful blog, you will have developed your own brand. A brand is not just your name, but can be anything that identifies you and your blog. A brand is not necessarily something you have full control of, as a brand is what other people perceive about you and your blog.

Above: Blogger Guido Fawkes has developed a unique brand and logo.

Securing Your Brand

A brand can become particularly valuable. Because of this, it may be worth protecting those things that denote who you are and help define your brand.

- **Your URL**: Your blog address could be particularly valuable. Make sure you protect your domain name and prevent other people from taking advantage of it.

> **Hot Tip**
>
> **To protect your brand identity, register other domains that include your blog name. If you have www.myblog.com, register www.myblog.co.uk, www.myblog.org and www.myblog.net.**

- **Your blog name**: Consider registering your blog as a trademark. This will prevent others from using it.

- **Logos and imagery**: You should also consider protecting any symbols, images and logos that reflect you and your blog.

PROFESSIONAL BLOGGING

For bloggers who have monetized their blog, success may mean there comes a time when they have to decide whether to become a full-time blogger. Earning a living from blogging can be extremely rewarding, but it means you have to start thinking about your blog as your business, not just a hobby.

Income Streams

While your own blog may be your main source of income, for many professional bloggers, finding other income streams is important to both expand their brand and ensure they have a viable and long-lasting career. Once you have become established in your field, you may find that you are paid to write guest slots for magazines and other blogs. This not only helps you generate other income streams, but also helps publicize your own blog.

Hiring Help

When you started blogging, you probably did everything yourself, from creating your blog and writing and posting your content to selling advertising space. However, when things really start taking off, you may find that you have to hire help to assist you with your blog. This may include employing other writers to help produce the content needed, web designers to maintain the blog, sales people to help sell advertising space or marketers to help promote your blog. All this can mean that you have to take on the responsibilities of a regular business, such as paying wages and handling employees.

Above: The Huffington Post, sold to AOL for $315 million, is a prime example of how blogs can accumulate high value over time.

SELLING YOUR BLOG

In 2012, popular financial blogger Martin Lewis sold his stake in www.MoneySavingExpert.com for

£87 million ($140 million), while recently, the news aggregation website and blog, *The Huffington Post*, was sold to AOL for $315 million (£200 million). While it is unlikely your blog will become worth as much as these examples, a blog can still become a valuable asset.

Valuing Your Blog

You may find that businesses related to your subject will demonstrate an interest in buying your blog, or you may decide to put it on to the general market. However, before you can sell it, you need to understand how much your blog is worth. This can be more problematic than calculating the cost of other assets such as property. A blog is essentially worth as much as somebody wants to pay for it, but some factors can help you understand its worth.

> **Hot Tip**
>
> **Websites such as www.sellmyblog.net can help evaluate, market and sell your blog.**

- **Earnings**: As with most businesses, revenue, profit and expenditure will determine a blog's value.

- **Traffic**: The number of people visiting your blog will affect its worth.
- **Sustainability**: Far more subjective is the long-term relevancy and future prospects of a blog.

Left: MoneySavingExpert.com is another example of a blog which was sold for a large amount of money.

Making a Sale

Whatever value you have attached to your blog, it may not be the same as what somebody else thinks it is worth. Before you sell your blog, make sure you are happy with the offer and conditions attached, such as any noncompetitive clauses, which may prevent you from starting another blog.

DIVERSIFYING

Once you have achieved your original goals, you may decide to diversify into other aspects related to your topic. An established brand, platform and experience can provide you with the tools needed to diversify into all sorts of other avenues.

- **Consultancy**: As a respected authority in your field, you may be able to provide consultancy services to related businesses.
- **Retail**: Expanding into a retail website could turn your blog into a large business.
- **Journalism**: Some bloggers become sought-after writers and earn a living as freelance journalists.
- **Starting a new blog**: If there is another topic that interests you, you could try to replicate your success with another blog.

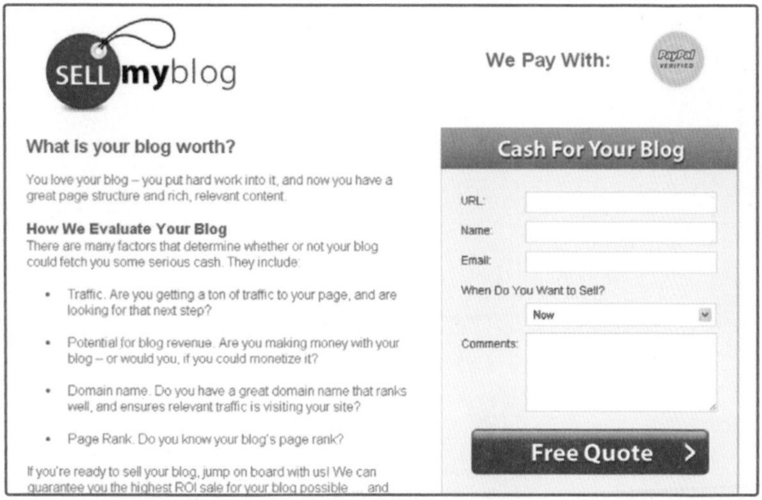
SELL myblog
We Pay With:
What is your blog worth?
You love your blog – you put hard work into it, and now you have a great page structure and rich, relevant content.
How We Evaluate Your Blog
There are many factors that determine whether or not your blog could fetch you some serious cash. They include:
Traffic. Are you getting a ton of traffic to your page, and are looking for that next step?
Potential for blog revenue. Are you making money with your blog – or would you, if you could monetize it?
Domain name. Do you have a great domain name that ranks well, and ensures relevant traffic is visiting your site?
Page Rank. Do you know your blog's page rank?
If you're ready to sell your blog, jump on board with us! We can
Cash For Your Blog
URL:
Name:
Email:
When Do You Want to Sell?
Now
Comments:
Free Quote

Above: Websites such as SellMyBlog.com simplify the process of marketing and selling your blog.

TAKING YOUR BLOG FURTHER

Once you have an established blog, you may wish to take it to the next level. Taking your blog further may mean reaching more people, maximizing your blogging income and improving the look and content of your blog.

REDEFINING YOUR GOALS

When most people start blogging, they do not have the long term in mind and just want a platform for their views and opinions. However, in order to take your blog to the next level, you need to establish a new set of goals.

What Do You Want to Achieve?

Now you have secured an audience, where do you want to go next? You may wish to expand your audience and become the number-one resource in your subject area. Alternatively, you may wish to make more money from your blog, or improve the content you are providing to your community. Whatever you want to achieve, taking your blog to the next level means going from a hobbyist to a serious blogger.

TAKING BLOGGING SERIOUSLY

Just because you are moving from blogging as a hobby to becoming more serious about it, does not mean you cannot have just as much fun, but you do need to move beyond the basics.

Self-hosted Blogging

While you may have started out using a free blogging platform, such as Blogger or WordPress, to take blogging to the next level, you really need to move to a self-hosted platform. This is for various reasons.

- **Domain**: A hosted URL looks less professional.
- **Freedom**: You have far more freedom and flexibility with a self-hosted platform, so can make your blog look how you want it to, and do exactly what you want it to do.
- **Support**: You have more plug-ins and support options with a self-hosted blog.
- **Control**: You do not have to abide by the rules of a hosted platform or worry about having your account deleted.

Hot Tip

Plan your move carefully. Ensure your audience knows what is happening. When you move, post a link on the old blog to the new.

Above: As your blog expands, you will want to shed yourself of a hosted URL. Self-hosted domain names appear more professional and come with more freedom.

EXPANDING YOUR REACH

Many bloggers find that their audience plateaus after a while. When this happens, it seems that no matter what you do, you simply cannot increase the number of visitors. If this happens, you need to improve your blog-promotion techniques.

Partnerships

Build partnerships with other bloggers. Swap advertising space to promote each other's blogs, provide mutual links and RSS feeds and do regular guest blogging.

Hot Tip

By far your best promotional tool is your audience. Make it easy for them to recruit new visitors to your blog by adding an 'Email this to a friend' button to your posts.

Advertising

Consider advertising your blog on industry websites. If you cannot afford the cost of advertising space, try to negotiate a quid pro quo arrangement by offering to host free advertisements on your blog or offer to write editorial pieces.

Newsletters

Newsletters can be an effective way of marketing your blog and reaching a wider audience. For a blogger, an email newsletter can summarize the blog posts for the month and contain links to the posts. In addition, you can provide information that you have not included on your blog.

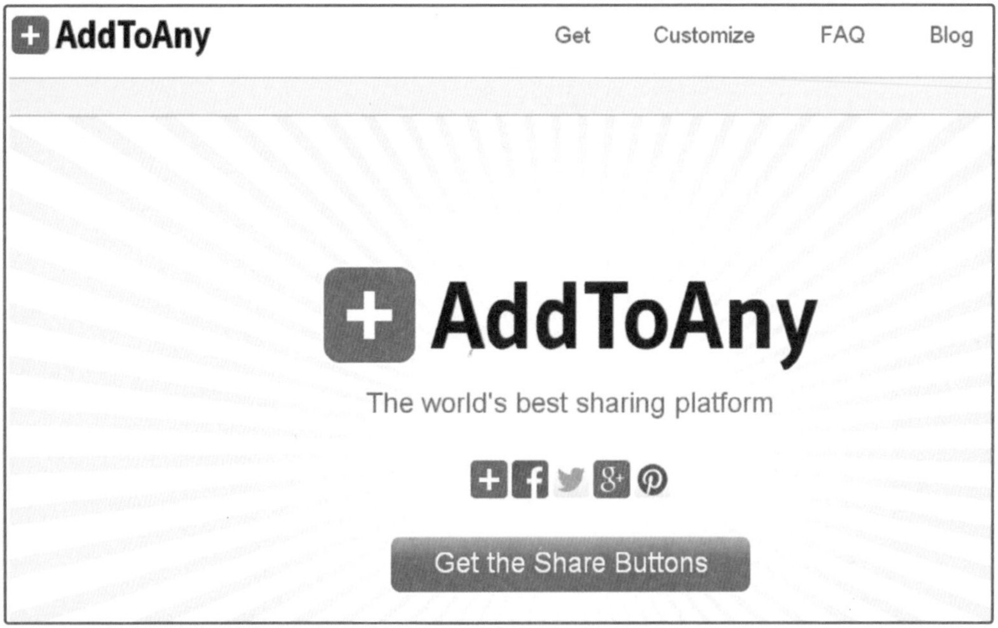

Above: Addtoany.com provides sharing buttons to make it easier for your audience to share your blog posts.

The great thing about newsletters is that people can forward them to others interested in the subject area. However, creating newsletters does require some thought.

- **Type of newsletter**: You can send newsletters as attachments or compose them as an actual email. Make sure you include links to your blog and a few images to catch the eye.

- **Content**: While you may want to summarize your blog posts, make sure you include extra content to offer an incentive for people to sign up to your newsletter.

- **Subscription**: You need to set up a 'subscribe' button on your blog. Most blogging platforms have newsletter plug-ins that you can use for this, or a simple contact form will do.

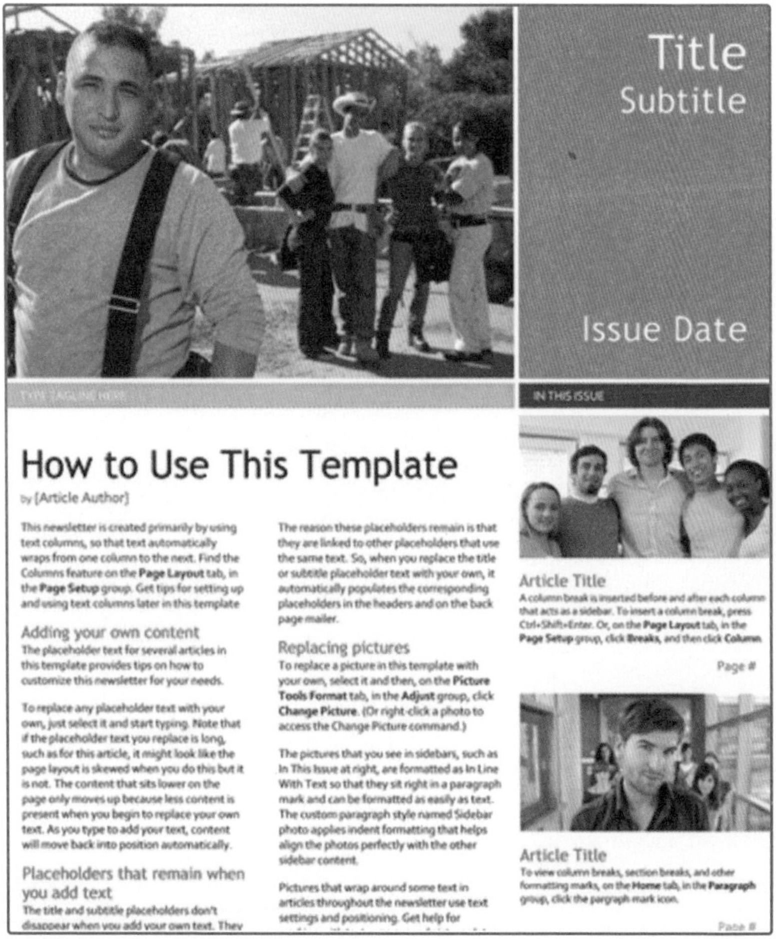

Title

Subtitle

Issue Date

TYPE TAGLINE HERE

IN THIS ISSUE

How to Use This Template

by [Article Author]

This newsletter is created primarily by using text columns, so that text automatically wraps from one column to the next. Find the Columns feature on the **Page Layout** tab, in the **Page Setup** group. Get tips for setting up and using text columns later in this template

Adding your own content

The placeholder text for several articles in this template provides tips on how to customize this newsletter for your needs.

To replace any placeholder text with your own, just select it and start typing. Note that if the placeholder text you replace is long, such as for this article, it might look like the page layout is skewed when you do this but it is not. The content that sits lower on the page only moves up because less content is present when you begin to replace your own text. As you type to add your text, content will move back into position automatically.

Placeholders that remain when you add text

The title and subtitle placeholders don't disappear when you add your own text. They

The reason these placeholders remain is that they are linked to other placeholders that use the same text. So, when you replace the title or subtitle placeholder text with your own, it automatically populates the corresponding placeholders in the headers and on the back page mailer.

Replacing pictures

To replace a picture in this template with your own, select it and then, on the **Picture Tools Format** tab, in the **Adjust** group, click **Change Picture**. (Or right-click a photo to access the Change Picture command.)

The pictures that you see in sidebars, such as In This Issue at right, are formatted as In Line With Text so that they sit right in a paragraph mark and can be formatted as easily as text. The custom paragraph style named Sidebar photo applies indent formatting that helps align the photos perfectly with the other sidebar content.

Pictures that wrap around some text in articles throughout the newsletter use text settings and positioning. Get help for

Article Title

A column break is inserted before and after each column that acts as a sidebar. To insert a column break, press Ctrl+Shift+Enter. Or, on the **Page Layout** tab, in the **Page Setup** group, click **Breaks**, and then click **Column**.

Page #

Article Title

To view column breaks, section breaks, and other formatting marks, on the **Home** tab, in the **Paragraph** group, click the pargraph mark icon.

Page #

Right: Microsoft Word provides users with an easy-to-use newsletter template.

IMPROVING YOUR DESIGN

When it comes to capturing new audience members, looks matter. The better-looking a website or blog, the more likely a visitor will hang around and read the content. While a basic theme layout may be satisfactory to begin with, to stay ahead of the game, you need to ensure your blog looks the business.

Hot Tip

To help reinforce your brand, consider hiring a designer to create a professional logo for your blog. Convert it into a favicon and use it on your social media pages, newsletters and emails.

- **Theme**: Consider a customized theme designed by an expert. While this may cost you money, the results will ensure your blog stands out from the crowd.

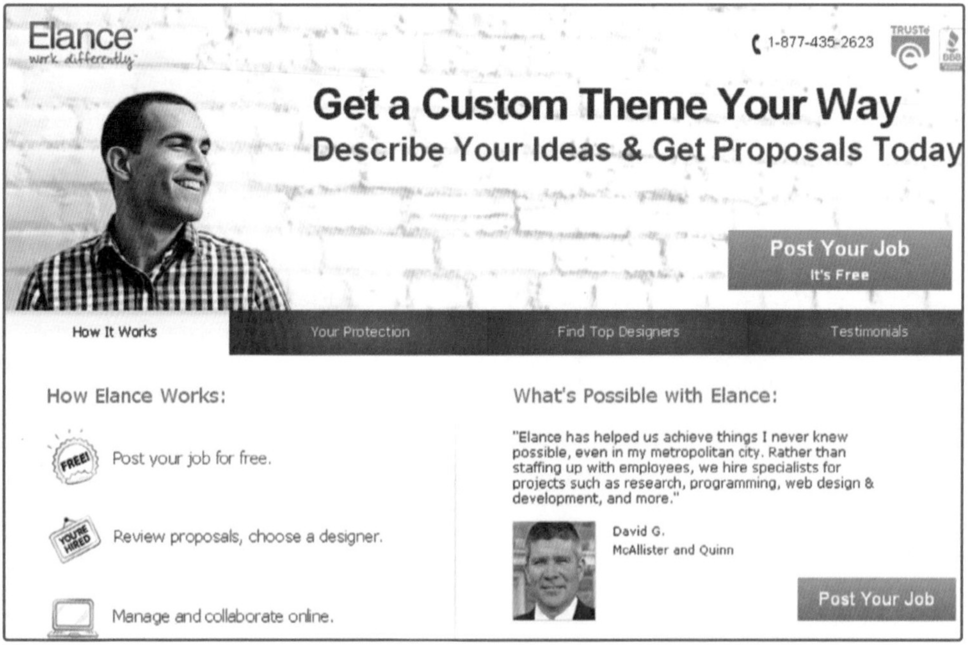

Elance
work differently
1-877-435-2623
TRUSTe
Get a Custom Theme Your Way
Describe Your Ideas & Get Proposals Today
Post Your Job
It's Free
How It Works
Your Protection
Find Top Designers
Testimonials
How Elance Works:
FREE!
Post your job for free.
YOU'RE HIRED
Review proposals, choose a designer.
Manage and collaborate online.
What's Possible with Elance:
"Elance has helped us achieve things I never knew possible, even in my metropolitan city. Rather than staffing up with employees, we hire specialists for projects such as research, programming, web design & development, and more."
David G.
McAllister and Quinn
Post Your Job

Above: Many theme designers advertise on Elance.com.

- **Streamline**: Too much clutter can get in the way, as can too much colour, overuse of fonts and unnecessary widgets and gadgets. Get rid of any unnecessary elements.

- **Typography**: Learn to adopt the most effective fonts. Understand which typefaces work best on the page, which are the most readable and when to use serif and sans-serif fonts.

ADVANCED LINKING

Most bloggers utilize links on their posts to help readers identify sources and find further reading, but for advanced blogging, linking needs to be done more discriminately. Not all sources are the same, and simply linking to an article that elaborates on a point you have made is not as effective as finding reputable and valuable resources.

Hot Tip

If you look at the bottom of a Wikipedia page, you will find the resources used to compile the article. Often, these are much more authoritative and go into more detail than the encyclopedia page.

Authoritative Sources

Finding authoritative sources to link to means looking beyond the usual blogs and encyclopedias such as Wikipedia. While these resources are fine for giving people a broad outline of a subject, they rarely go into much depth. What you need to find are articles written by expert sources that can provide added value to your readers interested in examining a subject further, rather than just providing a broad overview.

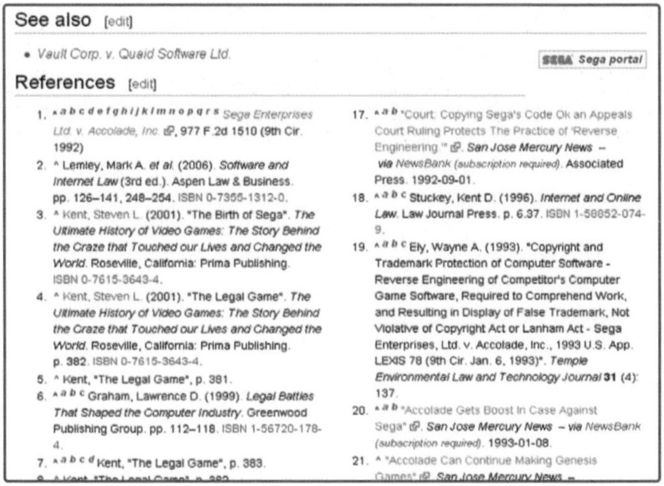

See also [edit]

- *Vault Corp. v. Quaid Software Ltd.*

SEGA *Sega portal*

References [edit]

1. ^ a b c d e f g h i j k l m n o p q r s *Sega Enterprises Ltd. v. Accolade, Inc.*, 977 F.2d 1510 (9th Cir. 1992)
2. ^ Lemley, Mark A. *et al.* (2006). *Software and Internet Law* (3rd ed.). Aspen Law & Business. pp. 126–141, 248–254. ISBN 0-7355-1312-0.
3. ^ Kent, Steven L. (2001). "The Birth of Sega". *The Ultimate History of Video Games: The Story Behind the Craze that Touched our Lives and Changed the World.* Roseville, California: Prima Publishing. ISBN 0-7615-3643-4.
4. ^ Kent, Steven L. (2001). "The Legal Game". *The Ultimate History of Video Games: The Story Behind the Craze that Touched our Lives and Changed the World.* Roseville, California: Prima Publishing. p. 382. ISBN 0-7615-3643-4.
5. ^ Kent, "The Legal Game", p. 381.
6. ^ a b c Graham, Lawrence D. (1999). *Legal Battles That Shaped the Computer Industry*. Greenwood Publishing Group. pp. 112–118. ISBN 1-56720-178-4.
7. ^ a b c d Kent, "The Legal Game", p. 383.

17. ^ a b "Court: Copying Sega's Code Ok an Appeals Court Ruling Protects The Practice of 'Reverse Engineering.'". *San Jose Mercury News* – *via* NewsBank *(subscription required)*. Associated Press. 1992-09-01.
18. ^ a b c Stuckey, Kent D. (1996). *Internet and Online Law*. Law Journal Press. p. 6.37. ISBN 1-58852-074-9.
19. ^ a b c Ely, Wayne A. (1993). "Copyright and Trademark Protection of Computer Software - Reverse Engineering of Competitor's Computer Game Software, Required to Comprehend Work, and Resulting in Display of False Trademark, Not Violative of Copyright Act or Lanham Act - Sega Enterprises, Ltd. v. Accolade, Inc., 1993 U.S. App. LEXIS 78 (9th Cir. Jan. 6, 1993)". *Temple Environmental Law and Technology Journal* **31** (4): 137.
20. ^ a b "Accolade Gets Boost In Case Against Sega". *San Jose Mercury News* – *via* NewsBank *(subscription required)*. 1993-01-08.
21. ^ "Accolade Can Continue Making Genesis Games". *San Jose Mercury News* –

Above: References sections at the bottom of Wikipedia pages are often useful for discovering authoritative sources.

HONING YOUR CRAFT

As blogging is about content, to take things to the next level, you need to up your game when it comes to the blog posts you are producing. You need to concentrate on both the content of your posts and how you are delivering them.

Content

Do not just rely on the internet to provide top-quality and insightful information. You need to find primary sources of information.

- **Contacts**: Speak to people in the industry. Build up a list of useful contacts who can provide you with information.
- **Press releases**: Make sure you subscribe to press releases from companies to ensure you get new and first-hand information.

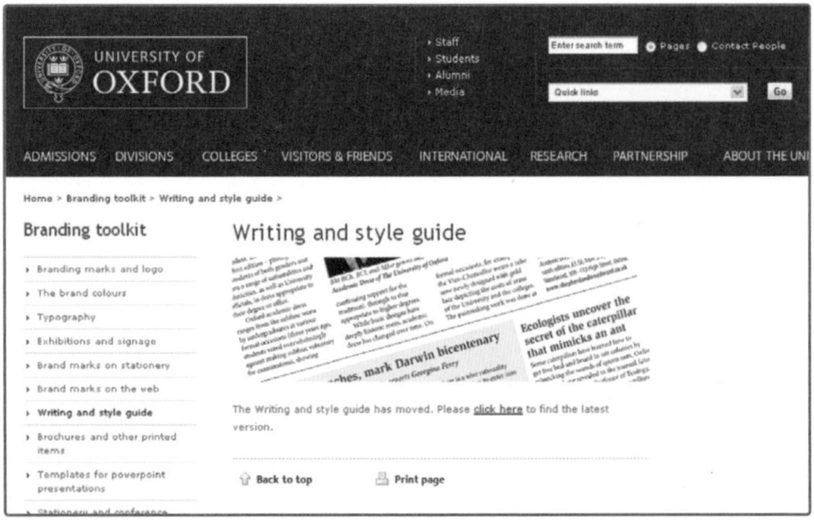

Above: Oxford University's style guide is a useful resource for individuals who seek to improve their writing technique.

- **Read**: Subscribe to periodicals related to your topic and read books. Become an expert in your field.

Style

Concentrate on honing your writing skills. Keep your writing concise and to the point. Learn to remove extraneous words and make sure you are always leading with the main points. If you have limited training, consider enrolling on a writing or journalism course or buy a book on style.

Editorial

How you deliver information can make a big difference to how much further you can take your blog. Think like a professional journalist. Come up with an editorial schedule. Review your posts every month to ensure you are keeping content fresh and not covering the same old ground. If your blog is mainly text based, start including more video, audio and multimedia on your blog. Be brutal with your editing and cut words and content that do not add value to your blog posts.

E-books

When you have been blogging a while, you may want to consider putting together a collection of your best blog posts and releasing them together as an e-book. Not only could this be an extra

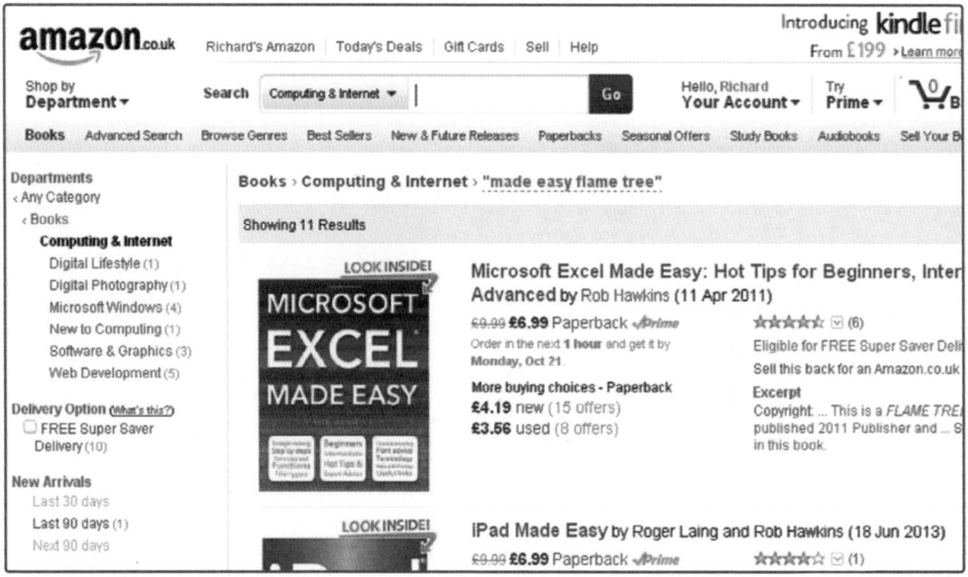

Above: If you decide to release an e-book, Amazon, one of the main e-book vendors, is the perfect place to market copies.

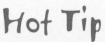

Above: Blog search bars make accessing posts on specific topics stress free.

revenue source, but it could also introduce new readers to your blog. You could sell your e-book through your blog or through some of the main e-book vendors, such as Amazon, Smashwords or Kobo. You could even give copies away as a means of attracting traffic to your blog.

CAPTURING NEW READERS

Once you have got the hang of some of the more intricate aspects of blogging, you can begin to design features aimed at enticing and capturing new readers to your blog. Many bloggers find they are getting a steady flow of new traffic from search engines but are failing to increase the size of their audience. Often, this is because new visitors are coming to a blog and then disappearing again because they cannot find what they are looking for.

Most Popular Posts

To retain new readers, you need to ensure they have easy access to the information they are looking for. If you have hundreds of posts on your blog, it can be arduous to click back through them to find relevant information. One way to make this process easier is to include a list on a sidebar of your blog posts that have had the most views.

Hot Tip

Most blogging platforms have a search bar facility, so make sure you include one on your blog. Make it prominent so it is not tucked away under all your sidebar features.

TECHNICAL DETAILS

Being an advanced blogger means learning some of the nitty-gritty aspects of blogging. Understanding SEO, CSS, HTML and other technicalities can help you enhance your blog and ensure you are maximizing its potential.

BLOGGING TECHNICALITIES

You do not need to be a programmer to be a great blogger, but a basic understanding of the technologies and systems that power blogs and bring in traffic can help you develop your blog beyond what the basic blogging platforms allow.

- **SEO**: Search Engine Optimization is key for bringing traffic to your blog. If you can develop you blog's SEO beyond just adding simple keywords, you can boost traffic and improve the visibility of individual blog posts.

- **CSS**: If you learn how to customize Cascading Style Sheets, you will have a lot more freedom to create the blog you want, make changes when required and add more functionality.

- **HTML**: Hypertext Markup Language is the language of the internet, so knowing how it works makes blogging much easier.

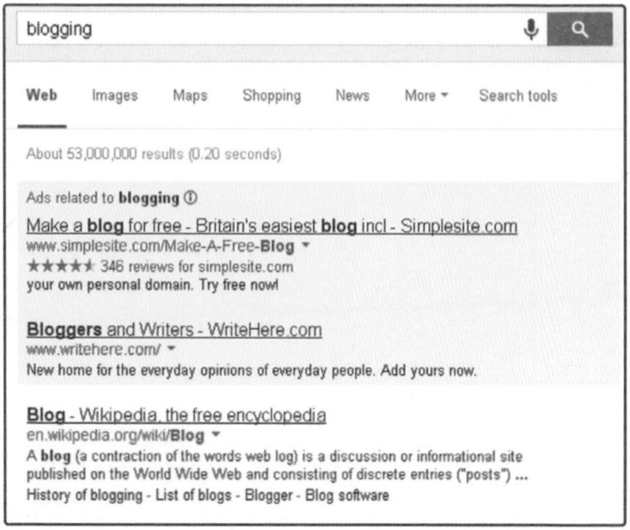

blogging
Web
Images
Maps
Shopping
News
More
Search tools
About 53,000,000 results (0.20 seconds)
Ads related to blogging
Make a blog for free - Britain's easiest blog incl - Simplesite.com
www.simplesite.com/Make-A-Free-Blog
346 reviews for simplesite.com
your own personal domain. Try free now!
Bloggers and Writers - WriteHere.com
www.writehere.com/
New home for the everyday opinions of everyday people. Add yours now.
Blog - Wikipedia, the free encyclopedia
en.wikipedia.org/wiki/Blog
A blog (a contraction of the words web log) is a discussion or informational site published on the World Wide Web and consisting of discrete entries ("posts") ...
History of blogging - List of blogs - Blogger - Blog software

Right: Search Engine Optimization can direct an abundance of visitors towards your blog.

SEARCH ENGINE OPTIMIZATION (SEO)

Despite the limitations of search engines, people generally trust results the higher up they appear, especially those on the first page. Rarely do people click on more than one or two pages of search results, hence the importance of SEO.

Optimizing Posts

Identify the pages that are getting the most traffic from search engines and optimize them.

- **Keyword density:** Cross-reference the keywords people have used to come across a post, then count how many times the phrase appears in the text. If it is just once or twice, add the keyword a couple more times to increase keyword density.

Hot Tip

Search engine traffic usually consists of people who have not visited your blog before but are those that are interested in the blog topic, so they could be future loyal readers.

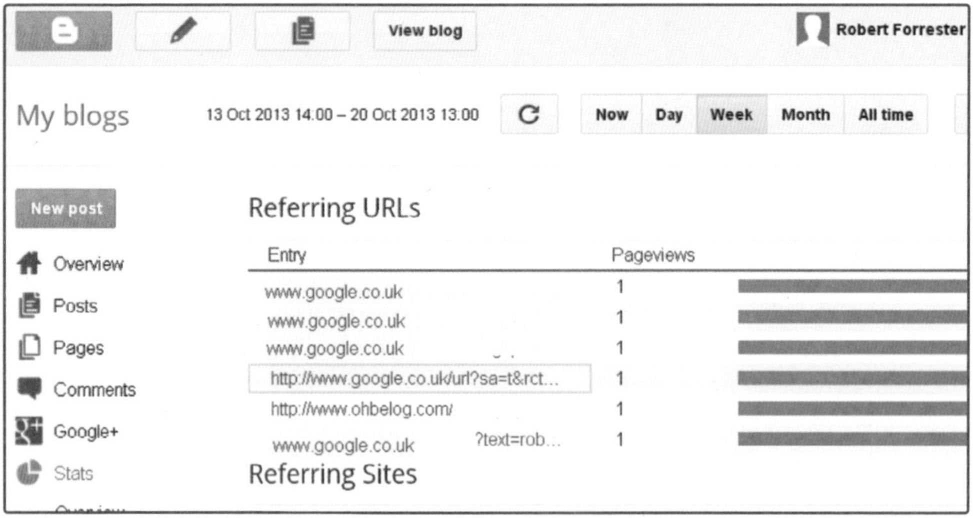

Above: Blogger stats pages are used to identify traffic sources and keywords.

- **Links:** Search engines love links, but only authoritative ones. Increase the number of links in your posts, but make sure they are good-quality sources. Do not forget to link to other posts on your own blog.

Related Content

Once you have an understanding of the types of pages that are getting the most search engine traffic and the keywords people are using, you can tailor posts that are optimized for this traffic. Think of other posts that you can write related to the keywords and search terms.

> **Hot Tip**
>
> **How often you update your blog affects how often search engines index it. If you add content regularly enough, new articles can appear in the rankings in just a few hours.**

Inbound Links

Links from other websites and blogs can really help promote your posts in the search engine rankings. However, inbound links have to be of good quality, from sites with high search engine rankings and from sites related to your content. Do not be tempted to buy links, as this can get you penalized by search engines. The best way to generate them is to write good-quality posts that other blogs and websites will want to link to.

Right: Adding links to websites and blogs is a good way to boost your posts in search engine rankings.

CSS

Many bloggers think understanding and learning to customize Cascading Style Sheets is daunting. On first glance, CSS does look complicated. However, plenty of resources on the internet can help you get to grips with the basics. Once you understand CSS, you will no longer have to rely on custom templates to stylize your blog and you can make all sorts of changes to your blog's appearance and layout, quickly and simply.

Understanding CSS

CSS stands for Cascading Style Sheets, which store all the code that governs the appearance of a blog or website. CSS controls how HTML elements are displayed on a page, such as colours, fonts, headers and placements for images. To edit a style sheet, you will need a CSS editor.

- **Notepad++:** Similar to the notepad text editor, only with added features for HTML and other source codes. Available for free at www.notepad-plus-plus.org.

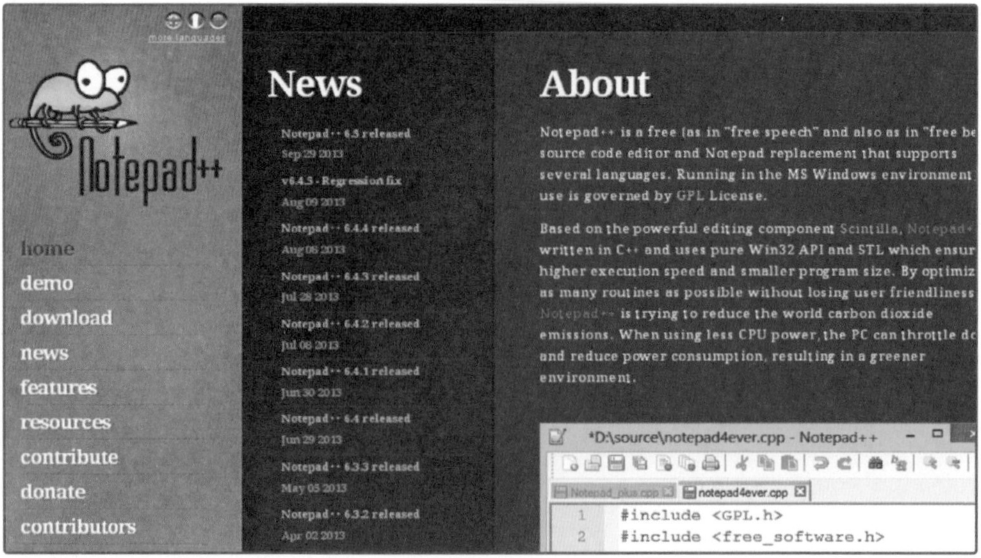

Above: Notepad++, a popular CSS editor, is free to use and includes features for HTML and other source codes.

- **PSPad**: Another simple-to-use editor that includes a spellchecker designed to highlight syntax errors in code. Available for free at www.pspad.com.

- **Rapid CSS**: Has both manual and assisted CSS editing. Available as a free trial from www.rapidcsseditor.com.

HTML

In order to edit style sheets and customize your blog, you will need an understanding of HTML beyond the basics discussed in Chapter Three. HTML, or a form of it, is the language used to create all websites and blogs. Spending time learning to code basic HTML will make blogging much easier and give you more freedom when it comes to the design and functionality of your blog.

Using HTML

Even if you are not using style sheets, understanding HTML can mean you can make changes to your blog posts to overcome problems caused by the way blogging platforms handle things such as images and spacing. For instance, you may have an image that is slightly too large or too small for your blog post, but your blogging platform will only let you reduce it in 10 per cent increments. With HTML, you can fine-tune image sizes as well as adjust spacing, justification, colours, fonts, text sizes and the general layout of your posts.

```
<!DOCTYPE html>
<html lang="en" class="home midcol">

<head>

    <meta charset="utf-8">
    <title>Notepad++ Home</title>

    <meta name="description" content="Notepad++: a free source code editor which supports several programming languages
running under the MS Windows environment."/>
    <meta name="keywords" content="Télécharger Notepad++, Telecharger Notepad++, Notepad, télécharger, téléchargement,
telecharger, telechargement, gratuit, free source code editor, remplacant de Notepad++, Notepad2, netpad, open source,
web editor, html editor, xml editor, php editor, asp editor, javascript editor, java editor, c++ editor, c# editor,
objective-c editor, NFO editor, VB editor, CSS, SQL, Pascal, Perl, Python, Lua, Regular Expression Search"/>

    <link rel="alternate" type="application/rss+xml" title="Follow Notepad++ with RSS" href="http://notepad-plus-
plus.org/feed.rss"/>
    <link rel="stylesheet" type="text/css" href="/assets/css/npp_c1.css"/>
    <link rel="stylesheet" type="text/css" href="/assets/css/fonts/droidserif.css"/>
    <link rel="shortcut icon" href="http://notepad-plus-plus.org/assets/images/favicon.ico" type="image/x-icon" />
    <!--[if lte IE 7]><link rel="stylesheet" type="text/css" href="/assets/css/ie67.css"/><![endif]-->



<script type="text/javascript">
window.___gcfg = {lang: 'en'};
(function()
{var po = document.createElement("script");
po.type = "text/javascript"; po.async = true;po.src = "https://apis.google.com/js/plusone.js";
var s = document.getElementsByTagName("script")[0];
s.parentNode.insertBefore(po, s);
})();</script>
```

Left: Understanding your blog's HTML code allows you to customize many formatting aspects of your page.

TROUBLESHOOTING

Bloggers can often run into trouble. Whether your blog has gone down, is not displaying properly or is slow to load, troubleshooting is an important aspect of maintaining a successful blog.

DISPLAY ISSUES

The most common problem bloggers face is their blog not displaying properly. This can be a real headache. Not only can pinpointing the problem be difficult, but display issues may also be restricted to certain browsers.

bloggingmadeeasyblog.wordpress.com/2013/10/09/how-to-write-a-killer-blog-post/
bloggingmadeeasyblog
Follow
Like
Reblog
Zoom: 125%
Reset to default
New Post
How to Write a Killer Blog Post
OCTOBER 9, 2013 | NEWBLOGGER1234 | 2 COMMENTS | EDIT
You do not need to be an expert writer to be a good blogger. What you are writing about is far more important than how you write it.

Above: Page size, or zoom, on a browser can often affect layout changes.

Browsers

Various internet browsers can display web content differently. This means that, while your blog may look neat and well laid out in one browser, it can be a complete mess in another. In addition, most browsers allow users to increase or decrease the sizes of pages, which can also make your blog look a mess. Always check your blog in different browsers and make sure none of the elements start clashing when you zoom in and out.

Layout

Sometimes, you can spend hours fiddling with the layout, yet your blog simply refuses to look the way you want it to. This is usually caused by HTML issues, so make sure your code is clean.

Hot Tip

HTML <font> and <span> tags set colour, size, typeface and many other aspects of formatting, so they can often be the cause of layout issues.

Backtrack

Most display issues occur after you have made changes to your blog. If things are not displaying correctly, think about recent changes. Adjusting one thing, such as the size of a sidebar, can often have a knock-on effect on other elements. If you cannot figure out the problem, backtrack to an earlier version.

SLOW LOADING

If your blog takes too long to load, you are going to lose visitors. People will not hang around for more than a couple of seconds waiting for a page to appear, so you need to ensure your blog loads quickly.

Server Speed

If you're having trouble with page-loading speed, it may be an issue with your hosting company. Check the connection speed and, if you are not getting the bandwidth you need, move to another host.

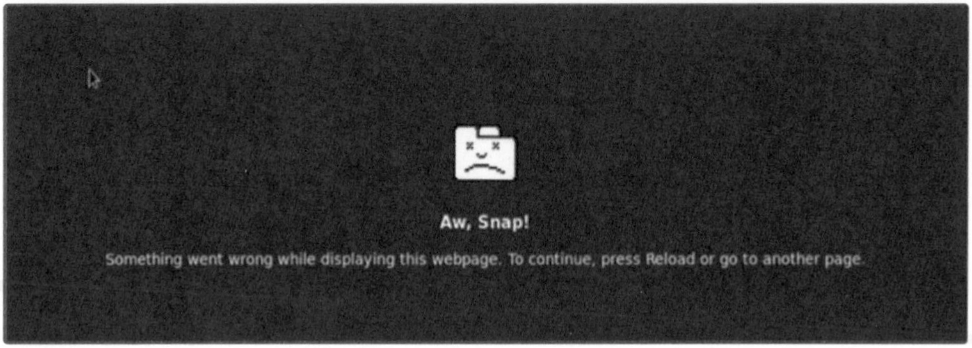
Aw, Snap!
Something went wrong while displaying this webpage. To continue, press Reload or go to another page.

Above: Error messages can be intimidating, though they are a vital part of identifying and solving technical issues that your blog may have.

Page Size

Sometimes, blog posts are so large they take ages to load. Check your images. Replace png, giffs and other files with jpegs, which take up less memory. If you are embedding external images, this may slow down your blog, so consider uploading images directly.

Hot Tip

Plug-ins like the Performance Profiler Plug-in, W3 Total Cache, WP-Super-Cache and WP-DBManager can help speed up page-loading times.

Plug-ins

Conflicting plug-ins can often be the cause of poor loading times. To pinpoint which ones are causing the problem, disable all plug-ins, then enable them one by one.

DISABLED BLOG

Worst of all is when your blog goes down. If visitors are faced with an error page, they may not bother coming back. In addition, if a blog is down for more than a few days, it will lose its search engine rankings.

Host Connection

If your blog has gone down, the first place to check is with your hosting company. Contact customer support and ask if there are any issues at their end.

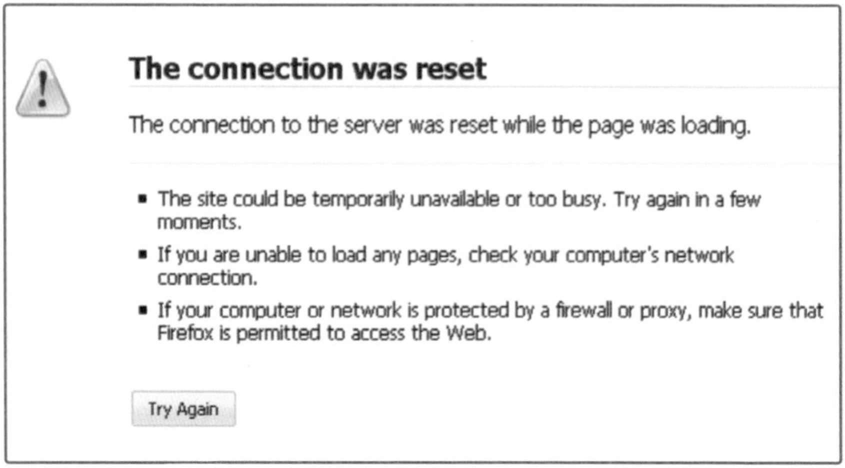

The connection was reset
The connection to the server was reset while the page was loading.
The site could be temporarily unavailable or too busy. Try again in a few moments.
If you are unable to load any pages, check your computer's network connection.
If your computer or network is protected by a firewall or proxy, make sure that Firefox is permitted to access the Web.
Try Again

Above: If you receive an error message like this, check with your hosting company to determine whether they are experiencing issues.

Blank Pages

Corrupted themes are often the cause of blank pages. This is especially true if you have migrated from another host, or have recently installed a new theme. To rectify this, change your theme back to a default, then reinstall the new one. If the problem continues, your theme file could be corrupt.

DROP IN VISITOR NUMBERS

A sudden and unexpected drop in visitor numbers can often be symptomatic of a problem with your blog. Make sure you monitor your statistics carefully and, if you notice a decline, troubleshoot your blog to ensure it is loading properly on all browsers and is displaying correctly.

Change in SERPS

Many bloggers have found they have had a sudden drop in visitors following algorithm changes made by search engine companies. Some blogs that were high in the search engine rankings (SERPS) have dropped down the rankings following these changes, which has resulted in reduced visitor numbers. Make sure you are not trying to play the system by spamming links or using 'black hat' (unethical) techniques to boost your rankings.

FURTHER READING

Cho, Joy Deangdeelert, *Blog, Inc.*, Chronicle Books, 2012.

Editors of The Huffington Post, *The 'Huffington Post' Complete Guide to Blogging*, Simon & Schuster, 2009.

Garrett, Chris and Rowse, Darren, *ProBlogger: Secrets for Blogging Your Way to a Six-Figure Income*, John Wiley & Sons, 2012.

Griffin, Zoe, *Get Rich Blogging*, John Blake Publishing Ltd, 2013.

Houghton, Robin, *Blogging for Creatives: How designers, artists, crafters and writers can blog to make contacts, win business and build success*, ILEX, 2012.

Macarthy, Andrew, *500 Social Media Marketing Tips: Essential Advice, Hints and Strategy for Business: Facebook, Twitter, Pinterest, Google+, YouTube, Instagram, LinkedIn, and More!*, CreateSpace Independent Publishing Platform, 2013.

Sullins, Angi and Toball, Silas, *Digital Art Wonderland: Creative Techniques for Inspirational Journaling and Beautiful Blogging*, North Light Books, 2011.

WEBSITES

basicblogtips.com
This website is a wealth of information divided into blogging tutorials, blogging forums, podcasts and YouTube videos, allowing you to get information from both experts and fellow bloggers.

bestbloggingtipsonline.com
A great site designed for bloggers, by bloggers. It covers design, themes and advice on how to grow your blog.

www.blogelina.com
Everything you need to know to get the most of out of your blog. Starting with the basics, this website even features an online blogging class.

www.blogger.com
Blog publishing tool from Google, for sharing text, photos and video.

www.bloggersentral.com
This site includes really useful SEO tools such as a speed checker, a rank checker and a reciprocal rank checker, together with a character counter.

bloggerspassion.com
More information about using multimedia and graphics in your blog.

www.bloggingtips.com
Great advice designed to help you to take your blog to the next level, including interviews with successful bloggers, case studies of building blogs, and a particularly good section on how to manage a small business blog.

www.blogs.com
A service that helps you find blogs by category and topic, or read daily blog roundups of some of the best blog content around the web.

www.blogtopsites.com
This site is a great way to keep up to date with the most popular blog sites. It enables you to search blogs by topic, which provides useful inspiration.

www.bluehost.com
Web-hosting site which allows you to register domain names and engage in e-commerce.

chitika.com
Online advertising network which produces widget-style adverts to suit your site.

crafterminds.com
An excellent advice centre for those looking to blog creatively, also offering a comprehensive list of further resources if you still have unanswered questions.

www.dailyblogtips.com
A great website offering daily blog tips in a myriad of areas including blog design, internet marketing, promotion and search engine optimization.

www.dailywritingtips.com
No matter what the format or layout of your blog, content is still king! This site has plenty of great advice so you can make sure your writing skills are up to scratch.

www.google.com/adsense
A widely popular resource when it comes to maximizing revenue from your online content.

www.movabletype.com
Content Management System, blog software and publishing platform.

www.mybloggertricks.com
From widgets and web-hosting information to case studies of highly successful blogs to inspire you, this site is a mine of information.

www.problogger.net
A website offering frequently updated blog tips to help you make money from blogging.

www.seobook.com
Further information on how to optimize your blog for different search engines. Also offers a training program and community forum.

www.spiceupyourblog.com
Excellent advice on how to make your blog stand out and serve its purpose. Includes great design tutorials and information on blogging gadgets.

www.squarespace.com
This website makes it easy for you to create your own website, including your own blog.

www.thebloghangout.com
Head to The Blog Hangout to learn up-to-date tips including advice on integrating your blog with other social media platforms and choosing plug-ins and themes.

www.typepad.com
High-quality blog platform featuring one-on-one support.

wallblog.co.uk
A blog covering digital marketing, digital media, social media, search marketing, e-commerce and email.

www.way2blogging.org
Information and templates for bloggers, particularly good information on integrating Pinterest into your blog.

weblogs.about.com
Comprehensive resource offering advice on starting, growing and monetizing a blog.

www.wordpress.org
This well-known blog platform offers an excellent variety of blog templates and themes for you to get started.

www.wpbeginner.com
A further resource for new WordPress users, featuring videos, forums and tutorials.

INDEX